THE PRINCETON JOURNAL

Thematic Studies in Architecture

Volume One

The Princeton Architectural Press

1 9 8 3

The Princeton Journal: Thematic Studies in Architecture
Volume One

Julia Bourke, *Editor*. Peggy Deamer and Lee Ledbetter, *Associate Editors*. Thomas Reed, *Assistant Editor*. Stephen Falatko, *Designer*. Susan Butcher and David Dymecki, *Business Managers*. Richard Martinez, *Production Manager*. Jennifer Aliber, Rico Cedro, Stephen Corelli, Joan Craig, Lois Nesbitt, and Brad Wales, *Editorial Board*. Eric Alch, William Georgis, and Deborah Gutowitz, *Production Board*.

Alan Colquhoun, Robert Gutman, Alan Plattus, and Anthony Vidler, *Advisors*.

Thanks to Patrick Burke, Randy Cloud, Julie Donoho, Ellen Dunham, Kevin Kennon, David Kowalski, Jin Lee, James Longenbach, Brendan Moran, Amy Philips, Marty Rowen, Steven Sivak, Maryann Thompson, Darrell Wilson, Penny Yates, and Andrew Zega. Also to William Taylor, photographer.

Special thanks to Robert Maxwell, Dean of the Princeton School of Architecture.

• • •

The Princeton Journal is published by the Princeton Architectural Press, Princeton, New Jersey.

Send editorial correspondence to *The Princeton Journal*, School of Architecture, Princeton University, Princeton, New Jersey 08544.

Send orders and business correspondence to The Princeton Architectural Press, 158 Valley Road, Princeton, New Jersey 08540.

Copyright © 1983 by *The Princeton Journal: Thematic Studies in Architecture* and The Princeton Architectural Press. ISBN: 0-910413-02-9.

Contents

EDITORIAL
Julia Bourke — 5

AN ALIMENTARY EXERCISE IN RITUAL: 1982 Princeton Esquisse
Competition and Dialogue — 7

RITES AND RITUALS
Fernando Montes — 22

SEQUENCES
Bernard Tschumi — 29

HELLENIC STUDIES CENTER
Stephen Corelli — 38

THE BATH AS A REITERATION OF THE COSMOGONIC ACT
George Gintole — 43

HOT SPRINGS HOTEL
Frank Moya — 8

RITUAL THEMES IN ARCHITECTURE
Michael Graves — 51

TABLE TALK: A Discussion of Michael Graves' Set for the Ballet *Fire*
Deborah Gans — 57

CLUB CHAIRS
Tod Williams and Billie Tsien — 66

RECEPTION DESK
Erich Marosi — 67

FANG ARCHITECTONICS
James Fernandez — 68

SERMON IN STONE
Robert Maxwell — 83

GEORGICA AND LEBRUN HOUSES
Diana Agrest and Mario Gandelsonas — 87

PASSAGES TO THE CITY: The Interpretive Function of the Roman Triumph
Alan Plattus — 93

THE RETURN TO THE ORIGINS: Rituals of Initiation in Late Eighteenth Century France
Anthony Vidler — 116

INTERVIEW WITH ANDO TADAO
    Toshio Okumura — 126

NEW YORK LOFT
    Peter Wheelwright — 135

HEARTH PROJECT
    Peggy Deamer — 139

A NAPA VALLEY WINERY
    Yossi Friedman — 144

PASSAGE AND ENTRY: An Artist's Loft
    Pe'era Goldman — 148

RITUAL AND THE LIBRARY
    Bruce Abbey and Robert Dripps — 151

MAYER HOUSE AND ALLEY THEATER
    Peter Waldman
    Text by Peter C. Papademetriou — 155

A TALL TALE OF URBAN STRATIFICATION: Men's Club, New York City
    John Maruszcak — 163

WATER FOLLY
    Gustavo Bonevardi — 167

ANCIENT MESOPOTAMIA AND THE FOUNDATION OF ARCHITECTURAL REPRESENTATION
    Peter Carl — 170

Note: The commentary accompanying the design projects and essays was written by the editors.

Editorial

The contemporary association of ritual and architecture is a matter of choice, involving the consent of both architect and participant. The rules which govern this association, although inextricable from tradition, are yet not commonly observed. In general, ritual as truth claim is rendered secondary to ritual as object of aesthetic appreciation. No longer necessarily in service to a particular ideology, architecture becomes the repository for a potentially wide range of meanings, and to come to a coherent judgment of a building depends more on the imagination than on any predetermined collective understanding.

The architect's desire to find a new kind of ritual comes in the wake of renewed interest in the past, and suggests an attempt to redress the balance, to counter the proliferation of mute form ("Moloch, whose eyes are a thousand blind windows") with an architecture that once again engages the participant on a primary level. The fear of ambiguity, of incommunicability, propels the search. This reaction has a parallel in early modern literature, in Baudelaire's invocation of ritual as the determinant of "crisis-proof form," in T.S. Eliot's deployment of myth as "a way of controlling, of ordering, of giving a shape and a significance to the immense panorama of futility and anarchy which is contemporary history." More important yet than symbolic form, ritual form is distinguished by use: in architecture, the functional imperative is transformed, and by this transformation it is validated in respect to the past.

The work of two distinguished contemporary architects, Michael Graves and Aldo Rossi, furnish strong examples of this effort to use ritual as a way of establishing communicable meaning and eliminating radically subjective interpretation. Both assert that ritual is the essential justification for the manipulation of form. In Graves' Pre-Romantic sensibility, the language of architecture becomes Adamic: having once called a system of mythic interpretation into play (ceiling is sky, column is tree), he relies on the assumption that each recombination of elements will be understood in that context. Furthermore, with every recombination, the vision of the "alternative landscape" becomes more firmly instantiated. Use confirms meaning, and the prescribed narrative (entry, procession, centering) traces the elements' overall unity.

Rossi shows a similar faith in the fixity of meaning; in his view, however, there is a discernible gap between meaning and its apprehension. He maintains the Romantic view that the past cannot be fully recovered; from this position the beauty of architecture is seen to be "made of ruins, collapses, super-impositions." The ritual gesture is necessarily flawed, incomplete. Ritual forms stir only the memory, only the expectation of ritual action. There is a sense of resignation, and a delight in the feeling of longing itself:

The widows' walks on the houses of New England recall the Greek ritual of scanning the sea for one who does not return—a substitution of ritual for pain, just as obsession is a substitution for desire. Similarly the repetition of the form of the tympanum on a building does not cause the event itself to recur. The event might not ever happen anyway. I am more interested in the preparations in what might happen on a midsummer night. In this way architecture can be beautiful before it is used; there is beauty in the wait, in the room prepared for the wedding, in the flowers and the silver before High Mass.

Rossi also points to the ritual aspect of artistic creation — an attempt to dispel the apparent arbitrariness of artistic choice by confirming the authority of tradition over the individual imagination.

These visions are compelling. In the end, however, the possibility of real belief is subverted by the persistence of competing truths, and ours remains an aesthetic judgment of an artistic work. Fixity is rather in the framework of the dialogue, in the acknowledgment that the work of art exists in its presentation. At this point where the architect, the language of architecture with its roots in tradition, and the observer all meet, the fear of arbitrariness is truly dispelled. Having once selected the appropriate system or game, we may proceed with the assurance that, in Gadamer's words, "all playing is a being-played."

Julia Bourke

An Alimentary Exercise in Ritual
1982 Princeton Esquisse Competition

The Brief. In April 1982, the editors sponsored a twelve hour esquisse or sketch competition based on the theme of this first issue of The Princeton Journal. *A familiar site in the Princeton vicinity, marked by the intersection of Route 27, the Delaware and Raritan Canal, and Lake Carnegie was the location chosen for this alimentary exercise. Students were invited to make an architectural intervention elucidating some aspect of ritualized eating, and to present their esquisse anonymously, on one panel, with an accompanying note of explanation.*

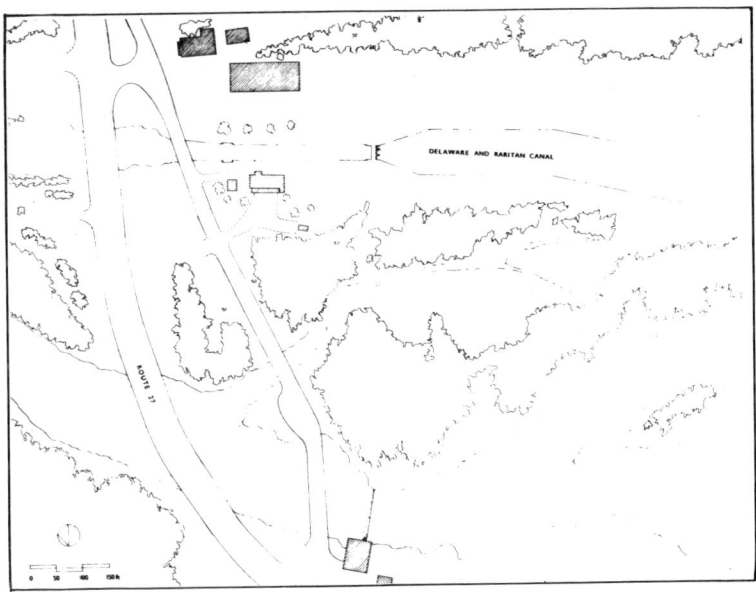

Competition site plan.

Five literary passages were offered to stimulate thoughts about rituals involving buildings and food.

In the dimness of the cafe, the manager is arranging the tables and chairs, the ashtrays, the siphons of soda water; it is six in the morning. He has no need to see distinctly, he does not even know what he is doing. He is still asleep. Very ancient laws rule every detail of his gestures, saved for once from the uncertainty of human intentions; each second marks a pure movement: a sidestep, the chair eleven inches out from the table, three wipes of the rag, half-turn to the right, two steps forward, each second marks, perfect, even, unblurred. Thirty-one. Thirty-two. Thirty-three. Thirty-four. Thirty-five. Thirty-six. Thirty-seven. Each second in its exact place. Soon unfortunately time will no longer be master. Wrapped in their aura of doubt and error, this day's events, however insignificant they may be, will in a few seconds begin their task, gradually encroaching upon the ideal order, cunningly introducing an occasional inversion, a discrepancy, a confusion, a warp, in order to accomplish their work: a day in early winter without plan, without direction, incomprehensible and monstrous.

Alain Robbe-Grillet, *The Erasers*

Now tonight, my body rises tier upon tier like some cool temple whose floor is strewn with carpets and murmurs rise and the altars stand smoking; but up above, here in my serene head, come only fine gusts of melody, waves of incense, while the lost dove wails, and the banners tremble above tombs, and the dark airs of midnight shake trees outside the open windows. When I look down from this transcendency, how beautiful are even the crumbled relics of bread! What shapely spirals the peelings of pears make — how thin, and mottled like some sea-bird's egg. Even the forks laid straight side by side appear lucid, logical, exact; and the horns of the rolls which we have left are glazed, yellow-plated, hard.

Virginia Woolf, The Waves

"...We had our bottle of wine, and under that seduction lost our enmity, and stopped comparing. And, half-way through dinner, we felt enlarge itself around us the huge blackness of what is outside us, of what we are not. The wind, the rush of wheels became the roar of time, and we rushed — where? And who were we? We were extinguished for a moment, went out like sparks in burnt paper and the blackness roared. Past time, past history we went. For me this lasts but one second. It is ended by my own pugnacity. I strike the table with a spoon. If I could measure things with compasses I would, but since my only measure is a phrase, I make phrases — I forget what, on this occasion. We became six people at a table in Hampton Court."

Virginia Woolf, The Waves

    And indeed there will be time
    For the yellow smoke that slides along the street
    Rubbing its back upon the window-panes;
    There will be time, there will be time
    To prepare a face to meet the faces that you meet;
    There will be time to murder and create,
    And time for all the works and days of hands
    That lift and drop a question on your plate;
    Time for you and time for me,
    And time yet for a hundred indecisions,
    And for a hundred visions and revisions,
    Before the taking of a toast and tea.

T. S. Eliot, "The Love Song of J. Alfred Prufrock"

Many years had elapsed during which nothing of Combray, save what was comprised in the theatre and the drama of my going to bed there, had any existence for me, when one day in winter, as I came home, my mother, seeing that I was cold, offered me some tea, a thing I did not ordinarily take. I declined at first, and then, for no particular reason, changed my mind. She sent out for one of those short, plump little cakes called 'petites madeleines,' which look as if they had been moulded in the fluted scallop of a pilgrim's shell. And soon, mechanically, weary after a dull day with the prospect of a depressing morrow, I raised to my lips a spoonful of tea in which I had soaked a morsel of the cake. No sooner had the warm liquid, and the crumbs with it, touched my palate than a shudder ran through my whole body, and I stopped, intent upon the extraordinary changes that were taking place. An exquisite pleasure had invaded my senses, but individual, detached, with no suggestion of its origin. And at once the vicissitudes of life had become indifferent to me, its disasters innocuous, its brevity illusory — this new sensation having had on me the effect which love has of filling me with a precious essence; or rather this essence was not in me, it was myself. I had ceased now to feel mediocre, accidental, mortal. Whence could it have come to me, this all-powerful joy? I was conscious that it was connected with the taste of tea and cake, but that it infinitely transcended those savours, could not, indeed, be of the same nature as theirs. Whence did it come? What did it signify? How could I seize upon and define it?

Marcel Proust, Swann's Way

The Review. Three winners were chosen by Professors Alan Colquhoun, Steven Harris, Alan Plattus, Michael Graves, and Judith Wolin. The following is a record of the jury's comments and of the general discussion which ensued.

Wolin: The comments which came to my mind first had to do with the problem of an *esquisse* in general. There are clearly things that were well-understood at the Ecole des Beaux Arts about how to win a brief competition like this, and in fact they're pretty much the way to win any competition — which is to rapidly come up with a very straight-forward visual idea, a very strong graphic idea — not a text, not an elaborate set of architectural rules — but one emblem-like move. That would take 45 minutes; then you would spend the next 23 hours drawing. The key is also to have a very strongly organized sheet or series of drawings which continue that emblematic quality so that the drawings themselves have a coherence which shouts the thematic solution.

Graves: The difference between a Princeton solution and, say, one from Illinois where they're skilled at this sort of thing, is that we would spend the next 23 hours doubting. [Laughter.]

Wolin: I think doubt is the kiss of death in an *esquisse*; so is revision. There's a problem with the humor here too. What seems awfully funny in the heat of an *esquisse* doesn't look so funny three or four days later. We all got a laugh out of the "Eating Club" scheme, but you can't give a prize to something like that — it's not an architectural solution.

Graves: Judy's comment that you might push one idea for the duration of the *esquisse* does not imply that that one idea should be a "one-liner"...though it was in that scheme.

Harris: Well, the "Diner" scheme is a "one-liner" too, but it's a better line.

Graves: But it brings to mind other things. You imagine yourself in it over a period of time.

Wolin: Yes, the "Diner" scheme was our unanimous choice. It has certain emblematic qualities, as well as a real sense of ritual in the arrangement behind that facade of a kind of sacred grove where all these ordinary things are arranged in an unordinary way. I mean a ham on rye would just not be the same.

Harris: It also has the ability to be very complex — to engage in other issues that have to do with the hermetic discussion of architecture — with the making of a facade relative to the plan which occurs behind it.

Wolin: Simple things like the use of light give it the potential of a magic quality. The facade is backlit like a diner but then the light becomes a set of lanterns in the woods.

Graves: I had hoped after seeing that, that there might be a transformation of the facade to let us into the world beyond... Perhaps a misspelling of "Dinner." [Laughter.]

Colquhoun: You wouldn't know it was a misspelling!

Wolin: I've given a studio which explored the problem of what makes a space sacred in architectural terms, that is, what architectural devices allow you to know that you do not bring your ordinary behavior with you into a particular place. You take your shoes off, straighten up, or take your hat off.... Some such devices could have been used in the schemes where one feels that the site planning strategy is basically very conventional. For instance, one could make a precinct, a walled

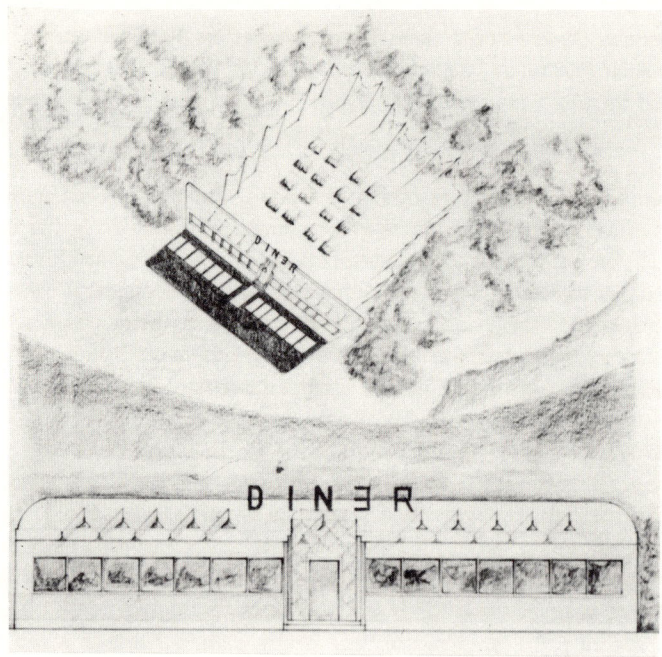

Diner

Ritual can exist on many scales: driving on a highway in New Jersey; seeing a billboard advertising fast food; stopping at a diner. The ritual can be identified by compressing and transforming its parts. The traveller understands the language. Once within the system the experience is limited only by the Proustian imagination.

Robert Marino

compound or a platform of some kind which isolates that piece of turf as existing on another plane, in a realm different from that outside, so that there's clearly a kind of "outside/profane" and "inside/sacred" quality to it — which is what the "Diner" does do.

Graves: That comes directly, I think, out of the Beaux Arts; when one is given a piece of paper 22"x 30" as the site, it produces that kind of isolation, that lack of contextual interest, that Judy was talking about. The ones that try to be contextual here tend to miss a bit. I suppose the contextual attitude is by nature more serious and takes longer.

Plattus: Yes, the site was a little bit distracting to everybody. They took the thing too seriously as if it were eventually going to be a six-week design problem and tried to somehow engage, or set up, an array of things that would eventually provide the framework for a vast set of architectural developments. What I would look at in terms of site information is less the site itself as an elaborate landscape condition, and more the place by the side of the road as something that one would characterize very quickly as one was driving past it. I'm almost surprised that I didn't see any picnic tables, because the distinction Judy was talking about between something that's ritualized or special and ordinary experience is really very subtle. It's not a matter of pumping it up ad nauseum, but of taking something that makes an immediate connection with ordinary experience and jarring it slightly.

Wolin: Charles Moore and a group of students did a project 12 years ago or so — a path that went down a very steep hill through untouched woodland. Instead of the path being naturalistic, it was painted safety-stripe yellow, and it was very, very narrow. So down through this natural woodland came this yellow stripe. It was really quite extraordinary, uplifting the idea of path so that one really felt the path was the "Way."

Plattus: There's a real question in most of these schemes as to whether the ritual is the architecture or something that goes on in relationship to the architecture, because in many of them the architecture in itself seems to be elaborated to the point where it acts out some idea of ritual, as opposed to providing a setting that is special, where one could imagine a rather unspecified ritual. I mean, we were not given anything as specific as a communion or a sacrifice — unless you invented it. I think in fact that a critical attitude toward ritual in a post-romantic period would have to be less than absolutely specific. One thing that's marvelous about Aldo Rossi's architecture is its ability to suggest aspects of the sacred and aspects of ritual by being non-specific — by saying that there is no precise correspondence between what goes on in this space and what this space can accommodate.

Harris: One of the values of the "Fishing Bridge" scheme is that it has a kind of generality about the nature of the ritual involved. One could imagine any number of things taking place there, but clearly it has a ritualistic aspect: the occupation of the centers of each one of those little pieces; the stairs to the water; the implication that there's some sort of sequential activity that has a particular meaning but which could be any number of a series of things.

Graves: It's also a bit like a dam... pavilions on top of a dam. It's quite nice because it also has suspension bridges which provide a double reading. It's a singular idea with several readings.

Colquhoun: It also has the idea of repetition, which is characteristic of ritual.

Plattus: It suggests that there are other kinds of ritual than those that are sequential, hierarchical, and route-oriented. One of the core assumptions about 75% of the schemes was that all rituals are about routes as opposed to something that might simply be a litany — repetitive and straightforward in that way.

Graves: What do you mean by "route-oriented"?

Plattus: The suggestion of a ritual in the movement from one place to the next either in a hierarchical fashion or a narrative fashion.

Graves: Unlike the "Fishing Bridge," many of the other rituals tend to be centroidal.

Harris: What makes the "Fishing Bridge" significant is that it accepts the fight between the linear and the repetitive.

Wolin: It also brings up the question of unison activity. That's another aspect of litany — if you get everybody together in a sacred house they will all do essentially the same activities, or the same non-activities.

Harris: If you compare the writing of Joseph Campbell to Eliade's, it seems to me that while Eliade is more interested in what makes separate myths specific, what gives them an independent character, Campbell, who's a bit out of fashion now, talks about what makes them general, what unites them all. Alan Colquhoun mentioned in a review that it was possible to make a building which was built as a monument but was occupied incidentally. I think what we're asking for is that the rituals maintain a generality where they could be any number of things — that their specificity be a secondary characteristic behind the more general aspect.

Fishing Bridge

This project focuses on the fishing ritual for its simplicity, familiarity, and appropriateness to the site. A series of twelve pavilions for the catching, killing, and eating of fish emphasizes the universality of this solitary act and suggests a possible choreography of the anglers' repeated casting rhythms. Strung across the dam which distinguishes Lake Carnegie from the Millstone River are the foundations of these pavilions, rising like buttresses against a wall of water and linked by a suspended footbridge. A parallel architectonic ritual is elaborated in the building and dismantling of a temporary shelter on one's chosen platform.

Julia Bourke and Jonathan Kirschenfeld

Wolin: Yes, there are certain specific generalities like initiation, crossing from one place to another, entering a sacred zone, going through repetitive acts, trials or progressing towards a center....

Colquhoun: A lot of the pieces were concerned with making the ritual specific with their scenarios; this was made evident in some cases by the tenuous connection between text and drawing. Architecture inevitably has its generalized portions. It's like music — it doesn't actually describe or insist on particular themes. Some of the schemes tried to make a direct connection between the story line and the building and inevitably didn't succeed. This makes the building an illustration.

Wolin: There's something about the sacred — that quality of a pre-existing form or culturally known form that transcends all the specificities of the site or program.

Plattus: Yes, everybody who tried it was very courageous because in some way it's more interesting, or more comfortable, to speculate about than to actually try to make.... In the end I suspect most of us realize that architects don't make rituals, just like they don't make types. It has to do with something rather deeply embedded in society and culture which is either there to be found and highlighted or not ; even resurrecting it in a direct and specific fashion makes you shake a little bit....

Mason Andrews: Could we have some further discussion about the relationship between ritual and architecture? There's something very seductive and powerful about the implication that we're tying our work back into some universal significance.

Colquhoun: This may be subjective, but one of the things I mean by a building that has ritualistic overtones is that it has a closed form; that the form can somehow be metaphorical; that it doesn't try to imitate, but simply says something. It creates a distinctive formal quality apart from the everyday flux of life, like Robbe-Grillet's description which presents, in very cold terms, the laying of tables, the formal organization of tables. To me, the whole idea of architectural ritual implies that kind of formality — that you create a world apart from the ordinary world, the everyday world; and that implies some kind of formal closure.... I don't think that the meaning of a *specific* ritual can be given architectural form at all. I think architectural form has different meanings according to different cultures.

Graves: A threshold has architectural form and it is at the same time significant to the collective body of society.

Colquhoun: ...But as a form and not as a specific ritual.

Graves: Well, the two things are synonymous in that case. They are synonyms or they become synonyms. The passage from out to in, or from one place to another around or through the membrane of the wall, is only possible because of the plane that one passes, and this is something that is commonly agreed upon. However, the passage to the stations of the cross, for instance, is an invention.

Colquhoun: That's the difference between metaphor and allegory. An allegory is something where the meaning is entirely conventional, whereas a metaphor is a motivated connection between form and meaning. If you look back in history, you invariably find both the structural meaning of what comes from, say, threshold, and another idea which is allegorical or conventional.

Harris: Isn't that an historical position? To recognize something as ritualistic without assigning the culturally agreed upon meaning of that ritual?

Colquhoun: We're no longer believers.

Plattus: It's a little bit like the modern notion of monumentality; it's not monumentalizing or commemorating, which is one of the original functions of all monuments — it's not commemorating anything in particular, but is turned into a general adjective — ritualized monumentality.

Wolin: I'm not inclined to take such an historical distance from it because in working with some of these problems with students, I found that certain of those ritual boundaries were inoperative while others still had the potency of taboo. The projects for religious retreats ended up looking like motels, but when we did a crematorium and mausoleum, we went to watch a body being cremated. At that moment some kind of special cultural and emotional significance was touched. Everyone agreed that in order to solve that particular problem we would have to acknowledge the current and real presence of taboo and fear and emotion. It became very clear to us that Modern architecture had failed to provide the scene for those kinds of real ritual situations.

Plattus: But I have to imagine that it's all up for grabs. It's merely convention: we're not talking about archetypes. You say that there are some that no longer have any meaning to students, and some that do. Now, is there some predictability about which ones do, or is it again a question of

In this project, ritual is interpreted as a clearly marked, habitual, public act. The basic, even primitive functions of catching, cleaning, and eating fish are each given a particular precinct and an elemental architectural expression. The three structures are versions of the same design in different states of enclosure and undress, thus suggesting the progression from fish hook to dinner plate. If this arrangement exceeds a functional solution, it is because the habitual act is allowed to attain self-conscious dignity. Rather than being obscured in the cloak of continuous action, habit is celebrated by places of repose.

James Von Klemperer

the cultural, social milieu and the conventions by which one operates?

Wolin: Well, it is up for grabs, but I'm asking: mightn't we still have an intact enough thing called Western culture? That is, aren't there certain rituals you can name?

Plattus: Well, that's an open question... maybe at RISD you do but....

Wolin: You watch a body being cremated and you will come out changed too.

Harris: Yes, but the Modernists would argue that an emotional response to a body being cremated reflects a Pollyanna sensibility, that the attitude toward death is for them no more meaningful than a motel.

Wolin: Yes, there's a level at which we can all adopt the attitude that it's just another term, another convention; but the fact is that some things still have an emotional charge which is being drained in part by the failure of architecture to handle those kinds of situations in a special way.

Colquhoun: Yes, but ritual is not to do with emotion. Art is the expression of emotion, but ritual is not. Ritual is an explanatory device. It's connected with myth. It explains a problem.

Plattus: It performs.

Wolin: Yes, you're right. Did you read *Purity and Danger*? There's an argument in contemporary anthropology that we have a whole set of myths within which we operate so unconsciously that only when somebody does something like leave a pair of dirty boots on the dining room table during a meal do we feel that sense of revulsion that comes with health and cleanliness — that our society's permeated not with religious myths but with notions of purity and danger — that the central myth is insecurity.

Colquhoun: I agree with that, but it's historicizing.

Harris: Purity and danger are both issues specific to the individual.

Plattus: What Judy's saying, or what Mary Douglas is saying, is that in Western culture, if you leave a pair of dirty boots on the dining room table, most people will react to it, whereas in the 17th century, courtiers didn't think anything of talking to Louis XIV while he was sitting on the can.

Hoke Slaughter: That's one level of talking about ritual, but a distinction has to be made between something that symbolizes ritual, like perhaps a plate or a table which might symbolize the ritual of eating, and a primary architectural element like a doorway. Does the doorway symbolize ritualized entry or is it simply the element that allows entry? It's both.

Wolin: I have a buddy who would say the doorway becomes ritualized when it's too big or too small.

Graves:...Through the modification of the thing we know, and only through that modification by mannerizing it.

Plattus: The curious thing about ritual is that it can take place, or it can insinuate itself, in the most adverse conditions. More often than not, rituals have persisted in a particular place because something happened there in a purely fortuitous way, and has modified the place, rather than having begun with favorable circumstances or with a built setting. In the everyday world of architecture, as opposed to cremation, you have to be able to have it in both ways; you have to be able to go in and out of that door fifty time a day and then the fifty-first time it might be special. What becomes problematic, at least for me, is when the architecture forces you to participate in the ritual fifty-one times a day instead of one out of fifty-one times.

Harris: But we're talking about two different levels of architecture. We're talking on the one hand about the mundane elements of architecture, and on the other hand about the iconic ones. Alan Colquhoun talks about "monument" and about a kind of image which we recognize as having historical significance. That's different than taking a door to which we do not necessarily ascribe any significance and changing that into something which begins to have a symbolic or ritualistic significance by distorting it.

Plattus: Hoke, I think you were talking about the not always real or absolute distinction between representation and performance..., between representation and use, in more mundane terms. The question is whether the primary function of the door is to represent itself or the idea of passage, or actually to create that situation. A door can have symbolic representational power even if it's not used, even if we just draw it on the facade, or build it and brick it up because nothing will ever pass through it again, the sacred having once passed through it. It's representation as an index of an act that once took place in real or mythical historic times. I'm talking about making a monument out of it, highlighting its representational powers, making it only a representation of something.

Colquhoun: But this has another aspect, because if all doors are ritualistic, no doors are ritualistic.

Harris: Not necessarily, Alan. Given that one obelisk is ritualistically symbolic, would it follow that if all are then none are?

Colquhoun: Well, a door is a different thing from an obelisk. An obelisk is completely useless. It starts off with a terrific advantage. [Laughter.]

Graves: The other crucial issue about the door or the threshold versus the obelisk is that the door has a craft tradition surrounding it. The threshold can also be called a sill, which in our language means craft while the other is poetic. You cannot do that to the obelisk or to the stations of the cross. It's meaningless there to talk about the craft associations versus the symbolic ones: the rheostat has been turned up so high on the symbolic that the mundane or the standard part of the language is out of the picture altogether.

Harris: There's a hierarchy of architectural elements which are more or less susceptible to ideas of ritual and symbol. The door is perhaps the most symbolic, but as soon as one admits that a door has an inherent ritualistic significance, one has to admit that the doorknob does, that the floor does, that the ceiling does, that every air-conditioning grill and light trim piece does.

Plattus: Well, I'm wondering to what extent you can make a set of distinctions derived from the elements: you can say that light is originally about hearths anyway. Where I don't quite follow you is when you say that because a door has a special kind of significance, so might a wall or ceiling: I think we're talking about different categories of things.

Graves: A wall absolutely does.

Wolin: I'm struck that you're all keeping this argument within the straight semiologic line, where units of vocabulary, like doors and windows, are the key carriers of meaning. Whereas it seems to me that one can also talk about spatial situations like being in the center or being forced to the edge — things which have not so much to do with units of vocabulary but with spatial location.

Graves: But I've got to have the location of the wall and the location of you and me talking to each other or somehow in relation to each other to know the center and edge.

Colquhoun: No you don't. For instance in North Africa there are primitive plays in which one or two actors a night do a mime in a little lit space. There's one crude lamp which lights up a circular area and they form a circle around that. There's no architecture at all. There are no buildings. This is ritualized space.

Wolin: Well, we're talking about architecture. We could talk about modern choreography — examples of choreographic space. In terms of talking about architecture one assumes that one is making the center of that space with architectural elements.

Colquhoun: Yes, but that's the whole point: once you talk about space you're not talking about architecture. You open the thing up to a whole possibility of choreographic space or theatrical space.

Wolin: That's an ideological watershed I'm not quite willing to step over.

Harris: What it comes down to is the issue of linear sequence. Why would you say a door potentially has more ritualistic significance as one passes through it and goes from one condition to another? It is based on procession and perception of a sort, on inside and outside, in a way that doesn't apply as easily to the wall.

Graves: The wall is inherently ritualistic because it's a boundary between two places. You can't have a door without the wall.

Plattus: This comes back to the question of whether architects in fact enforce or invent rituals. Whether simply by sheer architectural determination I can raise something to the level of ritual, be it door, wall, or window, and whether in doing so I'm either presuming or somehow taking for granted too much about that. In the end, it devalues what one understands as having originally been meant by ritual and its significance within society, its ability on particular days of the year, particular times of the season and particular times in one's life, to accentuate things.

Julia Bourke: Is ritual only enforced by repetition, by the fact that it's been done before, in time, in memory?

Plattus: It's potentially repetitive. It doesn't necessarily have to be something that is literally repeated over and over again.

Colquhoun: From the way you've just described it, it literally has to be repeated over and over again. You're saying that ritual has to be defined in terms of social custom, and in that case is always historical, which implies that it has been repeated.

Plattus: It implies that it could be repeated. In fact, in anthropological terms, the significance of ritual, or the efficacy of ritual, depends upon performing something in an absolutely precise way. The ritual doesn't work, the magic doesn't work, unless you go through certain motions, certain actions, in a particular way. The specification of that pattern absolutely implies that it be not only repeatable but that you or I could perform it as long as we were endowed with the necessary setting, power, etc. It must have potential cultural continuity. For instance, there can be another pope who can perform the same rites, because they are set down in that fashion. It's not private, in other words. There is something anomalous about the notion of private ritual.

Jamie von Klemperer: That brings to mind one of the texts that was included for our consideration — the passage from Proust in which he talks about a very private habit which you may or may not call ritual. You probably wouldn't call that ritual.

Colquhoun: I wouldn't call that ritual. And I wondered why the text was included....

Bourke: Well, it underscored the possibility of having private rituals in the modern age.

Harris: But if it's private then it's not a ritual.

Bourke: But if it has meaning for even one person, if a meaning is conjured up....

Harris: But you have different words for it at that point.

Bourke: What word would you give it?

Harris: I don't know; "fetish" perhaps.

Plattus: It's a literary device; it originates as a trope of exaggeration. It's putting two slightly incompatible things together. It's making a kind of metaphor.

Slaughter: I wonder whether this definition has an architectural parallel?

Harris: It's called "private language."

Slaughter: Does the definition of ritual automatically assume social acceptance? If we went to Webster's, would it cut out private ritual?

Plattus: No, I'm sure it wouldn't.

Colquhoun: Webster's dictionaries are concerned with normal usage. They're not concerned with etymology or with philosophical origins.

Slaughter: Does the etymological definition distinguish between ritual meaning among many people as opposed to one person? I mean, is there no such thing as private ritual?

Colquhoun: Well, there is if you believe there is.

Lois Nesbitt: That was my understanding of the Robbe-Grillet passage: he sees it as a certain hour of the day when he's in control of his existence. He's infusing that activity with the same kind of thing with which primitive cultures infuse their arbitrary ritualized activities. I think the fact that we only talk about having private rituals indicates that people substitute their own idiosyncracies because there is a need for ritual that our society doesn't provide.

Plattus: Well, whether that's true or not, it's still useful to make distinctions as opposed to blurring distinctions. It's useful to say that there is clearly something initially anomalous about talking in terms of private rituals... and very problematic from an architectural point of view.

Harris: Architecture doesn't have the opportunity to simultaneously call attention to itself and remain general, so in terms of making a private ritual public simply by putting it into new words or by some other convention, it doesn't have the advantages that other forms of art would.

Colquhoun: Historically the process is always the other way around. The initial event is always a public ritual. When we talk today about private rituals, we're talking metaphorically about private behavior that resembles what originally was collective behavior.

Harris: ...Private behavior to which we attach symbolic significance.

Colquhoun: Cleaning teeth, for example, is a very private thing and not a ritual act. I suppose it can have ritualistic elements to it, but that seems to be very metaphorical; it presupposes a private obsession. What has become a private obsession was at one time a collective obsession. It's a kind of degeneration of something that existed in a more paradigmatic form at a public level. When we talk about private ritual, we're referring obliquely to an earlier public ritual.

Harris: If one admits that our culture does not have, to the extent that it once had, institutions that are agreed upon in terms of their meaning and their value, then on the one hand you have what we've been calling private ritual, where particular connection from one individual to the next is not significant, and on the other hand a kind of structuralist position that allows you to use historically significant acts either hermetically, tragically, or polemically. They both seem to be flip sides of the same thing. I think the Modernists would call the individual ritualist Pollyanna. The structuralist says that a door is a pragmatic equation between two conditional spaces, and that the association of values that one attaches to being outside or being inside is a potentionally historically significant attribute, but not inherent in the value the ritual may have historically been understood to have.

Colquhoun: I don't agree with that. I don't think the structuralist sees the door pragmatically.

Peggy Deamer: It seems to me you were saying that if private language is supposed to be derived from public language it does have meaning. It's a variation of what used to be public, and therefore does have collective meaning; though we don't recognize it as that anymore. To investigate the notion of private ritual, then, is to investigate the idea that these rituals are in some sense public and shared. We have this general need to discover in a particular performance a larger public significance.

Plattus: You're saying that somehow these public rituals have become private and therefore they are the same thing or that they're the modern version of what used to be public rituals, that the distinction has become virtually impossible to make, at least in those terms. I still have to come back to the point that architecture, like most other art forms, does have the potential advantage of making distinctions about things instead of bending over backwards to obliterate them.

Harris: But it's how you view those distinctions, Alan, that's critical. You can use the distinctions as Truth, you can use them as referential, you can use them as tragic, you can use them relativistically.

Plattus: Yes, I think that's more difficult, because most of us don't attach truth values to those kinds of things anymore, although we might want to, just as most of us have a difficult time telling when somebody's being witty or ironic even though they might intend us to understand the meaning. But we can understand when a basic distinction in an architectonic sense has been made, as opposed to rubbed out.

Colquhoun: Couldn't you say that one definition of architecture might be its ability to make distinction, like language? It makes it available for public meaning.

Wolin: Going back to the projects themselves, the things we appreciated about the "Fishing Bridge" scheme was that there were many rituals that people could associate with. Distinctions like "this is what you do, and this is when you do it" hadn't been made — it was the openness, the possibility, that was nice.

Harris: I think what makes it compelling in part is its slightly overscaled and polemical gesture. The idea of having things of that sort to fish from has an ironic cast to it.

Wolin: To me, in that particular project the ritual has really very little to do with the fishing. You know that by the repetition and by the crossing of the water, by the monumentalization of that, by the occupation of the centers, one can project a series of — I wish I could use another word besides ritual — of symbolic, codified acts.

Michael Stanton: I think Alan Plattus made a very interesting point when he said that there's a crisis of definition in that we can now confuse public and private ritual; I think that crisis of definition also affects architecture: the notion of private and public, the idea of the Barcelona pavilion, and of the brick country house by Mies, which are almost the same type formally, but used in distinct ways and applied to different programs, is a very 20th century thing. And I think this crisis of definition is part of what Modernism is about.

Deamer: I'm interested in knowing what Alan would prescribe for architects today. Is it to make the distinctions very clear — "yes, ritual and its relation to architecture should really be that which has direct implications for the enactment of a certain kind of procession or ceremony" — or does it mean that "well, we're in this dilemma and architecture mirrors for us this dilemma."

Plattus: On a cultural level I probably have many of the same doubts that anybody else has about the efficacy of inventing ritual or even pretending to house ritual and I think that it also has to do with another characteristic confusion — that is between theatre and architecture, between stage set and architecture. To me, the legitimate relationship between those two modes of expression is one that is not as isomorphic as it is in the theatre. When there is a literal translation of the stage set for a specific event into architectural terms, I think architecture is devalued or at least misused.

Graves: I don't accept Michael Stanton's remark. I think there is a similarity between the spatial disposition of the brick country house and the Barcelona Pavilion. The Barcelona Pavilion acts as a surrogate house. And I don't think it's a 20th century distinction. What about a 1st century triumphal arch acting as a facade for a Renaissance church?

Stanton: But those events occur a millenium apart, whereas the brick country house and the Barcelona Pavilion are concurrent.

Graves: It's a spatial concurrence or convention that is being established there, rather than "house" versus "pavilion". Talking about de Stijl space, we're talking about spatial rotation or dissolution — essentially abstract space.

Colquhoun: But isn't the whole thing about de Stijl space that it is anti-ritualistic?

Graves: Absolutely.

Colquhoun: It's characteristically modern; it's anti-ritual.

Plattus: The issue with Mies is to make two buildings that are both about space rather than both of them being about what they represent in society.

Wolin: That leads me back to something I've become a little uneasy about, and that's the consensus that you can't invent ritual. Certainly I agree, but it does seem to me that it is within the power or the realm of an architect to observe and isolate and make visible those things which are embedded or ritualized, which we now live with in a mythic sense.

Colquhoun: Such as?

Wolin: Well, for instance, for me Rossi's cemetery project holds up a mirror to the world in a way which illuminates certain things about the conventions and the patterns of our lives, those hierarchies which we assign to certain things in our lives. I think architecture *can* do that. I do not think it is so entirely internal to itself that it cannot illuminate and reveal those things which exist in our culture that we are normally blind to.

Plattus: In a way that's what I was saying. There's a difference between that though and somehow turning something into ritual. The cemetery is a very special example.

Harris: I agree it has meaning and allegory, but I don't think it's ritualistic. When we use ritual as language, it merely sets up and makes a comment upon....

Wolin: Which is what I said. I said architecture has the ability to reveal ritual.

Harris: It doesn't in and of itself have any immediate symbolic value. It's one remove from it; it is commenting upon it. It's entirely possible to make things which are allegorical, which are ritualistic, which conform to historically justifiable ideas about ritual... and believe them. But I don't think that any culture in the world can believe them.

Plattus: Architecture is inevitably naive about many of these questions. To engage in a problem requires a certain naivete, a certain willing suspension of disbelief, whether in the case of the continued existence of public rituals, which is questionable, or whether in the case of the accessibility and meaningfulness of private rituals, which I think is also in a critical sense questionable. The trick is not in the end that you pick something that is absolutely and logically defensible at the starting point. Architecture gives it a certain level of necessity that it didn't have as an act of faith. I really think that at a critical level the whole question of ritual in a contemporary context has really been, since Nietzsche or before, so thoroughly laid open to every level of deconstruction that to use it in a meaningful sense architecturally really does involve the suspension of disbelief.

Harris: Or a cultural critique.

Plattus: There's a big difference between a cultural critique and the kind of positive embracing of something like that. I don't think it's a meaningful cultural critique to say, "Oh, we don't have any public rituals but we all wish we did so I'm going to make them work or bring them back."

Wolin: That begins to sound like you're speaking a private language again and you're almost trying to create some kind of private ritual that only somebody in the know is going to understand. But I still think there are plenty of viable public rituals around if you look.

Harris: The other alternative to the solution is to say, "No, our culture does not have public rituals, therefore I will make architecture about a culture which does not have any public rituals." And that allows a tragic sensibility.

Plattus: Yes, and then we're back into that realm where you need a text to know the intention....

Rites and Rituals

Fernando Montes
Translation by T. S. Faunce

AFTER THE CURE of mythological detoxification brought about by the Modern Movement, to speak of ritual in the architect's work borders on bald provocation, dubious esotericism or half-baked reaction. How, after all, can we avoid assimilating ritual to the nostalgia for the academical? How, furthermore, can we dissociate ritual from a heavy, painful institutionalization of architecture which is so costly in terms of creativity?

Nevertheless, we assume these risks advisedly, without any particular sense of bravado, and lay claim to the ritual element in architecture.

Why?

For the same reasons that as architects we cannot afford to neglect developments in cinema, painting, literature, photography — that is to say all available forms representing space. And rite is particularly rich in this regard.

Without any argument the golden age has passed, the golden age when the architect, facing his sheet of paper alone and with unshakeable confidence in his art's capacity for redemption, believed he could furnish a meaning for the project with one devastating flourish of the pencil.

From misunderstandings and failures the architect has learned to be more humble and distrustful, to question the world more closely. Before unleashing one of his new creatures on the world he is bound today by moral contract to look around, in front and behind himself. "Avant-garde architect" is no longer synonymous with apprentice-sorcerer or ingenuous experimenter. It is rather the contrary: the obstinate artisan capable of restoring to a building a minimum of its lost reality, the builder capable also of imagining a staged performance.

Since ritual is nothing other than the sublimation of use, everything that calls for use — product or service — is automatically a potential subject for ritual. In terms of architecture, I would define rite as the preferential use of a space which is typologically constituted. From this point of view, the probability of the ritualistic appropriation of a space will thus be a function of its degree of recognition: the more singular the space, the less conducive it is to ritualistic practice. As an illustration of this, let us note that by its inherently emblematic nature a public building will foster preferential use more than will a private dwelling.

All spaces and all products are not ritualized to the same extent. The level will depend on the greater or lesser generalization of the product in a society and on the social profile of the society in question.

The widespread belief that primitive societies are more open to rites than modern societies is

---

1. Campus Autiosus. Jaime Azocar, Edouard Boucher, Catherine Clarisse, Takis Koubis, Richard Scoffier, and Lionel Thomann, *Assistants.*

doubtless based on fact. But this ethnological truth must in no case lead to the false conclusion that rite is the expression of an attitude of simplistic fetishism.

Since Levi-Strauss we know that there is nothing more deliberate and less simplistic than a "primitive" society. Moreover, we must not ignore the fact that what characterizes these societies is the small number of manufactured products surrounding everyday life. It is therefore not surprising that one finds in such societies an extraordinarily intense relationship between the community and its objects.

Entirely unlike primitive societies, ours are societies of consumption where the range of products, their variety and the speed with which they are replenished, are key factors in the successful operation of the economy. Under such conditions preferential and generalized attachment to a given object, a prerequisite for all ritualization, is all the more improbable.

The forms which ritualistic practice may take are consequently more diverse insofar as the raison d'être of rite (that is, identification in a group) is other than an urgent need for survival. The most common of modern rituals is fashion, a system which consists in playing on the increase in an object's potential for communication by the modification of its characteristics in order to distinguish the user.

In architecture the phenomenon of fashion stands out perhaps more clearly than elsewhere. This is due to the breakdown of the aesthetic norms of discipline, to the "all is possible" which emerges from periods of crisis. Architectural permissiveness fertilizes fashion which tends to occupy the position of an unavoidable norm. It is up to us to know how to place ourselves in the narrow stretch of territory separating the functionalist's discourse of needs from the ritualist's discourse of desires.

Campus Autiosus

This is not an archaeological restoration, but rather an architecture project which is as current and normal as all my projects. It asks only to be regarded as such; it seeks no justification whatsoever in any link with a supposed architectural science of the ancients under the tutelage of archaeologists. In this case, the buildings are intended to accommodate a center of tourism at Trequenac in Brittany.

This project uses, in filtered form, the text of Pliny's letters, in the same way that all architectural projects refer to a program. Programs, furthermore, have their history as well as their drafters: a low-income housing unit has just as much of an ethnological origin as a vacation home, since it has slowly defined itself according to human use.

My interest in this project comes from the fact that for centuries Pliny's letters have been an exercise of interest to architects much in the same way that competitions of improvisations have been for organists. They have been a form of training and a personal test adapted to the profound nature of the architect's work and calling on his gifts of perspicacity, interpretation, and synthesis to translate an order given by word or text into a practical, measured, economical, and comfortable building.

Well before Butor and Robbe-Grillet, Pliny describes a concrete world made up of sequences, circuits, stopping-places, connections, and sensations. As a describer of space he feeds and challenges our architectural imagination; as a writer he succeeds in speaking of his house in universal terms.

His house, whether real or fictitious, is a dream space in the manner of Baudelaire's Parisian palace or Katherine Mansfield's miniscule facade. Like these, it has its arcades and wells. It is not a founding house like Solomon's Temple, nor is it a residence attached to another existence such as that of Tournier's Robinson (Robinson Crusoe), a potential "museum of the human" where fig leaves are arranged as slate. Rather it is a house of plenitude, of balance and stability.

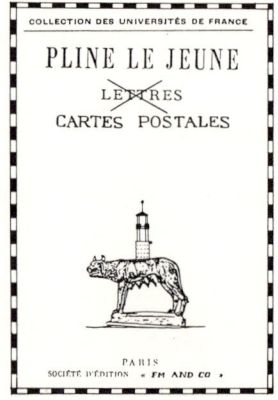

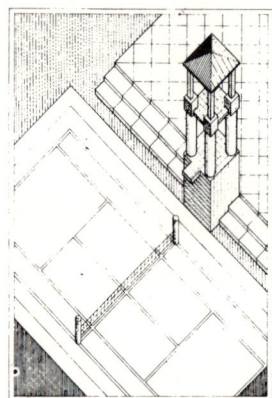

1. Campus Autiosus (project), 1982. Postcards. Clockwise from upper right: Porticus in D litterae simitudinem circumactae, quibus paruola, sed festiva area includitur *(a D-shaped colonade around a small but charming court).* Cubiculum *(room).* Est et alia turris hortum (videt) procul sphaeristerium *(there is also another tower which looks over the garden near the tennis court).*

"I would like there to be stable spaces, spaces which would be immobile, intangible, untouched and almost untouchable, unchangeable, firmly rooted; spaces which would be references, points of departure, sources."

This is not Pliny speaking in another letter, but rather Georges Perec (*Espèces d'espace*) for "such spaces do not exist, and it is because they do not exist that space becomes a question, that it ceases being self-evident, ceases being incorporated, ceases being appropriated. Space is a doubt: one must endlessly distinguish it, designate it ... it is never given; one must fight for it...."

The house of Pliny's letters, if only because it is entirely contained in a text, is like the catoptric room which Calvino imagines after the *Ars magnae lucis et umbrae in mundi* (1645) of Athanasius Kircher: the multiplication of its image, the house into which he can vanish at will.

Submitted to the test of the text, Pliny's house becomes a ruin. In this space of figuration its functional organization loses force and slips into metaphor. Pliny's description, beginning at the entry and conducted in conformance with topological succession, as in a guided tour, takes on the aspect

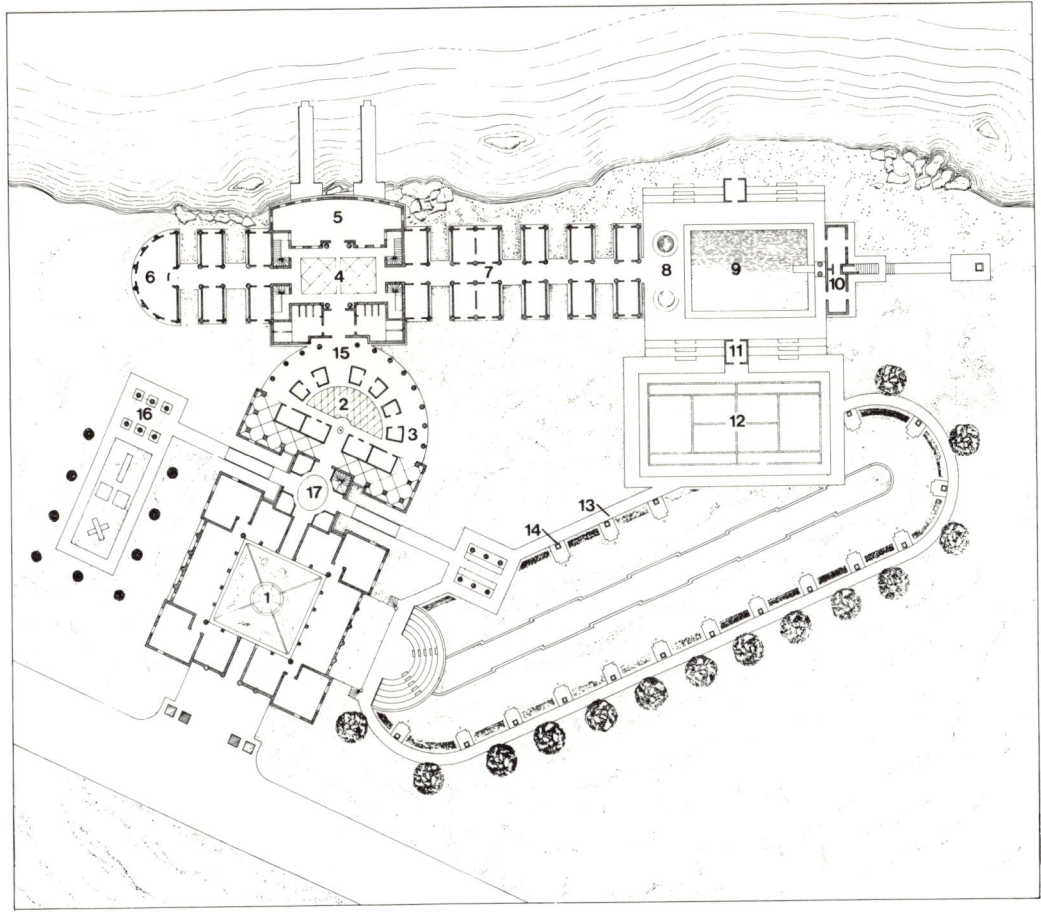

2. Campus Autiosus. *Ground plan.*

1. Atrium - *parking* 2. Porticus in D - *"D" shaped portico* 3. Parvula sed festiva area - *changing rooms* 4. Cavaedium hilare - *dance floor* 5. Triclinium satis pulchrum - *dining room* 6. Bibliotecha [cubiculum in hapsida curvatum] - *library/television room* 7. Cubiculi - *rooms* 8. Cella frigidaria [duo baptisteria] - *two cold plunge baths* 9. Calda piscina - *swimming pool* 10. Turris - *diving tower* 11. Alia turris - *another tower* 12. Sphaeristerium - *tennis curt* 13. Via tenera - *mini golf* 14. Pliny's models 15. Solarium 16. Gymnasium 17. "Amores mei" - *Pliny's pavilion*

of an initiatory journey. External time is abolished, replaced by an internal time, that of pleasure. Let us make no mistake, however, about the reversibility of his voyage. If the text undeniably contains an architectural program which is sufficient to produce new representations, it nonetheless draws as extensively as possible on literary privileges: little or no scale, dimensional relativity, complete fluidity of movement which has no thought of sputtering, grating, or grinding to a halt because of a bad joint.

All of the equipment which Pliny uses to draw us into his dream has not resisted with equal success the passing of time. Despite the fact that architecture relies on archetypes, certain of them are more durable and universal than others; certain ones remain unchanged while others are diverted or disappear. The atrium of the Roman house did not have the same fate as the cavaedium. It is precisely here that the architect and archaeologist differ. Whereas the former has the task of elaborating a current project, making allowance for wear and tear as well as modifications brought about by culture and techniques, the latter must tend to the restoration of an original whole.

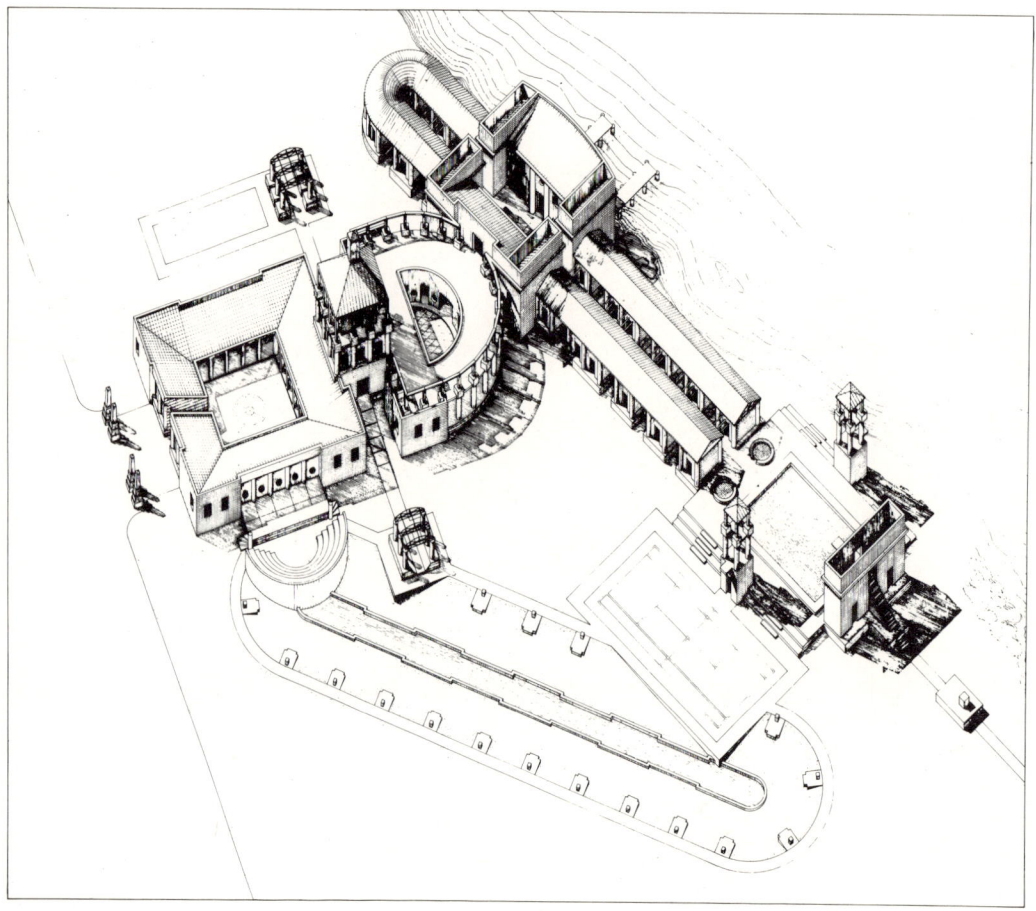

3. Campus Autiosus. *Axonometric view.*

Little does it matter whether the house of Pliny, the Ambassador of the Grand Turk, or Hamlet, did or did not exist in Rome, at the Court of Louis XIV, or in the Kingdom of Denmark. Now they exist everywhere, and it is indeed because of this that we are interested in them.

We found Pliny's house at Trequenac, a beach on the Breton Finistère coast. Today it is one of the many beach clubs which have sprung up as a result of paid holidays and tourism. We didn't look elsewhere, but it seems quite likely that the European coast is dotted with Pliny's houses.

Our research has shown that Pliny is a Breton country gentleman who inherited an elegant seaside estate. Having no income, he was forced through the years to sell part of the original seventy-five acres in order to subsist. On the few remaining acres he thought of building a grand residence which would serve to replace, little by little, the family residence in Quimper which was in a state of disrepair and highly expensive to maintain. Since he had always been interested in architecture (his father had left him an extensive library which he was able to enrich with purchases made during several visits to Italy after the war), he drew up fairly ambitious plans.

He was forced by lack of means to proceed gradually. The first stage was constructing a simple, three-storey villa in the form of a tower, which he christened "Amore mei" (words with an equally Latin and Breton ring) and where he used to spend several weeks each year. The second stage was planting a garden adjoining the villa, where he arranged sixteen pedestals intended for as many

4. Campus Autiosus. "Amore mei," Pliny's pavilion.

statues, but which he began crowning with models of the future house. At the end of the Sixties, experiencing yet another period of financial difficulty and seeing all hope of completing his work vanish, he accepted a proposal to transform his property into a resort, converting the existing villa into a house for the Resident Director and transforming — with slight modifications — the initial plans, as represented by the models in the garden, into the parking lot, lobby, coat room, baths, dance floor, bar & grill, pier, t.v. and reading room, bungalows, kiddy pool, pool with high-dive, playground, tennis courts and 18-hole miniature golf course.

Today, after a decade of the resort's success, Pliny has retired and accepted employment as Resident Director of the resort, where he lives once again in "Amore mei."

■   ■   ■

Montes' delineation of the Laurentian Villa of Pliny the Younger affirms and advances a long tradition begun in the late Renaissance by Scamozzi. To undertake this project is itself a ritual act: the cumulative attempts by so many individuals to interpret Pliny's evocative yet incomplete description in architectural terms has confirmed the rules of the rite and distinguished the initiates. Even the most personal reading is inscribed in a horizon of expectation, necessarily governed by the tradition of the letter's reception;

ineluctably, all readings participate in the collective validation of classical culture, and of the classical elements of architecture.

As Montes explains, Pliny's impressionistic narrative pulls us into a dream world—idealized, unchangeable, removed from time and space. Gallus, to whom the letter was addressed, was invited to enter that other realm of pleasure and relaxation embodied in Pliny's retreat in the Roman campagna, to escape the obligations of urban life—the conduct of negotiam—in his haven by the sea. Subsequent readers might effect that same transformation within the realm of the imagination, but the obligation of the "interpreter," as defined by the exercise of reconstruction, is to take the process one step further—to effect a double transformation.

The reading thus becomes an "initiatory journey" from which both reader and text emerge transformed. While contained by the written word, Pliny's world is complete. When subjected to the exacting demands of visual interpretation, however, it becomes a fragment, a "ruin," for Pliny offers no description of the villa's general configuration or "parti," nor does he elaborate the details of construction and ornament. The exercise of reconstruction cannot then be seen as an attempt to recreate the villa. An index of this is the remarkable range of expression within its autonomous history, accommodating the archaeologist, antiquarian and architect alike. For the latter it has served as a statement of personal style, a model for villa or palace construction, a test of compositional ability (or classical vocabulary,) and simply an intellectual game.

"Campus Autiosus," as Montes makes clear, is not an archeological project, but rather a free interpretation framing a contemporary program. This modification of the program sets Montes apart from his predecessors and suggests an architectural problem peculiar to the twentieth century: the preoccupation with the programmatic imperative. For Montes, this problem is embodied in the relation of a given type to the functions accommodated within it. While the lifestyle described by Pliny applied equally well to the villas and palaces of the seventeenth and eighteenth centuries, in our own time country retreats on such a scale most often take the form of hotel resorts. What the villa was to Pliny, the resort is to Montes, and presumably to us as well. Though the type remains constant, the program is modified from private to public service, thus reinforcing Montes' claim that "the ritualistic appropriation of a space will be a function of its degree of recognition."

Sequences

Bernard Tschumi

Bernard Tschumi divides sequences into three categories: transformational, spatial, and programmatic. He is concerned primarily with the latter two, and it is in their prescribed simultaneity that ritual lies. To explain the nature of sequences and how they interact, Tschumi draws on Russian Formalist theory. The placing of ritual in this context is particularly interesting given that Formalism, being essentially a reaction to Symbolism, dismissed all notions of transcendent significance, including those normally associated with ritual. Tschumi, however, is not addressing ritual's intrinsic or spiritual significance; he is exploring the means by which ritual illuminates the fundamental but mundane significance of the sequential spaces and events that are its framework.

Tschumi believes that sequences of spaces and sequences of events are independent systems. He is primarily interested in how the "narrative" causes the two systems to intertwine and define each other. As he describes in Manhattan Transcripts,[1] the aim is "to maintain these contradictions in a dynamic manner, in a new reciprocity and conflict," an approach which recalls the Formalist process of defamiliarization in which new relationships, initially appearing awkward, actually make overly familiar material perceivable again. Ritual, as understood by Tschumi, opposes this process: it is a pre-determined form of narrative with an exaggeratedly structured program which "orders events, movements, and spaces into a single progression that either combines or parallels divergent concerns." In the end, the dominance of this program overshadows the particular character of spaces and events that comprise it: "the route is more important than any one place along it."

Another level on which the association of ritual and narrative is illuminating, but which is only implicit in Tschumi's discussion, is the Formalist understanding of narrative as both story and plot. The story is here seen as "the action itself" while the plot is "how the reader learns of the action." The story, with its natural, chronological sequences — "they met, they parted, they met again, they married" — provides the excuse for the self-conscious and artful mastery of the telling. Defamiliarization in this context calls attention to itself as a device, as formal manipulation. Tschumi's Manhattan Transcripts is an excellent example of this aspect of defamiliarization and the dominance of plot. The initial stories of murder, pursuit, fall, and game-playing that describe the action are not the real motivation for the text. The logical, formal, and artistic manner of presentation — the plot — is. In this case, ritual takes on a different significance. It is not merely a narrative that joins the sequences of events and spaces in a pre-determined manner; it is rather a self-conscious display of formality that calls attention to its own contrived nature.

1. Manhattan Transcripts (New York: St. Martin's Press, 1982).

> *Although it does not defamiliarize the spaces and events that take place, it nevertheless does defamiliarize our normal behavior and calls attention to our own need to abstract what might otherwise be "natural" activities. This then might be the second and implicit meaning of Tschumi's statement that in ritual, "the route is more important than any one place on it": when the route refers to plot, to the unfolding of the artistic devices, everything is subordinate to the formal manner of presentation. Spaces and events are merely devices for ritual display.*

■　　　　　　　■　　　　　　　■

ANY ARCHITECTURAL SEQUENCE includes or implies at least three relations. First, an internal relation, which deals with the method of work; then two external relations, one dealing with the juxtaposition of actual spaces, the other with program (occurrences or events). The first relation, or *transformational* sequence, can also be described as a device, a procedure. The second *spatial* sequence is constant throughout history; its typological precedents abound and its morphological variations are endless. Social and symbolic connotations characterize the third relation; we shall call it for now the *programmatic* sequence.

●　　　　　　　●　　　　　　　●

One customary mode of architectural drawing already implies a transformational sequence. Successive layers of transparent tracing paper are laid one upon another, each with its respective variations, around a basic theme or *parti*. Each subsequent reworking leads to or refines the organizing principle. The process is generally based on intuition, precedents, and habit.

●　　　　　　　●　　　　　　　●

This sequence can also be based on a precise, rational set of transformational rules and discrete architectural elements. The sequential transformation then becomes its own theoretical object, insofar as the process becomes the result, while the sum of transformations counts at least as much as the outcome of the final transformation.

●　　　　　　　●　　　　　　　●

Transformational sequences tend to rely on the use of *devices*, or rules of transformation, such as compression, rotation, insertion, and transference. They can also display particular sets of variations, multiplications, fusions, repetitions, inversions, substitutions, metamorphoses, anamorphoses, dissolutions. These devices can be applied to the transformation of spaces as well as programs.

●　　　　　　　●　　　　　　　●

There are closed sequences of transformation as well as open ones. Closed sequences have a predictable end because the chosen rules ultimately imply the exhaustion of a process, its circularity or its repetition. The open ones are sequences without closures, where new elements of transformation can be added at will according to other criteria, such as concurrent or juxtaposed sequences of another order — say, a narrative or programmatic structure, juxtaposed to the formal transformational structure.

●　　　　　　　●　　　　　　　●

Roland Barthes, in the "Structural Analysis of Narratives," defining a sequence: "A logical succession of nuclei bound together by a relation of solidarity: the sequence opens when one of its terms has no solitary antecedent and closes when another of its terms has no consequences."[1]

---

1. Roland Barthes, "Structural Analysis of Narratives," in *Image-Music-Text* (London: Fontana, 1977).

Sequences of space, *configurations-en-suite*, *enfilades*, spaces aligned along a common axis — all are specific architectural organizations, from Egyptian temples through the churches of the quattrocento to the present. All have emphasized a planned path with fixed halting points, a family of spatial points linked by continuous movement.

• • •

Sequences of transformation and sequences of spaces rarely intersect, as if architects carefully distinguished means of inception from end product through a sort of discreet restraint that does not reveal the maker's artifices in the final result, and favors the certainty of a well-defined axis over the passionate uncertainties of thought.

• • •

If spatial sequences can be obviously manifest differences of geometrical *form* (the Villa Adriana), they can also differ by *dimension* alone, while maintaining similar geometrical form (the Ducal Palace at Urbino). They can even steadily increase in complexity, be constructed, step by step — or deconstructed — according to any rule or device.

• • •

Spatial transformations can be included within the time sequence — for example, through continuous scenery such as Kiesler's 1923 space stage set for O'Neill's *Emperor Jones*.

• • •

Luigi Moretti, writing on Palladio's Palazzo Thiene in Vicenza: spatial sequences and abstract relationships: "In their pure dimensions, the sequences can be equated graphically as circles whose radii are proportional to the sphere corresponding in volume to each surrounding and whose center coincides with the center of gravity of the volume itself and is marked at the distance which in proportion this center has from the base plane of the spaces, that is from the level of the plinth."[2]

• • •

Spatial sequences can also display mixed formal devices. Moretti, again, writing on Palladio's Villa Rotunda: "in the density of light, the volumes go from portico to hall in the order of maximum to minimum, while in dimensions, the order is medium, least, greatest."

• • •

Yet architecture is inhabited: sequences of events, use, activities, incidents are always superimposed on those fixed spatial sequences. These are the programmatic sequences that suggest secret maps and impossible fictions, rambling collections of events all strung along a collection of spaces, frame after frame, room after room, episode after episode.

• • •

Is there ever a causal link between a formal system of spaces and a system of events? Rimbaud wondered whether vowels possessed colors, whether the letter "a" was red or blue. Similarly, do cylindrical spaces go with religion and rectangular ones with industry? Is there ever a homology between systems, a one-to-one relationship between space and event, between "form" and "function," two systems that evoke and attract one another?

• • •

Adding events to the autonomous spatial sequence is a form of *motivation*, in the sense the Russian Formalists gave to motivation, ie., whereby the "procedure" and its devices are the raison d'être

---

2. Luigi Moretti, "Structures and Sequences of Space," *Oppositions*, 4, New York, 1974.

of literature, and "content" is a simple *a posteriori* justification of form.

• • •

Alternately, is adding space to the autonomous sequence of events a reverse form of motivation? Or is it merely an extended form of *programmation*? Any predetermined sequence of events can always be turned into a program.

• • •

Program: "a descriptive notice, issued beforehand, of any formal series of proceedings, as a festive celebration, a course of study, etc.(...), a list of the items or 'numbers' of a concert, etc., in the order of performance; hence the items themselves collectively, the performance as a whole ...."[3]

• • •

Programs fall into three categories: those which are indifferent to the spatial sequence, those which reinforce it, and those which work obliquely or against it.

• • •

Indifference: sequences of events and sequences of spaces can be largely independent of one another — say, assortments of exotic stalls among the regular columniation of the 1851 Crystal Palace. One then observes a strategy of indifference, in which formal considerations do not depend on utilitarian ones. (The battalion marches on the fields.)

• • •

Reciprocity: Sequences of spaces and sequences of events can, of course, become totally interdependent and fully condition each other's existence — say *"Machines à habiter,"* ideal Werkbund kitchens, space age vessels where each action, each movement is designed, *programmed*. One then observes a strategy of reciprocity in which each sequence actually reinforces the other — the sort of architectural tautology favored by functionalist doctrines (The skater skates on the skating rink.)

• • •

Conflict: sequences of events and spaces occasionally clash and contradict each other. One then observes a strategy of conflict, in which each sequence constantly transgresses the other's internal logic. (The battalion skates on the tightrope.)

• • •

In themselves, spatial sequences are independent of what happens in them. (Yesterday I cooked in the bathroom and slept in the kitchen.) They may coincide for a shorter or longer period. As sequences of events do not depend on spatial sequences(and vice-versa), both can form independent systems, with their own implicit schemes of parts.

• • •

Spatial sequences are generally structural; that is, they can be viewed or experienced independently of the meaning they may occasionally evoke. Programmatic sequences are generally inferential; conclusions or inferences can be drawn from the events or the *"decor"* that provide the sequence's connotative aspects. Such opposition is, of course, quite artificial; these distinctions do not exist separately.

• • •

Events "take place." And again. And again.

---

3. *Oxford English Dictionary.*

The linearity of sequences orders events, movements, spaces into a single progression that either combines or parallels divergent concerns. It provides "security" and at least one overriding rule against architectural fears.

• • •

Not all architecture is linear, nor is it all made of spatial additions, of detachable parts and clearly-defined entities. Circular buildings, grid cities, *as well as* accumulations of fragmentary perspectives and cities without beginnings or ends, produce scrambled structures where meaning is derived from the order of experience rather than the order of composition.

• • •

Mies van der Rohe's Barcelona Pavilion: dissociation, fragmentation of unitary space. There is one sequence of direct vision, and one for the experience of the body where a set of indeterminate and equivocal articulations suggests a multiplicity of readings. Its spatial sequence is nevertheless organized around a *thematic* structure, a series of variations around a limited number of elements which play the role of the fundamental theme — the *paradigm*.

• • •

By order of experience, one speaks of time, of chronology, of repetition. But some architects are suspicious of time and would wish their buildings to be read at a glance, like billboards.

• • •

Sequences have emotional value. Moretti, again, discussing St. Peter's: "pressure (access doors), limited liberation (atrium), opposition (atrium walls), very short pressure (basilica doors), total liberation (transversal of nave), final contemplation (space of central system)."

• • •

Like snapshots at key moments in the making of architecture whether in the procedure or real space). Like a series of frozen frames.

• • •

If the spatial sequence inevitably implies the movement of an observer, then such movement can be objectively mapped and formalized — sequentially. Movement notation: an extension from the drawn conventions of choreography, it attempts to eliminate the preconceived meanings given to particular actions in order to concentrate on their spatial effects: the movement of bodies in space (dancers, footballers, acrobats).

• • •

For Lautréamont, to move is never to go from one place to the next, but always to execute some figure, to assume a certain body rhythm. "He is running away ... he is running away." Or "the mad woman who passes by, dancing."

• • •

S	E	M
Space	Event	Movement

• • •

The final meaning of any sequence is dependent on the relation space/event/movement. By extension, the meaning of any architectural situation depends on the relation S E M. The composite sequence SEM breaks the linearity of the elementary sequence, whether S, E, or M.

But architectural sequences do not mean only the reality of actual buildings, or the symbolic reality of their fictions. An implied narrative is always there, whether of method, use or form. It combines the presentation of an event (or chain of events) with its progressive spatial interpretation (which of course alters it). Such, for instance, are *rituals* and their routes of initiation where, from point of entry to point of arrival, successive challenges await the new candidate. Here, the order of the sequence is intrinsic. The route is more important than any one place along it.

•   •   •

A ritual implies a near-frozen relationship between space and event. It institutes a new order against the disorder it aims to avoid. When it becomes necessary to mediate the tension between events and spaces and fix it by custom, then no single fragment must escape attention. Nothing strange or unexpected must happen. Control must be absolute.

•   •   •

Partial control is exercized through the use of the frame. Each frame, each part of a sequence qualifies, reinforces, or alters the parts that precede and follow it. The associations so formed allow for a plurality of interpretations rather than a singular fact. Each part is thus both complete and incomplete. And each part is a statement against indeterminacy; indeterminacy is always present in the sequence, irrespective of its methodological, spatial, or narrative nature.

•   •   •

Gap / closure / gap / closure / gap / closure / gap / closure
•   •   •

Is there such a thing as an architectural narrative? A narrative not only presupposes a sequence, but also a language. As we all know, the "language" of architecture, the architecture "that speaks," is a controversial matter. Another question: If such architectural narrative corresponds to the narrative of literature, would space intersect with signs to give us a *discourse*?

•   •   •

The ability to translate narrative from one medium to another — to translate *Don Juan* into a play, an opera, a ballet, a film or comic strip — suggests architectural equivalences, equivalences that are not made by analogy to an architectural strip of course, but through carefully observed parallels. Terragni's *Danteum* does not tell us a story of events, but reminds us about the temporality of a search — the impossibility of being at several places at the same time — a special type of allegory where in every element initially corresponds to a physical reality.

•   •   •

The use of a plot may suggest the sense of an ending, an end to the overall organization. It superimposes a conclusion to the open-endedness of the transformational (or methodological) sequence. Whenever a program or "plot" (the single-family house, or "Cinderella") is well-known (as are most architectural programs), only the "retelling" counts: the "telling" has been done enough.

•   •   •

Sequence (after J.L. Godard): "Surely you agree, Mr. Architect, that buildings should have a base, a middle and a top?" "Yes, but not necessarily in that order."
•   •   •

In literature and in the cinema, sequences can be manipulated by such devices as flashbacks, crosscuttings, close-ups and dissolves. Are the inclusions of baroque details in the modern architectural sequence ... temporary flashbacks?

Forms of composition: collage sequences (collisions) or montage sequences (progressions).

• • •

Contracted sequences fragment individual spaces and actions into discrete segments. In this manner, we might see the beginning of a use in a space followed immediately by the beginning of another in a further space. Contracted sequences have occasionally reduced architecture's three dimensions into a single one (Le Corbusier's Villa Stein at Garches). The *expanded* sequence makes a solid of the gap between spaces. The gap thus becomes a space of its own, a corridor, threshold or doorstep — a proper symbol inserted between each event (John Hejduk's Wall House). Combinations of expanded and contracted sequences can form special series, either coordinated or rhythmical.

• • •

All sequences are cumulative. Their "frames" derive significance from juxtaposition. They establish memory — of the preceding frame, of the course of events. To experience and to follow an architectural sequence is to reflect upon events in order to place them into successive wholes. The simplest sequence is always more than a *configuration-en-suite*, even if there is no need to specify the nature of each episode.

• • •

Frame: the moments of the sequence. Examining architecture "frame by frame," as through a film-editing machine.

• • •

Frames are both the *framing device* — conforming, regular, solid — and the *framed material* — questioning, distorting, and displacing. Occasionally the framing device can itself become the object of distortions and the framed material be conformist and orderly.

• • •

The frame permits the extreme formal manipulations of the sequence, for the content of congenial frames can be mixed, superimposed, dissolved, or cut up, giving endless possibilities to the narrative sequence. At the limit, these material manipulations can be classified according to formal strategies such as repetition, disjunction, distortion, dissolution, or insertion. For example, devices such as the insertion of additional elements within the sequence can change the meaning of the sequence as well as its impact on the experiencing subject, as in the well-known Kuleshov experiment, where the same shot of the actor's impassive face is introduced in a variety of situations, and the audience reads different expressions in each successive juxtaposition.

• • •

Parameters that remain constant and passive for the duration of the sequence can be added and transferred, as when a given spatial configuration (the "circle") repeatedly passes from frame to frame, from room to room: a *displacement*.

• • •

All transformational devices (repetition, distortion, etc.) can apply equally and independently to spaces, events, or movements. Thus we can have a repetitive sequence of spaces (the successive courtyards of a Berlin block) coupled with an additive sequence of events (dancing in the first court, fighting in the second, skating in the third).

• • •

Alternatively, of course, architectural sequences can also be made strategically disjunctive (the pole-vaulter in the catacombs).

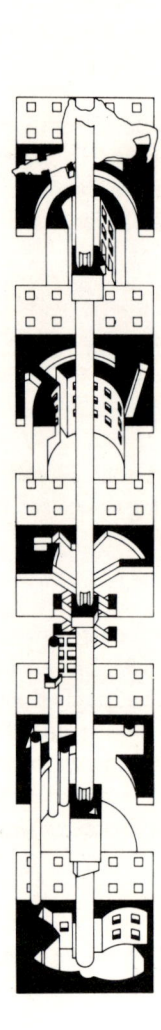
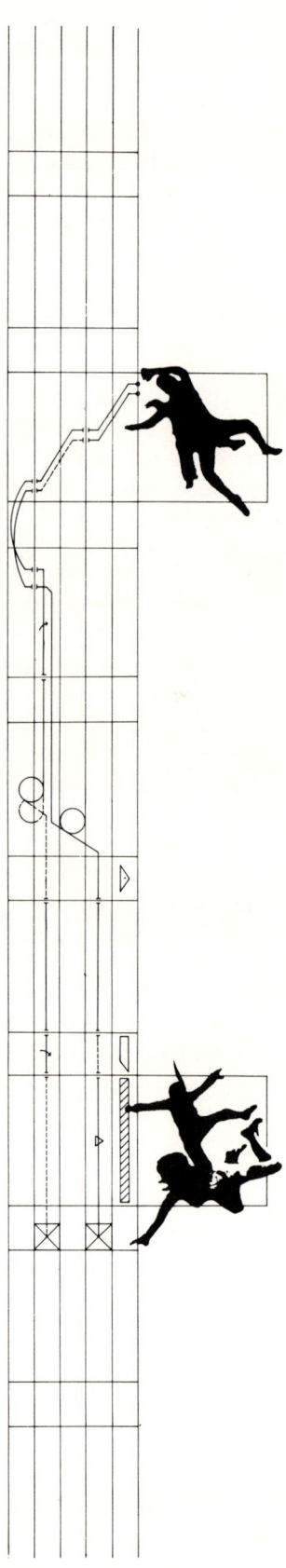

"The Fall" (Excerpts from the Manhattan Transcripts,1981) *illustrates the drawn and photographed notation of a murder. The formula plot of the murder — the lone figure stalking its victim, the murder, the hunt, the search for clues building up to the murderer's capture — is juxtaposed with an architecture inextricably linked to the extreme actions it witnesses. A special mode of notation underlines the deadly game of hide and seek between the suspect and the ever-changing architectural events. Photographs direct the action, plans reveal the alternatively cruel and loving architectural manifestations, diagrams indicate the movements of the main protagonists. There, attitudes, plans, notations, movements are indissolubly linked. Only together do they define the architectural space of "The Tower" (The Fall).*

Hellenic Studies Center

Stephen Corelli

THIS PROJECT, an Hellenic Studies Center added to an existing art museum in Princeton, can be seen on one level to be a resolution of a range of programmatic requirements, including the separation of exhibitions from academic studies, and a response to a constrained but beautiful site. On another level, however, the architectural organization can be understood as the representation of an extremely significant Hellenic myth which describes the cycle of the seasons

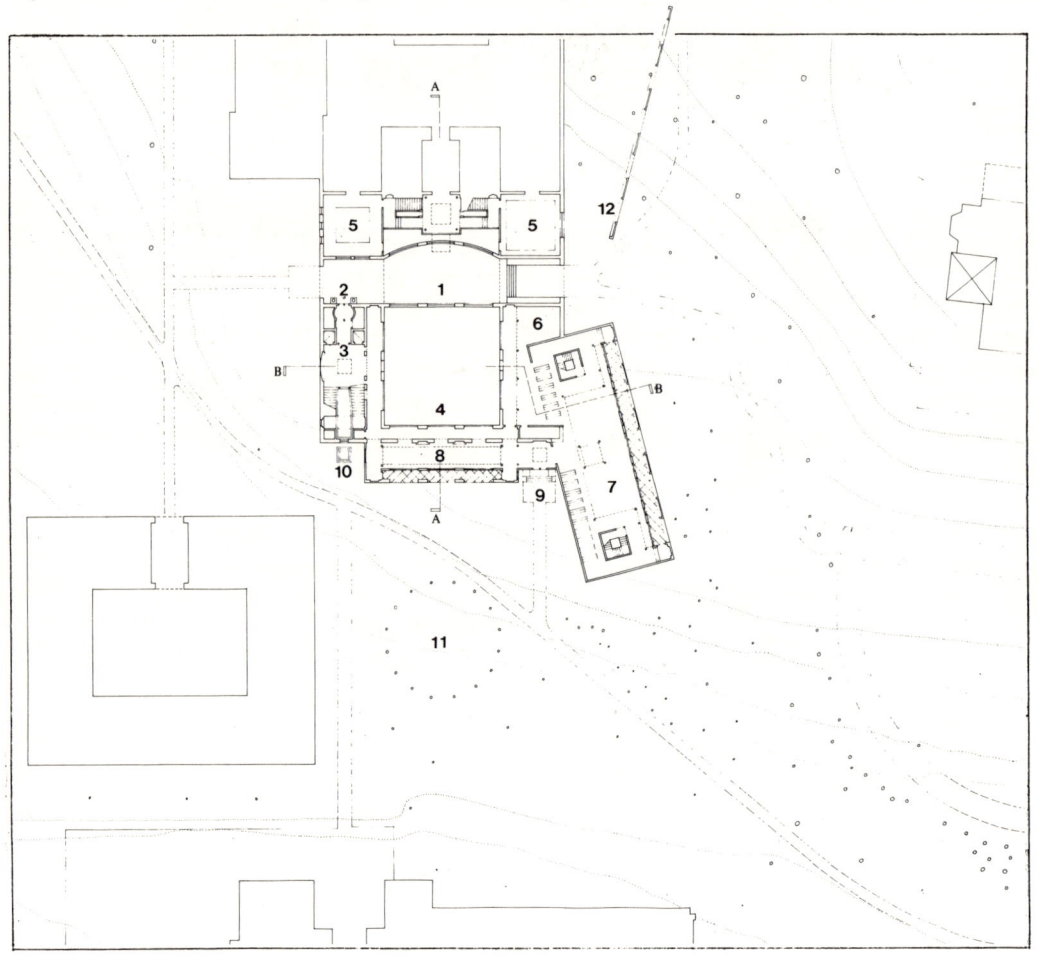

1. Hellenic Studies Center (project), 1980. Ground plan.

1. Passage 2. Entrance 3. Lobby 4. Permanent exhibition below 5. Temporary exhibition 6. Catalogue and workroom 7. Library 8. Student lounge 9. Garden entrance 10. Statue of Demeter 11. Outdoor exhibition 12. Lattice screen

and explains the secrets of planting and harvesting. The myth is found in the Homeric hymn to Demeter and is the basis of the Eleusinian Mysteries, a ritual of initiation into the cult of Demeter which culminated in a celebration within an enclosed temple, the telesterion. Square in plan, this building was the only interior temple-type in Greek architecture. Sacred objects were shown there and "secret" knowledge imparted to initiates.

The Hellenic studies center is organized about a central, interior exhibition space. This space is a transformation of the telesterion; its elevations recall the unusual irregular bay structure of the original plan, and maintain its perimeter dimensions. The objects displayed within it hold "secrets" analogous to those contained in the original telesterion: they are fragmentary clues to the knowledge of the past. This element of secrecy is enforced by the fact that access to the exhibition space and its artifacts is only possible from the existing art museum.

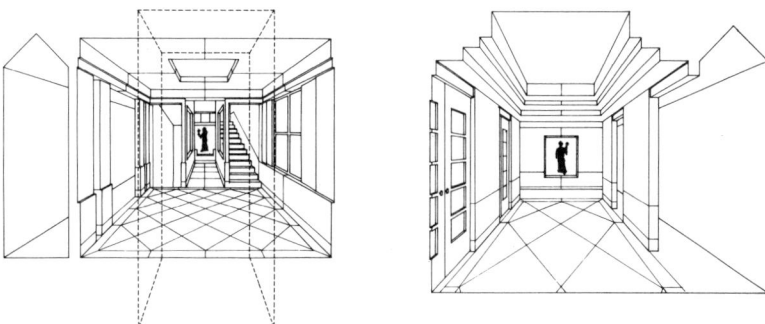

2. *Views through lobby and garden room.*

On the axis of the entry to the building is a window which frames a profile view of the statue of Demeter: the frontal view can only be obtained by penetrating to the garden room which is held between the exhibition space (the reconstituted telesterion) and an outdoor exhibition area defined by a ring of trees. This garden, as a literal description of planting, growth, and decay, represents in an immediate way the cycle of the seasons evoked in the myth of Demeter. Like the building as a whole, it situates itself between and has windows onto both metaphorical and literal texts.

With this particular strategy I have attempted to "bridge the gap" between abstraction and representation, while avoiding some of the current preoccupations with style.

3. *Hellenic Studies Center. Section B-B.*

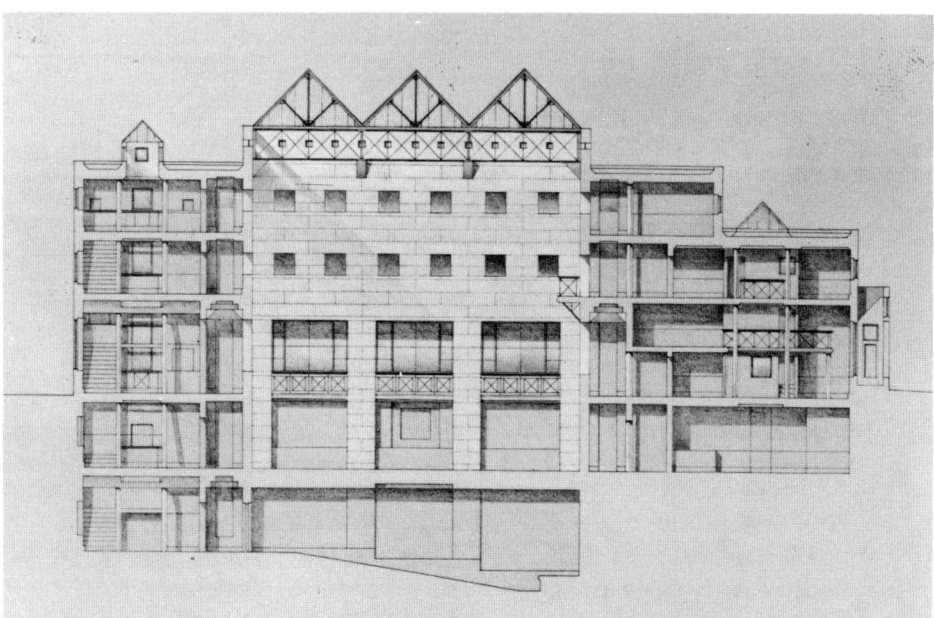

4. Hellenic Studies Center. South elevation.

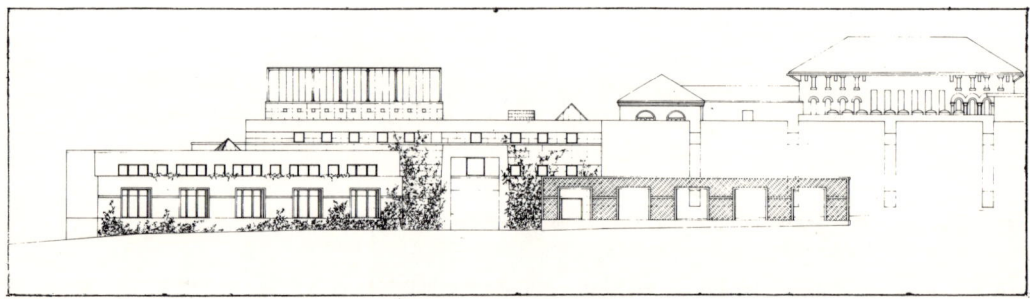

5. Hellenic Studies Center. East elevation.

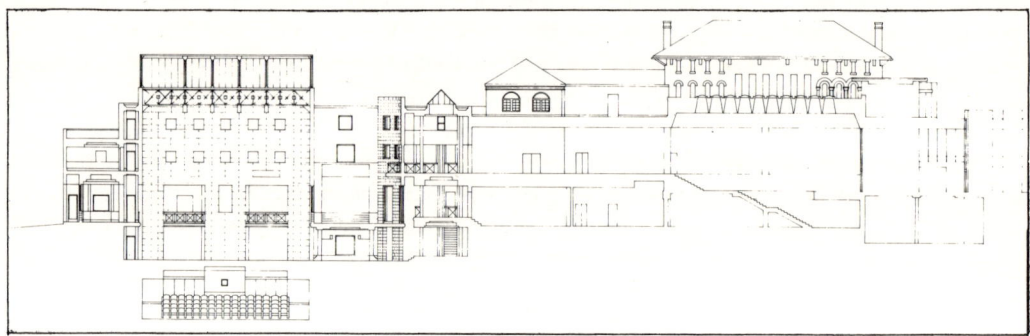

6. Hellenic Studies Center. Section A-A.

■   ■   ■

While on one level this project may be read as a straightforward response to program and site, Corelli asserts that its generation and final significance lie in its reference to the ancient Greek ritual of the Eleusinian Mysteries, and to that ritual's architectural setting — the telesterion. This association implies a judgement about the nature of the program: as our limited understanding of the Eleusinian Mysteries suggests, the study of history must necessarily conform to fragmentary evidence. Furthermore, just as we cannot fully re-create the past, we cannot re-enact ancient rituals.

The central court containing the display of artifacts embodies this interpretation in an immediate way by its physical inaccessibility from the surrounding rooms. As an abstracted representation of the telesterion, it also suggests metaphorically that knowledge can only be possessed by the "initiate" who knows the "clues," for the meaning of the building only unfolds in direct relation to the pursuit of knowledge within. In this context, learning may be seen as an ordeal analogous to that of the ancient neophyte: only with solemn, painstaking research may the "secrets" of Hellenic culture be penetrated.

The Mysteries are further elaborated in the literal representation of their subject: the workings of nature. But this "literal" representation should still be understood as metaphor, or more exactly as a form of metonymy; the ring of trees is nature taken out of its "natural" context to symbolize the cycle of the seasons. Thus, what used to be discovered ritually is merely represented symbolically.

Interestingly, the hermeneutical process is here the reverse of the ancient myth: originally, the telesterion was the actual embodiment of the rituals performed within and required no interpretation as such, while the "secrets" of nature were never overtly given and required interpretation through the enactment of the rites. In Corelli's project, the building is not what it appears to be, but is instead a metaphor for something that only students of Hellenic studies will understand, while "nature" is physically represented as nature to initiate and non-initiate alike.

A third level of metaphorical meaning arises in the use of the statue of Demeter. While it is the most symbolically literal clue to the significance of the square-planned central room, its initial presentation in profile, and hence the difficulty of identifying it immediately, demands that the user/viewer move through the entirety of the building in search of the frontal view. On the way, he or she would be exposed to other "hints" yielding a fuller understanding of the building: it is a hermeneutic treasure hunt that has its own prescribed ritual route.

The Public Bath

Symbol and myth have become one of the dominant concerns in architecture, and this is appropriate to an art which is entering what appears to be a strongly romantic period. Both Frank Moya's project for the Baños de Coamo and George Gintole's Padua Bath involve designs which are only understandable through ritual. For Moya, who draws on local legends about the search for the Fountain of Youth, and Gintole, who finds in the nearby Padua Botanic Garden and Prato della Valle a reference to the Genesis story, the essence of architecture is the mediation between the present part and the absent whole. Symbol bridges reality and the void. Put another way, what characterizes this kind of architecture is precisely that which separates the meontic from the mimetic. The mimetic is representational, it cuts across different periods, demonstrating the continuity of perception and thereby stripping away the feeling of solitude and alienation. In contrast, the meontic is an imitation of what is not there; offering a vision of wholeness, its purpose is therapeutic. As Thomas McFarland has written, "the mimetic arrests the loss of being, the meontic restores the loss of being."[1] These baths, as ritual architecture, are meontic; they try to answer the yearning for wholeness.

Modern society has de-ritualized the bath. We live amongst community pools and health spas, Nautilus centers and country clubs. Giedion attributes this twentieth century destruction of the public bath's symbolic value to mechanization and the "democratization of comfort."[2] However, some private baths retain the feeling of a discrete restorative experience. There is, for example, the familiar image of Le Corbusier's bathroom "landscape" at Poissy. The man-made metaphors of nature — the bath as a natural pool, the chaise lounge a natural silhouette — encourage contemplation and heighten the meaning of everyday actions. But Moya and Gintole are concerned with reinstating the public bath, not transferring its ancient meaning to a private ceremony.

The choice to undertake a public bath is at once an indictment of our loss of ritual and a reassertion of the necessity for a discourse of the imagination in architecture. The challenge of tradition is taken seriously in both projects, and although it is true that each forms a language game unto itself, with its own rules and its own definitions and its own hierarchies of significance, they are also both part of the romantic quest for a common language, in which the meaning of art is located in its transformation into structure.

1. Thomas McFarland, Romanticism and the Forms of Ruin: Wordsworth, Coleridge, and the Modalities of Fragmentation (Princeton: Princeton University Press, 1981), p.417.
2. Siegfried Giedion, Mechanization Takes Command: A Contribution to Anonymous History (New York: Oxford University Press, 1948), p.661.

The Bath as a Reiteration of the Cosmogonic Act

George Gintole

THIS THESIS PROJECT emphasizes two basic ideas: physical contextualism and thematic contextualism. The site of the intervention is Padua, Italy, adjacent to the Prato della Valle. The program consists of a public bathhouse, housing, and retail shops.

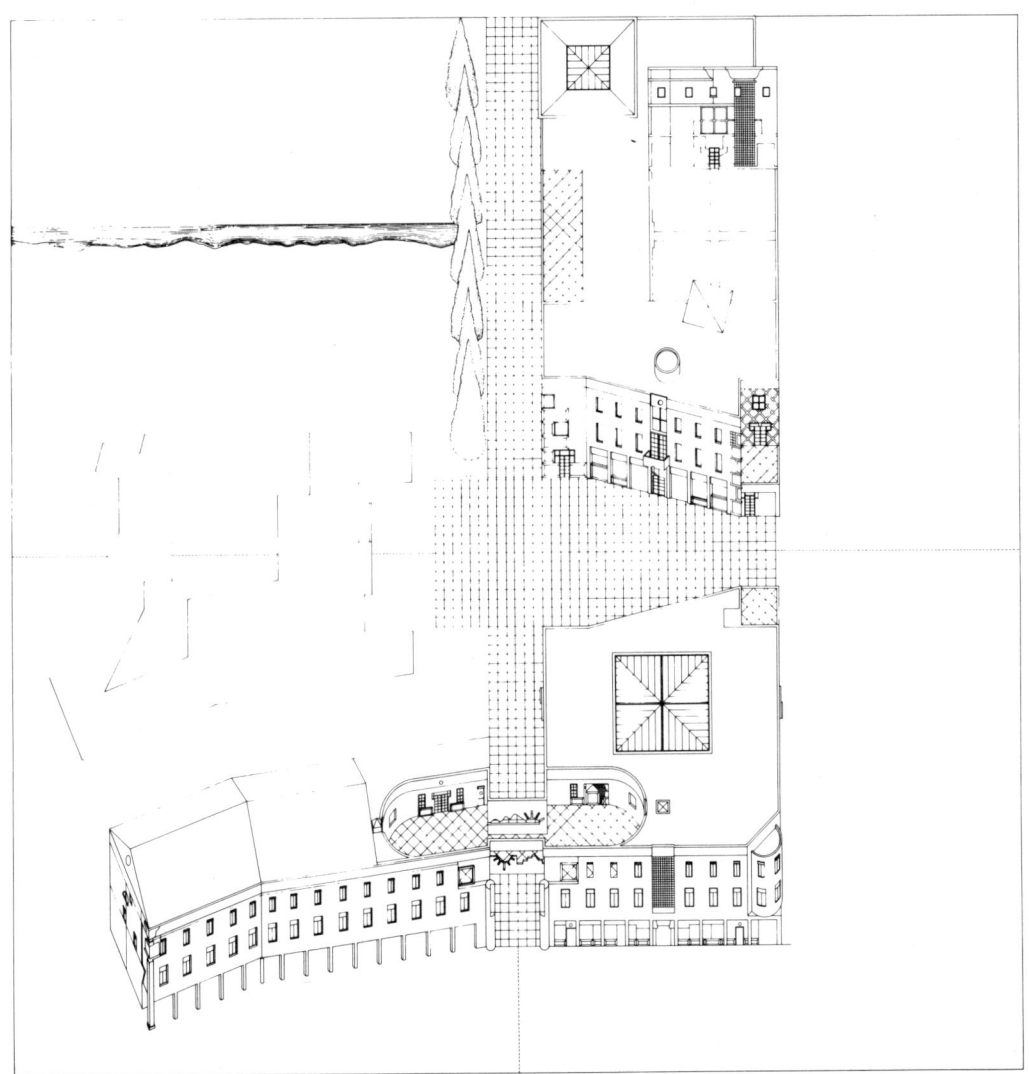

1. Public Bath (Master's thesis), Axonometric view.

The elliptical Prato della Valle, redesigned in 1775 by Domenico Cerato, was developed as a "green," in appearance somewhere between a square and a park. The popularity of romantic primitivism and the Rousseauvian return to nature explains the introduction of large planted areas and trees into the townscape in the late eighteenth century.[1] The classical form of the Prato depends for its inspiration on the ambitious endeavors at Caserta and Stupinigi; however, its quadripartite form is undoubtedly drawn from the Botanic Garden in its immediate vicinity. The Botanic Garden, founded in 1545, is the oldest of its kind in Europe. Represented as a perfect circle divided into four parts with a fence circumscribing its boundary, the garden is the paradigmatic image of the Garden of Eden.

Throughout the Middle Ages it was believed that the Garden of Eden had not been eradicated by the Flood. Relying on the Genesis account, in which trees bore fruit continuously in a perpetual spring, explorers searched for lands that had equal diurnal and nocturnal time.[2] Although the Spanish and Portuguese geographical missions failed to unearth the Garden's existence, the plants they

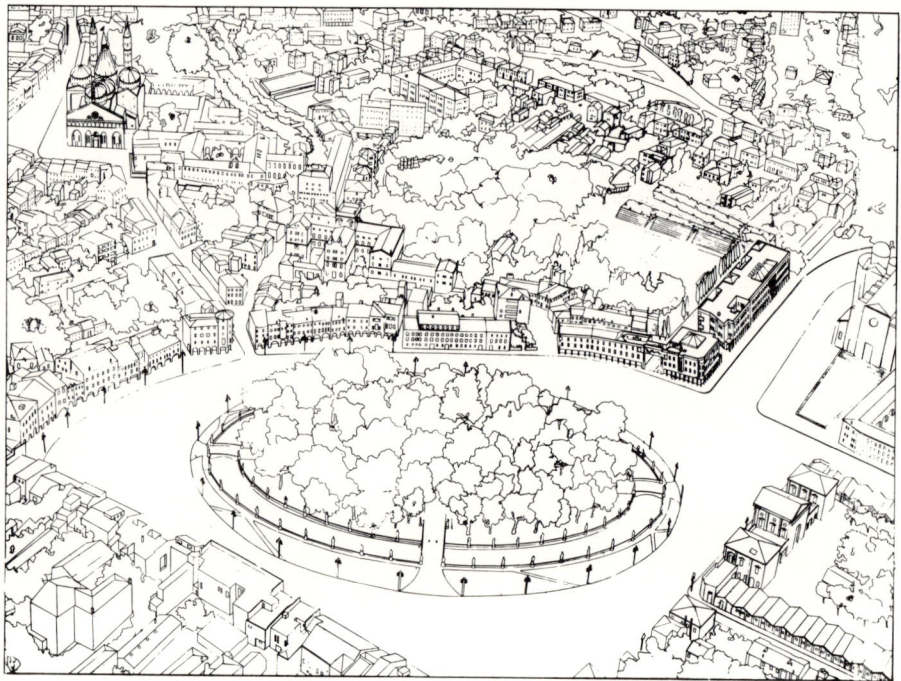

2. Public Bath. Aerial view of context.

brought to the European continent created a new interest — that of capturing the "world in a chamber" (in the words of an early curator of Padua's Botanic Garden).[3] Since all plants were believed to possess curative properties, the extensive collections of the botanic garden assumed a sort of magico-religious importance.[4] The Botanic Garden founded in Padua therefore became an encyclopedic chamber, whose highly ordered design was an abstraction of the Garden of Eden, and not an actual representation or likeness.[5]

A bathhouse seemed to be the logical accompaniment to this garden. Water enables our return to a state of naked innocence and is an integral part of the regenerative cosmogonic act, representing

1. P. Zucker, *Town and Square: From the Agora to the Village Green* (Cambridge: MIT, 1970), pp.160-162.
2. See J. Prest, *The Garden of Eden: The Botanic Garden and the Re-Creation of Paradise* (New Haven: Yale, 1981).
3. G. Porro, *L'Horto dei semplici di Padora* (1591), cited by J. Prest, p. 44.
4. J. B. Jackson, *The Neccessity for Ruins* (Amherst: University of Massachusetts, 1980), p. 40.
5. J. Prest, op. cit., p. 42.

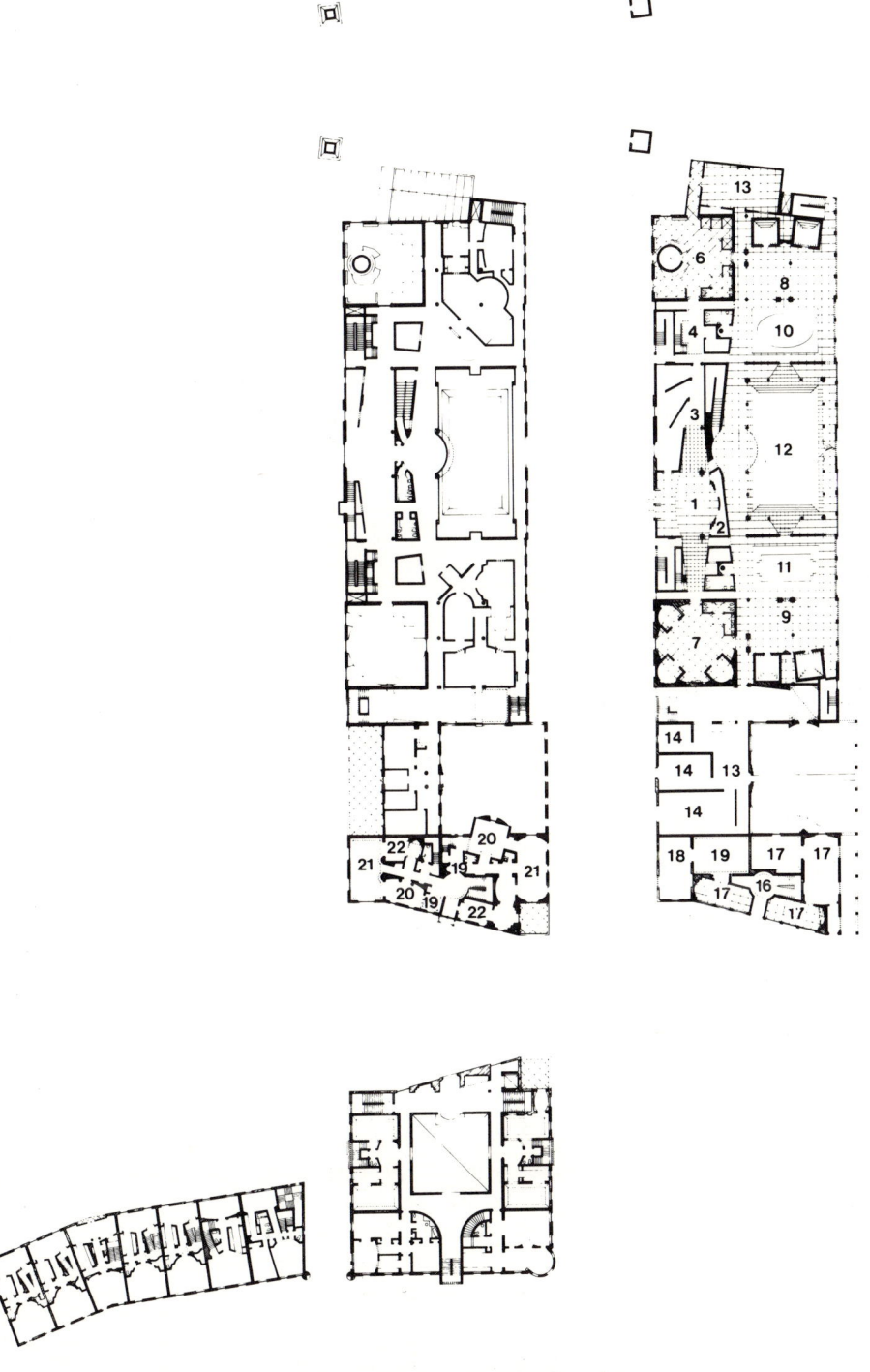

3. Public Bath. Second and first floor plans.

1. Entry 2. Registration 3. Barber 4. Men's towels 5. Women's towels 6. Men's divesting hall 7. Women's divesting hall 8. Men's air bath 9. Women's air bath 10. Men's cold water plunge 11. Women's cold water plunge 12. Common pool 13. Men's weight room 14. Offices 15. Courtyard 16. Entry to duplex units above 17. Retail 18. Garden obelisks 19. Entry foyer 20. Living 21. Dining 22. Kitchen 23. Bathroom

a return to preformal conditions. In Genesis, water is the primal substance: "Let there be a firmament in the midst of the waters." In many religions, emersion has come to symbolize a repetition of the act of creation, endowing water with the power of regeneration. As Mircea Eliade has said, water "precedes all form and upholds all creation,"[6] and, as in baptism, water regenerates, restores, purifies.

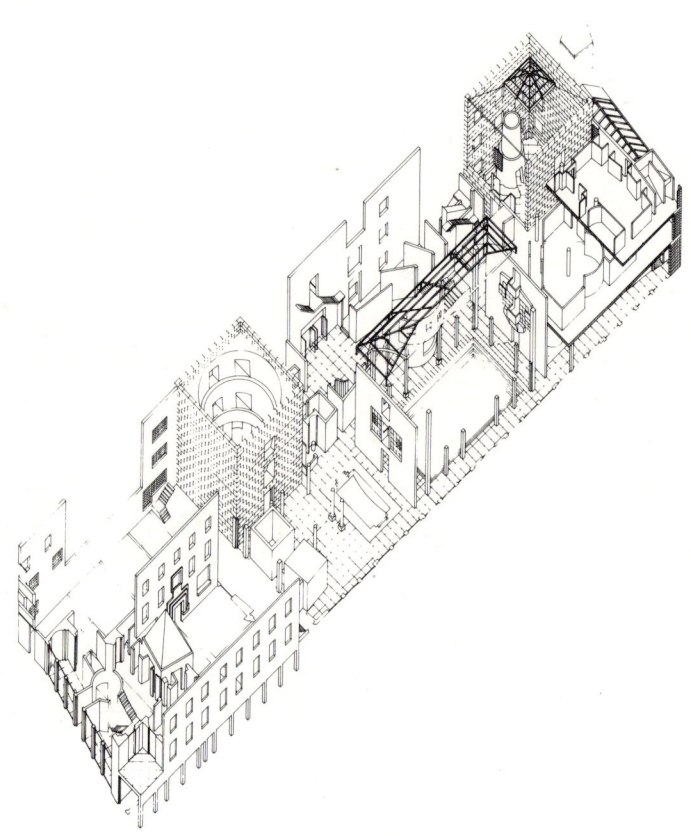

4. Public Bath. Axonometric view.

An examination of the bath's morphological evolution as a place for social intercourse sets up the polar notions of the bath as either a context for total regeneration, in both its mythical and physical constructs, or merely a private facility for external ablution.[7] This project explores both: in the housing complex, the bath is designed after the late Nineteenth Century English model — as a "room" where the sanitary fixtures are disposed as furniture at dignified distances, in contrast to the American conception of the bathroom as an expedient cell whose breadth is determined by the length of the tub.

The bath as public institution undergoes transformations from the Greek technified *gymnasia* to the Roman *thermae*, whose archetype is found in the Islamic *hammam*.[8] The bathhouse for Padua

---

6. M. Eliade, *Images and Symbols*, tr. P. Mairet (New York: NAL, 1974), p. 188.
7. See S. Gideon, *Mechanization Takes Command*, (New York: Norton, 1969), pp. 628-634.
8. Ibid.

represents a confluence of the spatial and programmatic conditions present in the Greco-Roman model and the Oriental or Islamic model. The ritual of entry, initiation, divestiture, anointment, immersion, and emersion are orchestrated with respect to the allegory of Eden. Conceptually, the bathhouse may be divided in half longitudinally into a dry area on the north side and a wet area on the south side. The entry is deliberately placed west of center such that the distance traveled by men from the point of entry to the divesting hall is slightly longer than the distance women must travel — thus acknowleging the Biblical account of Adam's existence on earth prior to Eve's. The function that absorbs the extra distance is the barber's quarters, reminding us that the only difference between the genders is that typically men are more hirsute than women. Entering the divesting hall, a twilight-lit cubic volume reminiscent of the *maslaks* or rest halls of the Eastern *hammam*, one undresses under a perforated domed ceiling representing the stars in the celestial *soffit*. Exiting the divesting hall one is anointed at the paired columns bearing a mitered arch, whose configuration is a kind of flattened *aedicula*. This threshold then is a way of signifying anointment as the "stain" of the burden after the expulsion from the Garden of Eden. (The ancient Romans were anointed after exercising and prior to the bathing ritual.)[9] In the bathhouse the dry area is representative of mankind's prelapsarian state, and the wet area, of his antediluvian state of existence: the common pool is symbolic of the Deluge. The placement of the pool in the geometric center of the bathhouse proper, equidistant from both men's and women's functions, is also a reminder of the egalitarian nature of existence: only upon immersion in the water do we achieve cosmological unity.

9. Vitruvius, *The Ten Books on Architecture*, tr. M. H. Morgan (New York: Dover, 1960), p. 160.

Hot Springs Hotel

Frank Moya

IN THIS PROJECT, the ruined resort of the Baños de Coamo in Puerto Rico provides both a real and a conceptual foundation for the elaboration of the bathing ritual within the program of the Coamo Hot Springs Hotel. The theme of water, with all its symbolic and mythical connotations, generates the new *parti* in a narrative which carries the bather to the bath and the spring water to the bather. The use of water here transcends immediate physical necessities; it correlates the cleansing of the body with the cleansing of the soul.

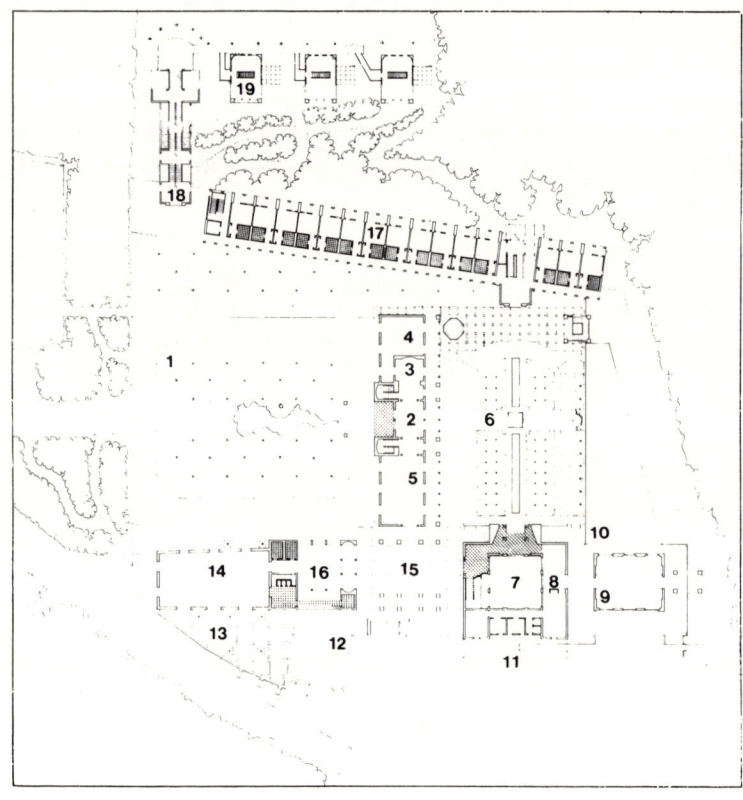

1. Hot Springs Hotel (Master's thesis), 1982. Plan.

1. Entrance court 2. Lobby 3. Front desk 4. Office 5. Lounge 6. Formal garden 7. Bathcourt below 8. Therapist's office 9. Bath below 10. Swimming pool below 11. Reservoir at termination of aqeuduct 12. Service yard 13. Terrace 14. Dining room 15. Cocktail lounge 16. Patio lounge 17. Guest room 18. Fountain stair 19. Guest cabana

Distinctive creation myths establish water as the origin of life and the essential source of nourishment for both the body and the mind. In Greek mythology, the Spring of Hippocrene is the source of poetry and intellectual life. The same tradition also stresses the bathing ritual as a means of spiritual and physical restoration, and proposes the first principles of physical planning for the public bath, the distinctive elements of which were simply planned chambers with steam, and warm and cold baths, mostly underground and usually in close proximity to a spring.

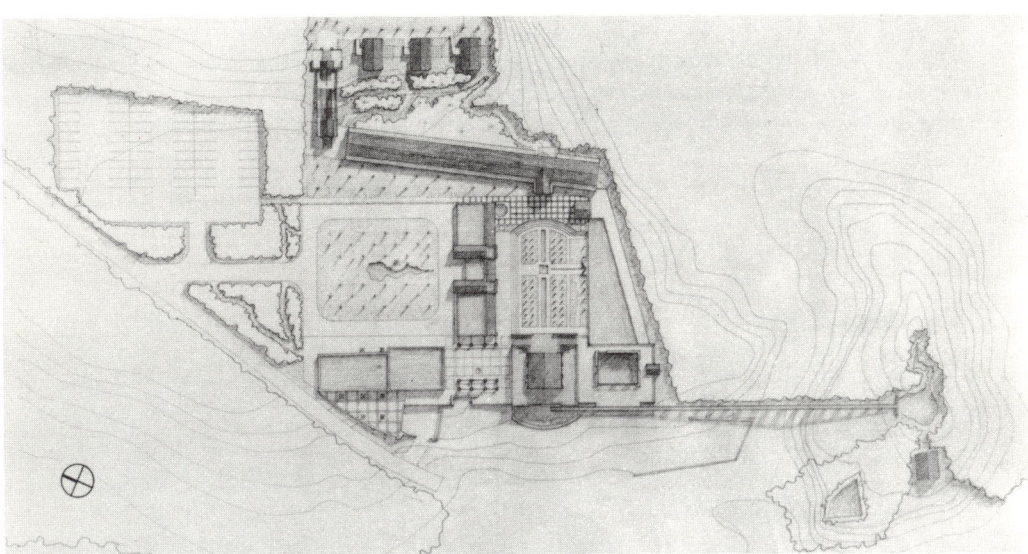

2. Hot Springs Hotel. Site plan.

In much the same way, the Coamo Hot Springs Bath is located close to a spring of hot sulphur waters once favored by the pre-Columbian natives and sought as the elusive "Fountain of Youth" by the Spanish conquistadors. (Ponce de Leon, Governor of Puerto Rico, mistakenly searched for the waters outside the island and in the process discovered Florida.) These springs form a natural pool which was used for three centuries by the natives and the Spaniards until a bath resort was built in the 1850's. The present project incorporates what remained of this resort after its abandonment in 1958 — the Neo-classic dining-hall and adjoining monumental wall.

The original parti consisted of a linear series of buildings oriented towards the spring, yet not connected to it, with the baths built into the foot of the hill along the wall. The new project is also arranged sequentially, but with water as its unifying element.

Coming in from the main road, we are confronted with the astringent odor and permanent mist of sulphur vapor signalling the proximity of the baths. In the entrance forecourt, among tall, red *Flamboyan* trees, a "natural" pond directs the view towards the receiving gates of the compound. Once beyond these gates, the natural landscape is forgotten. A formal garden, whose order is

3. Hot Springs Hotel. West elevation.

accentuated by pools of water crossing on axis, redirects the promenade towards the bath building. This central, temple-like structure encloses a three-storey court, where the muffled roar of cascading water invites us to descend. At the lower level we discover the "source," its presence signaled by the fall of sulphurous water from the impressive aqueduct just outside. The actual route

4. Hot Springs Hotel. Perspective view of entry.

of the invisible spring is framed by an axial view through the baths. This spring, the mythical origin of life and locus of the restitution of body and spirit, remains the *symbolic* focus, while the aqueduct brings the water within the formal confines of the precinct.

5. Hot Springs Hotel. Perspective view of bath.

At this point men and women enter separate steam rooms to the left and right, then re-unite at the entry to the sulphur bath, where spring water and bathers finally meet. The process of regeneration is finalized with the breaking of the axial sequence. The bathers must leave the warm pool and re-enter the outside world on the left, closing their pores with a therapeutic cold plunge.

An Architectural Idyll

The fullness of Graves' vision of the "alternative landscape" appears to depend equally on image, building, artifact, and text. This suggests both its limitations — from a strictly conceived architectural standpoint —, and its richness as an effort of the imagination. The landscape of Graves' imagining is a lyrical arcadian setting populated by a benign collection of de-historicized architectural fragments: a colonnade, a small pavilion, an urn, a table, an ordered grove of trees, all contribute to a mythic conception of architecture as the symbolic expression of Dasein, being-in-the-world. While the landscape image itself is somewhat fanciful and not without a touch of humor, it must ultimately be seen as one part of a seriously conceived structure of belief. As Alan Colquhoun observes:

> [Graves'] thought is permeated with a kind of eighteenth century deism and a belief that architecture is a perennial symbolic language whose origins lie in nature and our response to nature.... The frequent use in his writings of the words "sacred" and "profane" shows that he regards architecture as a secular religion which is in some sense revelatory.[1]

Like the masonic architects of the Enlightenment (see Vidler's essay, "The Return to the Origins "), Graves develops an expressive, didactic architecture which offers a re-creation of the past and, in consequence, a stabilization of the present: his architecture absorbs the exigencies of change within a well-balanced asymmetry. The fragments of history, the accidents of experience are acknowledged and ritually orchestrated. Just as Vidler observes of the eighteenth century revolutionary architects, Graves too offers a "lived utopia" — yet we might well ask "under what guise?"

Graves cites the backdrop for the ballet "Fire" and the recently designed Sunar showroom in Dallas as illustrations of "ritual themes" in his architecture. While set design provides an obvious opportunity for the delineation of the "alternative landscape," a furniture showroom might seem an unlikely medium, fixed as it is in commerce and consumerism. Yet for Graves, architecture is clearly assumed to transcend its immediate function. As an extension of Joseph Ryckwert's claim that "all form has symbolic meaning," we might say that for Graves all subjects are open to symbolic understanding. Although the specific program generates the design, pragmatic considerations are subsumed by the poetic vision. In the end one cannot ignore this disjunction. Graves is in a difficult position not unlike that of the poet laureate: he must truly believe in or subtly subvert the system he is bound to represent.

1. Alan Colquhoun, "From Bricolage to Myth," in *Essays in Architectural Criticism: Modern Architecture and Historical Change* (Cambridge: MIT Press, 1981), p.180.

Ritual themes in Architecture

Michael Graves

THE QUESTION OF RITUAL became particularly interesting to me some years ago when I was asked to give a seminar on the thematic content of architecture. It has always been apparent to me that while literature is involved with text and narrative, architecture, in its abstract nature, is not necessarily bound by story-telling but instead by the enactment of rituals. Rituals may represent general narratives or even the aspirations of society, but by nature they are inconclusive. Because of this, we realize both their importance and their fragile character in any composition. Though we may speak of hierarchy in architectural compositions, we do do not think of hierarchy in terms of the compositions' thematic content. Instead, I think its safe to say, the thematic struc-

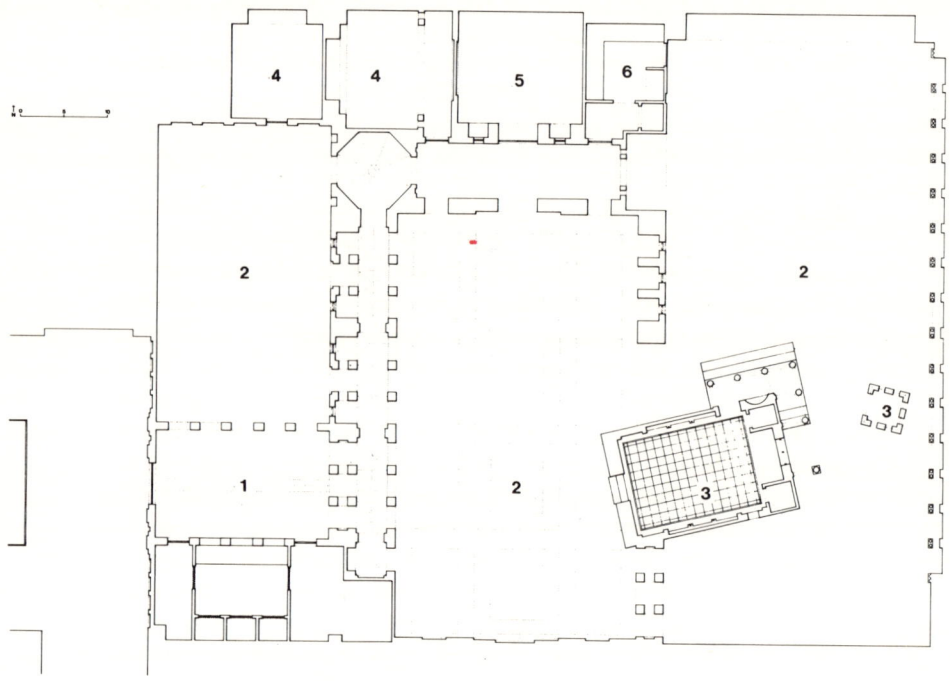

1. Sunar showroom, Dallas, Texas, 1982. Plan.

1. Entrance 2. Office systems display 3. Textile pavilion 4. Office 5. Conference room 6. Kitchen

tures of architecture rely on the elevation and suspension of ritual elements to provide a resonance of meaning.

The physical elements or gestures of enclosure that compose an architectural surround are capable of embodying both pragmatic and poetic elements. While the window might originally have relieved the wall for the practical benefits of light and air, the same light and air become poetic when we find ourselves physically and emotionally renewed by these natural phenomena. I would

---

1. Dallas Sunar Showroom. Steven Harris, Theodore Brown, *Job Captains*.
Fire Backdrop. Yossi Friedman, Natalie Fizer, Mason Perkins, and Anita Rosskam, *Assistants*.

2. Sunar showroom, entrance

3. Sunar showroom, loggia

also suggest that while light may enter the room from the outside, our gaze and our "light" given back to the landscape force the window to respond in an equal but opposite direction. It is this tautness of the wall membrane pierced by the window that we suddenly understand and represent as a ritualized threshold. Once we see the incredible potential in viewing the elements of an architectural enclosure in a thematic sense — for example, ceiling as sky, floor as ground —, we may reduce the abstractions of architecture to allow for the richness of ritual.

To illustrate this, we might examine one of the dominant themes of architecture, the ritual of procession, the promenade or *marche*. This aspect of movement can be seen in a recent showroom designed for Sunar in Dallas. After passing through the front door — a facade onto a public corridor —, the visitor enters an ephemeral space portrayed by a tent-like roof. This roof contributes to an idea of instability, to the sense that this is an equivocal place, at the edge of public and private realms. The location of the receptionist in this area also helps to establish the plane dividing public and private spaces.

I have assumed that light, and especially linear light overhead, acts as an enticement, leading us from beginning to end. Where the plan establishes peripheral and linear movement, then, skylights have been used to heighten the difference between passage and room. Proceeding straight ahead along

4. Sunar showroom, entrance to textile pavilion *5. Sunar showroom, textile pavilion*

the peripheral passage of the Sunar showroom, it is possible to enter a number of hierarchically arranged spaces. In this case and for this program, the hierarchy has to do with size as appropriated to use, with the largest and most public space in the center, and the smaller, more private offices at the end of the axis. At the same time, the themes of threshold and spatial character are embraced as part of our ritual sensibilities.

Fabric display, as distinct from furniture display, is separated into smaller pavilions within the larger organization or field. The two textile pavilions are arranged in plan in a somewhat picturesque manner off the grid of the rest of the composition. This both reinforces our understanding that textiles precede furniture historically and gives a sense of historical texture to the Dallas Merchandise Mart which seems to have been "built yesterday." The entrance to the main textile pavilion is described by a swag of fabric on the front face and casement garlands on the back porch. These "architectural" suggestions of swag and garland add to the ritual importance of entry. The garland was the element that decorated the temple at times of celebration, and the swag was originally made of fruits and vines and draped as an invitation to the internal garden. Light is also employed ritualistically in the interior of the fabric pavilion, again to exhibit its loose fit within the plan of the whole as well as to provide the pragmatic illumination of the textiles.

Architectural promenades allow both linear and cyclical narratives to unfold as we pass through variations offered by the plan. A single painted surface, however, offers another conceptual base. While the architectural or three-dimensional promenade suggests the literal unfolding of ideas over time and space, single painted surfaces develop such temporal and spatial sequences through other devices such as linear perspective. Further we are taught, through Cubism and through paintings such as Piero della Francesca's "Flagellation," that the strength of individual figurative or narrative elements can interrupt our perception of perspective depth. By setting up a tension between perspectival devices and objects or figures found in the painted field, the text or ritual narrative of the painted field may be understood with some degree of simultaneity. This phenomenon is illustrated in the stage set I designed for Laura Dean's ballet *Fire* (fig. 7).

The narrative for the ballet was first proposed by Ms. Dean and touches on the theme of the "bacchanal." Her previous choreographic compositions were to a large degree without narrative or text. They were highly organized, abstract patterns of formal content without literary references. In a collaboration between the two of us, she wanted a more associative composition. She also felt that there could be a strong relationship between the formal attitudes of her previous compositions and a basic, or archetypal, structure for this dance. The archetypal structure would free the dance from nostalgia and misapplied sentimentality. The dance was given the title *Fire* as a reference to its archetypal roots, for Ms. Dean makes characterizations of our beginnings in the broadest sense. There appears also to be a correlation between fire and the extremely physical, somewhat frenzied choreography for which she is known.

The bacchanal, though thought by some to expose an overly indulgent, decadent society, was originally simply a celebration of the first harvest, a ritual enactment of thanks to the gods for sustaining the society. This ritual dance of thanksgiving is also thought to be the setting for the first "theater." The dance allowed the society's collective participation, and represented the harvest by the use of garlands, wreaths, and other floral motifs. The garlands, which offered a circumferal binding for the dancers, were gathered from the vineyard, and the wine was thought to be the drink of the gods.

In describing this ritual act pictorially we tried to understand the limitations of the physical surrounding of the stage and to make positive use of them. Although the original setting for the bacchanal was outdoors, we intended to underscore the fact that this dance would be performed within the indoor theater. Rather than seeing the stage and its boundaries as a limitation, we imagined that the dialectic between internal and external conditions would place the performance within a contemporary aesthetic context. The literal space where the dancers perform, the stage, and the virtual space represented pictorially by the backdrop are what we might expect from an orthodox spatial sequence. However, these traditional spatial roles are transferred when the dancer is seen in profile against the silhouette of associated artifacts presented in the backdrop. Early Cubist experiments provide the aesthetic model for such role transferrals. The artifacts found in the backdrop are propelled into the space of the stage by virtue of the dancer's engagement with them. In addition to representing foreground and background, the backdrop is a diptych, its division reinforcing the choreographer's interest in experimenting with the "partnering" or pairing of male and female dancers. While my intention was not to make one side strictly male and one side strictly female, the backdrop suggests such a division.

The altar, one of the more literal elements of the pictorial representation, is paired with the most ephemeral figure, the empty easel. The altar traditionally symbolized our ritual of offering. The empty easel asks the question of the future. Rather than being located in the foreground and back-

6. *Fire. Costume study.*

gound, these two elements are placed on opposite sides of the central dividing column to further engage the space around them. The figures of two small pavilions occupy the middle ground of the backdrop. The roof of one is cleft, the other erect. In their singular nature, both buildings are seen as temples. Their plans are assumed to be simple and unified, and their exterior configuration is accessible to use, in that their singularity of space implies a unified sacred attitude. We are asked, for instance, to ascend the edge of the buildings to gain access first to the point of entry and subsequently to the place of arrival.[1] The pavilions may thus be read, traditionally speaking, from outside to in.

The double opening provided by the legs of the stage, left and right, and the central paired columns produce a sense of the interior, as if one were within a loggia or semi-enclosed space looking out to the landscape beyond. The artifacts found on that loggia or stage space, primarily the easel and the altar, are comfortably associated in our consciousness with an interior. It is at the crucial junc-

---

1. Cf., Peter Carl's unpublished essay, "Psychoanalysis and the Place of Arrival."

7. Set design for Laura Dean's ballet Fire

ture between the gray floor of this loggia space and the imagined landscape beyond that the spatial "crisis" takes place; for at one moment we think of the space developed through the perspective rendering of the landscape to be deep. However, the framing provided by the base, or floor, the swagged soffit, the column on one side and the wall on the other, suggests a stability that renders the wall of the landscape as flat, as only an allusion to ideal depth. By and large, through this conflict of deep and shallow space, of backdrop and literal stage, I hope to provide a more believable frame for our contemporary interpretation of the ancient bacchanalian rite.

Table Talk

A Discussion of Michael Graves' Set for the Ballet *Fire*

Deborah Gans

> Q: Why didn't you make it larger so that it would loom over the observer?
> A: I was not making a monument.
> Q: Then why didn't you make it small so that the observer could see over the top?
> A: I was not making an object.
>
> *Tony Smith on his sculpture "Die"*[1]

In *FIRE*, a dancer is exactly as high as a table. For the ballet by Laura Dean, Michael Graves has painted a landscape filled with curious structures. He has populated the middle distance with pavilions of indeterminate size, somewhere between object and monument. In the foreground, where the backdrop meets the stage, he has placed a table, an easel, a board held up by a stick, a flight of stairs. These objects disturb by virtue of their size and position; they are gigantic pieces of furniture that do not clearly belong to a land of giants. They might belong to the world of the dancers, for they occupy a room on the edge of the stage, except that their size denies them any functional value within that world. In the relation of the dancers to their furniture lies a larger dialogue between the aesthetics of Laura Dean and Michael Graves (fig. 1).

Both Dean and Graves are acclaimed post-modernists. This shared epithet is not so specific, however, as to imply an easy alliance; in fact its meaning in dance differs from the concerns of post-modern architecture and requires explanation.

Post-modern dance followed on the heels of Modernism. As defined by Clement Greenberg, Modernism called for the delimitation of each art according to the essential parameters of its medium and its primary illusion. Thus the problem of modernist painting was the simultaneous presentation of the virtual flatness of the canvas and the suspension of this fact in optical depth. Modernist dance, as codified by the generation of Merce Cunningham and George Balanchine, stripped away the narrative of ballet and the emotional and psychological motivation of movement found in the early modern dances of Martha Graham, Mary Wigam, and Doris Humphrey. It purged also the elements of ritual and primitive form that the first modern dancers had used to structure their free flowing and expressionistic works. The objective became to explore movement for movement's sake, to discover its syntax and internal logic. The choreographer's task was to admit the virtual reality of the stage and of the dancers and simultaneously to suspend the material presence of both in the illusion of weightlessness and of shifting space.[2] Cunningham achieves the illusion of impermanence by making the dancer's body the only point of reference. As one critic notes, "rapid shifts of weight and direction make any fixed focus except for the dancer's own body ineffective."[3] Dancers enter and exit the frame of the stage constantly and so transform the static, centralized proscenium into a fragmented, centripetal composition. Cunningham explains his space as "a field

---

1. Tony Smith, in Robert Morris, "Notes on Sculpture," *Minimal Art: A Critical Anthology*, Gregory Battock, ed. (N.Y.: E.P. Dutton & Co, 1968), p. 228.
2. A comprehensive discussion of modernism in dance is provided by David Levin, "Balanchine's Formalism," *Dance Perspectives 55*, 14 (1973), p. 40.
3. Arlene Croce, "A Time to Walk in Space," *Dance Perspectives 34*, 9 (1968), p. 25.

1. Fire, choreography and music by Laura Dean, set and costumes by Michael Graves. World premiere December 30, 1982. Patricia Brown and Luis Perez, dancers.

without a center of interest, all parts being of equal usage."[4]

Post-modern dance takes the propositions of Modernism to an internally logical conclusion, but in doing so subverts their original premise. Movement is perceived not only as abstract and without internal motivation, but also as objective. Movement is a thing — like a coat or a box — with a literal presence only. This attitude parallels the aesthetic of Minimal Art which celebrates the physical attributes of objects and space. As the minimalist sculptor Donald Judd argues, the literal presence is "intrinsically more powerful and specific than illusionism."[5] In dance, illusionism is destroyed through the reduction of the vocabulary to basic, axiomatic elements, to the movements that occur in life as well as art. Repetition and unison emerge as two of the post-modern choreographer's most powerful devices. As Yvonne Rainer explains, "repetition enforces the discreteness of a step — its beginning and ending — and hence makes it more object-like. Unison makes movement as a unit easier to see by isolating it in its own context."[6]

In their revision of formalist content, the post-modernists restore to dance one of its original intentions — the aspect of ritual. The first generation of modern choreographers incorporated ritualistic forms into essentially theatrical compositions. For example, Ruth St. Denis quoted loosely from Indian religious dance in *Incense*; Doris Humphrey borrowed the patterns of American transcendentalist ceremony in her *Shakers*. Rejecting this historicism, post-modern dance recaptures the *process* of ritual. From the cults of the Greeks to the revels of the Elizabethan masque, rituals establish a specific and immediate relation between the performers and audience. The participants in the rite are members of the same primal group as the beholders, and they occupy a shared stage. (At the climax of revels, for instance, the royal performers descended into the hall to dance with the audience.) Post-modern dance differs from traditional ritual in the content of the common vocabulary of simple movements: it eliminates the duality of the mundane steps and their spiritual intent. Repetition and unison lead not to transcendence but to an affirmation of the power within their material bounds.

---

4. Merce Cunningham, *Changes: Notes on Choreography* (N.Y.: Something Else Press, 1968), p. 90.
5. Donald Judd in Milton Glaser, "Questions to Stella and Judd," *Art News*, Vol. LXV No. 5, September 1966.
6. Yvonne Rainer, "A Quasi Survey of Some Minimalist Tendencies in the Quantitatively Minimal Dance Activity Midst the Plethora, or an Analysis of Trio A," *Minimal Art: A Critical Anthology*, Gregory Battock ed. (N.Y.: E. P. Dutton, 1968), p. 271.

2. Tympani, *Laura Dean dancers.*

Laura Dean began as a post-modernist choreographer renowned for her dances of spinning. In early works such as *Tympani*, the dancers walk and skip for extended periods and then break from the unison of the group and begin to spin (fig. 2). The spinning builds a peculiar momentum as the dancers group and regroup, but then simply stops. Unlike the spinning of the dervishes or Dionysian bacchants, it leads neither to ecstasy nor death but to cessation. It is as blank as movement can possibly be. Much of the power of Dean's early work arises from its sheer size and gestalt. A former Dean dancer explained to me that in order to really *do* Laura's dances he had to imagine himself to be gigantic. He had to pretend that the stage was too small for him and that when he reached to either side he could touch the wings. The soul of the work, he said, lay in this gigantism, in the use of monolithic blocks of movement, and in the conceptualization of the stage as one vast place without any smaller parts (fig. 3).

Fire marks a departure for Dean from this reductive aesthetic. She now broadens her spectrum of movement to include even the language of ballet. She endows her dance with a context and atmosphere allied with the figural language of Graves' backdrop. She compromises the generality of blankness and the colossal scale for specificity of meaning.

The character of *Fire* emerges from Dean's and Graves' complementary use of cultural reference. The music of the Pan-like flute, the pastel tunics of the dancers, the pastoral color and light, the landscape with its primitive temples, all evoke the sense of a proto-classical world. From the depictions of dancers on Greek vases Dean borrows the silhouette, the hieratic gesture, and the linked chains of movement. These images belong to an extensive tradition of "tunicked" ballets, from nineteenth century frolicking naiads, to the innocent freedom of the Golden Age evoked by Isadora, to the sophisticated neo-classicism of Balanchine's *Apollo*. But Dean's attitude toward the mythic past most closely resembles that of Nijinsky, who saw in the Greeks a Dionysian combination of the erotic and formal which he explored in both *Afternoon of a Faun* and the darker *Rite of Spring*.

As in her earlier work, Dean structures *Fire* with a series of discrete sections, each with a simple geometry and a dominant movement, yet here she modifies her minimalist sensibility to create a progression with a particular direction and content. In part one, the dancers describe a large rectangle which simply reiterates the boundaries of the stage. Initially, they stand rigid with their arms and legs outstretched and their weight evenly distributed. Their first movements are limited and

3. Tympani, Laura Dean dancers.

static. Then the dancers gradually begin to bend their knees and shift their weight from side to side. The rhythm of the drum changes from a relentless one-two to a triplet with lyric potential. The dancers join hands and begin a simple chain step. The section ends with a brief episode of spinning — the only spinning in the piece. In part two, after having executed rather complicated patterns of passing, the dancers with a simple folk step in the round define the primary figure of this section. A change in drumming signals part three. Suddenly the dancers find partners and launch into volatile duets filled with *penché* arabesques, dips, and bends. Formations of two supplant the unity of the group. In part four, the chorus reassembles to perform almost courtly figures. The couples march in a column down the center of the stage, split, and rejoin the formation. They stand in a line across the back of the stage and watch as individual dancers emerge, perform acrobatic feats in a huge circle, and then return to the line. Finally the incessant drumming stops, the group disbands, and a single couple stands on stage embracing to the strains of the flute.

In this sequence, the choreography builds from an initially limited vocabulary of movement to one of greater complexity. It progresses from mundane and earth-bound steps to aerial and acrobatic ones, from abstract and anonymous dance to gesture laden with emotional content. Beyond a formal progression, these shifts establish a narrative which remains open to interpretation: they could suggest both a history of dance and a human history. Dean introduces the dancers as primitive beings with a stiff, geometric presence. The gradual emergence of bending knees and shifted weight recounts the evolution of *contraposto*. As in the history of classical sculpture, the human image develops from the archaic stance of the *kouroi* to the dynamic balance and grace of the Hellenistic figure. The next stages of the dance might describe social development of these newly awakened beings. They emerge as individuals from the tribe when they perform their acrobatic feats. They master a more sophisticated understanding of group interaction in their execution of courtly figures, discovering their identities as men and women when they suddenly couple. Here the partnering of ballet provides a codified and decipherable language of human relations which Dean uses in a rudimentary way. The arabesque is always the ultimate display of the ballerina's "line" and hence of her feminine power. In *Fire*, the ballerina swoops down and kicks her leg high in the air; she is kept from falling only by the strong grasp of her partner. Her darting energy and thrust in this arabesque signifies the erotic, while the support she requires in order to perform it suggests her dependent relation to her partner. An emerging consciousness and sexuality supplants an inital stage of harmony. In the end the group breaks down; one couple stands alone. They no longer dance but merely embrace, united to each other but severed from the chorus, their primal group.

Despite the stark simplicity of its final image, Fire seems unresolved. The couple's caress can be read as poignant or pathetic, optimistic or despairing. It lacks the conviction of the opening moments of the dance and suggests that Dean herself is ambivalent toward the ending she has created. She seems to doubt the value of a process of increasing complexity that results in the destruction of unity and loss of gigantism. We can only grasp the full sense of the final gesture from its relation to the backdrop.

4. Setting for Luminalia, or the Festival of Light, scene 1, Night. By Sir William Davenant. Performed 1638.

As with Dean, Graves draws on the history of his medium. In his backdrop for Fire, he conflates the two major traditions of stage design, the emblematic and perspectival set, presenting an ambiguity which parallels the struggle contained in the choreography.

From its inception in ancient Greek culture to its codification in the Renaissance, the perspective set evolved from the depiction of multiple and fragmented illusionistic scenes within a complex facade to the creation of a competing reality. The achievement of the late Renaissance was to apply

5. Setting for Oberon's Palace in Oberon, the Faery Queen. Performed 1611.

the new understanding of space as unified, continuous, and infinite to stage design, subordinating the drama's narrative flow of time and events to the creation of spatial singularity. A large central opening gradually came to replace the multiple windows within the architectural facade, and the variety of landscapes within those windows gave way to a scene with a single vanishing point. As the central portal was widened, illusionistic space was further revealed and the performance area was aligned with the depth of the perspective. Thus the facade became identified with the other traditional open frame, the proscenium curtain. In the early seventeenth century, it was joined with the proscenium at the front edge, while the painted landscape reached across the back of the stage. Because its viewpoint was now coordinated with the single vanishing point, the audience could empathetically enter the alternate world that now completely embraced the stage (fig. 4).

Whereas the perspective set simulates another reality, the emblematic set symbolizes it. Typically, the sets of this tradition are architectural objects composed of an assemblage of signs and structures placed at the center of the stage. One scene might combine castle turrets with a triumphal arch, the whole embellished with garlands and trees. Because of the multi-valent nature of the imagery, its meaning could shift from scene to scene according to the context supplied by the narrative. The tower might represent a castle in one act and an entire walled city in the next.

Furthermore, by varying and amalgamating a stock repertoire of signs, the designers transformed the meaning of the individual parts. Emblematic devices such as temples placed on mountains and castles on elephants worked both as gestalt objects with a single impact and as compendia of signs (fig. 5).

6. *Partial proscenium and castle towers as wings, Il falso amor bandito, Turin, 1667. Formal façade at back shutter, showing small perspective scene either painted on shutter or built on inner stage.*

In the history of set design, the two traditions of perspective and emblem often stand side by side. In the *tableaux vivants* of the early Renaissance, for example, emblematic objects are found in perspective settings (fig. 6). In the backdrop for *Fire*, on the other hand, Graves allows these traditions to collide. At first glance the space of the backdrop seems harmonious and continuous, the objects within it calmly situated. A deep landscape is framed by a delicate painted proscenium. A shallow interior space connects the floor of the stage to the illusion represented on the canvas. The narrow architectural space with its valence and attenuated column evokes Pompeiian wall murals just as the landscape suggests a classical world. Within the landscape, the buildings are placed along two diagonal lines which converge with the horizon at opposite ends of the canvas and so imply a simple system of two-point perspective. This coherence is merely a veneer, however. The triangular arrangements of the buildings only suggests perspective. Individually the pavilions follow their own spatial law: an axiomatic order that does not extend beyond the bounds of each object's perimeter. The central column, like the window frame in a proto-Renaissance set, implies that the views to either side are self-contained. In the neutral zone of the gap within the double column, the horizon is erased altogether.

This play with perspective occurs symbolically within the buildings themselves: each contains a triangle which is the shape of a rectangle seen in depth. The inverted roof of the pavilion on the right is a void triangle. The other pavilion has a triangular opening or door. The pyramid is a dwarf perspective cone. By repeating the shape of perspective on a small scale and placing it in different orientations, Graves changes it from an ordering device to an object. In instances where the triangles are larger, they actually begin to subvert the sense of perspective diminution. The canted legs of the table and the profile of the stairs get larger as they seem to recede. The figure inscribed by the buildings in the landscape reads as an inverted perspective cone with its apex at the double column and its base at the horizon.

In using the buildings to disrupt the unity of the landscape, Graves employs his own symbolic language to contravene the perspective tradition. Like emblemata, the buildings stand isolated from one another and independent of any larger spatial order. They are composed from a kit of architectural pieces and parts that strongly resemble the grammar of the early Renaissance. The tops of the two largest pavilions sit like huts or temples on podia suggesting mountains or legs. The inclusion of an image of Stonehenge near the horizon directly recalls its use by Inigo Jones in his sets for the Stuart masques. Jones employed it as a symbol for the Golden Age, for it was believed to be a temple of the ancient Britons and proof of their descent from classical culture. But Graves treats even perspective emblematically. The triangle becomes a multivalent sign: a roof, an object, and a shorthand notation of the cone of perspective. One senses that all of the pieces could so be analysed in both traditionally emblematic terms and within the specific language of Graves.

This schism between space and objects is more than a commentary upon history. In the dialogue between the Renaissance values of unified perspective and the emblematic mode of understanding through totem, Graves sets up a confrontation between his primary interest in architectural humanism and attitudes more akin to Dean's early objectivism. The backdrop captures the tension found in Dean's attempt to remain true to her original aesthetic and yet move beyond minimalism.

According to Michael Fried in his seminal article "Art and Objecthood," minimalism is inherently theatrical.[7] Minimal art needs the actual circumstance of its environment and its relation to the beholder to complete itself. Thus it requires a stage and an audience. Rejecting a structured anthropomorphic relation among parts, it favors the power of an object's gestalt which also depends on the entrance and presence of the spectator. In this way, it attempts to break down the bounds between art and life and to replace the proscenium with a frame which includes the beholder within the event of art. The devices which Minimal Art uses to establish its immediate relation to the viewer are size and location. The larger the object, the more distant we tend to keep it in order to see it as a whole and to reduce its potentially threatening presence. Correspondingly, as objects approach human size we allow them closer to our personal space. Fried describes the territorial imperative of men in relation to life-size objects. Sculptures of human size, like the boxes of Tony Smith and Richard Artswager, suggest actors standing on a stage that is also the space of the beholder. The key to the establishment of this situation is what Fried labels "hidden anthropomorphism." Despite their blankness and undifferentiated form, the boxes of minimalism are surrogate persons. They have the stature of humans. Their enclosing surfaces suggest hollowness and hence a life within (figs. 7,8).

The subject-object relation of Minimal Art exists between the set and the dancer in stage design, a relation best exemplified in the sets made for the Cunningham Company during the 1960's. Although essentially modernist in his own attitude toward movement, Cunningham chose to commission sets by minimalist artists. He believed in a type of total theatre where the disciplines of music, dance, and art stood side by side as equal and independent objects. In Robert Rauschenberg's

---

7. All quotes from Michael Fried from "Art and Objecthood," *Minimal Art: A Critical Anthology*, Battcock ed., pp.116-147.

7. "Die," Tony Smith, 1962. Steel, painted black. 72 × 72 × 72"

8. Untitled, Richard Artschwager, 1966. Formica on wood. 59 × 18 × 30".

set for *Nocturnes* for example, a white rectangular pier of twice human height, blank and opaque, stood as a minimalist sculpture on stage. During the course of the dance it began to glow from within and so revealed its hollowness and its inner light or life. In the set for *Tread* by Bruce Naumann, floor fans stood equidistant across the stage, their round heads hovering just above human height on top of skinny poles. As the dancers moved insouciantly among them, absorbed in their abstract patterns, the fans began to spin, motivated, as in *Nocturnes*, by some internal anima. In both pieces the objects stood as surrogate actors within the field of the dance. The audience experienced the connection of subject and object in two ways: empathetically, because they identified with the dancers in their relation to the set, and literally, because they sat within the arena of the Minimal sculpture.

Within the deep space of Graves' landscape and behind the blatantly anthropomorphic masks of the pavilions lurks the aesthetic of minimalism. Although Graves' use of illusionistic depth is at odds with the literalist sensibility of the minimalists, he approaches a theatrical understanding of both objecthood and duration. Fried finds the antecedent for the minimalists' sense of time in surrealism, a movement which has clearly influenced Graves as well. As Fried explains, "the sense at bottom of temporality and simultaneity approaching and receding as if apprehended in infinite perspective contradicts Modernism which is wholly manifest attachment and has no duration." Minimal Art exists temporally, like theater, rather than synchronically as a composed relation of parts. In Graves' backdrop, as in de Chirico's landscapes, where distance is one with memory, the perspective moves back in time as it moves in space, back to Stonehenge and the pyramid. The triangular shape which the buildings inscribe on the landscape correspond exactly with the situation Fried describes. The double column can be read as the central point in the foreground from which the perspective lines recede. It can also be read as the vanishing point from which the perspective lines expand for a space with its picture plane at the horizon. Thus the space in Graves' set simultaneously advances and recedes in telescoping perspective. Axonometric projection possesses this same ability to flip between receding and advancing space. The parallel lines of an axonometric object can seem to move either forward or backward. Because the pavilions appear in axonometric, the spatial progression within the landscape becomes even more ambiguous.

Both the pavilions and the furniture are clearly surrogate actors. In Graves' original conception they were constructions standing on stage; and although as executed they are mere images, they have great physical presence, much like the animate objects of surrealism. The parallel lines of their perimeters refuse to converge, asserting the power of their corporeality over the law of illusion. The localized shadows endow them with solidity in the midst of the optical pastel landscape. They possess human stature and latent sexuality. The receptive kylix crowns the table's shapely leg. Although many of the pieces of their physiognomy come from a traditional architectural vocabulary, these objects belong to the new generation of more abstract surrogate beings. Despite their anthropomorphic structure they are as blank, mute, and intransigent as minimalist sculpture. The eyes of the pavilions are dots, holes, or slits. Their life seems buried deep within their solid structures. Perhaps the easel best expresses their nature: it is a *tabula rasa* — blank, blind, without memory.

As in Minimal Art, the objects which inhabit Graves' room also define it. In Graves' architecture, the room is of primary importance as a closed figure with a place for man at its center. In Minimal Art, the room has a clandestine importance. As Fried writes, "it is equal to space. 'It is in your space' is the same as 'it is in the room with you." In the set for *Fire*, the sense of room drifts toward this non-figural reading. Although the valence, a traditional stage symbol for an interior, indicates that the green floor of the backdrop is a room, this zone actually depends on the objects within it for its shape. Without the furniture to form a back wall, and the right hand column to anchor the outer edge, the landscape behind and the real stage in front would overwhelm it. Even so, the zone seems to continue beyond the wings of the stage, more like an endless horizontal strip than a complete room. The floor may also be read as a vertical element coincident with the picture plane, thus collapsing the space of the room entirely. It then becomes a podium for the furniture which hovers on the edge between the stage and the illusionistic landscape like a tribune of elders watching the acrobatic feats performed before them.

The dance takes place in an arena that belongs both to the special zone of the furniture and to the audience. Graves has not placed the valence like a Renaissance proscenium between the performance and the audience; rather, he uses it to separate the landscape from the realm of the dance. The audience and the furniture face each other across this realm as if they were seated on opposite sides of an amphitheatre. Together they define the edge of the performance space and imply that the stage exists like an arena in the round, bounded by observers on all sides. As in minimalist dance and art, the subjects and objects define a shared territory in which the ritual event occurs.

Michael Graves and Laura Dean tell similar histories but draw different conclusions. The dancers with their weight evenly placed between their straight legs seem the children of the squat pavilions. They share the same static attributes of objecthood. As the spatial qualities of the landscape counter the totemic presence of the furniture, so the progression of movement offsets the initial ritualism of the dance. When the dancers begin to explore movement and their relation to one another, however, they leave the world of the set behind. The scale of the furniture becomes more and more alien to the dance as the corps breaks down and the couples occupy the stage. Where the table initally stands as high as a member of the group, it finally towers over the individual gesture. The power of gigantism remains in the set but not in the dance. In the last scene, when the lone couple embrace on stage aware of their own isolation in the landscape, the furniture has grown awesome. The only way Dean finds to restore a sense of balance and to focus her final image of the couple's humanity is to darken the set and spotlight the dancers — to extinguish the life of the objects.

1. Club Chair, 1981. Study.

Club Chair

Tod Williams and Billie Tsien

THIS CHAIR is about ritual. In groups of two or four, the chair creates an interior place where experiences of a more silent nature may occur. A wall with an impenetrable face is presented to those who arrive. A bronze grill serves as a window for those who are already present. A figural dais, described by the grey/gilt base, serves as platform to the plush lining of the seats. When the chair is considered as a single piece, its asymmetry suggests rotation and the fragmentation of the protective cabinetry of the back. This is a cubistic deformation of the "throne" archetype.

The chair is a palanquin, a refuge, a room, a confessional, a mystery, a building.

Materials are: laminated wood finished in lacquer and gold leaf, with brass fittings. Seat cushions are suede leather.

2. Club Chairs.

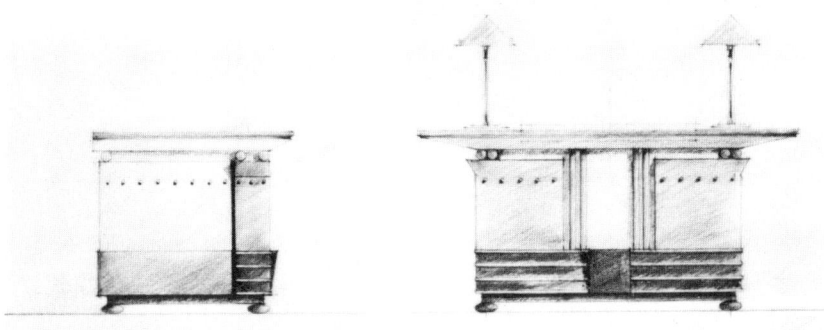

1. *Reception Desk, 1982. Elevation studies.*

Reception Desk

Erich Marosi

THIS DESK was designed for the reception room of a large law firm occupying three floors of a high-rise office building. Given the lack of public image and spatial definition of the typical commercial floor, it was felt that the desk should provide the client with a memorable point of reference — a symbolic image of the whole. Conceived as part of the entire office renovation by the Montreal architect Peter Rose, the desk uses materials and a language which are elaborated throughout the scheme. The ceremony of reception begins with entry at a lower floor. The desk terminates the axis of the processional stair which the client would ascend to reach the lawyers' offices. Moving up, he or she would first see the brass lights framing the receptionist, then the niche with its flanking brass columns and supporting keystone. The complete view presents a facade with cornice and rusticated base, divided horizontally in a tripartite arrangement.

Materials are: light and dark stained oak with solid brass fittings and ornament. Lamps are matte-finished brass.

2. *Reception Desk.*

Fang Architectonics

James Fernandez

From our cultural perspective, the precise and frequently playful rituals of an African tribal society may seem remote, yet the human needs they provide for, and the patterns they trace are completely familiar. In Fang Architectonics, James Fernandez describes the gradual "decentering" of an African culture in the face of colonial pressures, a centrifugal motion which affects the society and its conception of space. He distinguishes the natural process of decentering, where centripetality is cyclically recovered, from a sense of irrevocable distancing from the center, a process imposed by uncontrollable external forces.

In an interview with Maryann Thompson, Fernandez emphasized that the built environment is not his primary concern. In fact, he resisted using the word "architecture" during the discussion because of its too specific implications of enclosure. Fernandez prefers the term "architectonics," which implies "an extension of the built environment to include the entire affective quality of organized space in its relation to the cultural system as a whole." The dialectic between centripetality and centrifugality is basic to Fernandez' theory of architectonics. As he notes, for hunting and gathering nomads decentering was a way of life, and, although the Agricultural Revolution enabled the attachment to territory that we now know, the early centrifugal stage of human development still finds expression in the patterns of contemporary life. As evidence of this "ancient two-vectored wanderlust built into our humanness," he cites the yearly pilgrimage from Paris to the Church of Santiago in Compostella, Spain. Marking the pilgrim's destination is a triumphal portico — its dividing column the ultimate centering device, worn by the touch of thousands of worshippers. One is reminded here of a similar gesture made by the Fang as part of the Bwiti religion. In the face of the disintegration of order on a material and social plane, such symbolic decenterings and recenterings provide a compensatory sense of certainty in the spiritual realm.

■   ■   ■

*Ndok dulu a ne kison
mintangan a bizima*

The passion for journeying
ends in the white man's
towns and in soldiering.

IN THIS PAPER I propose to discuss various aspects of the Fang representation of space.[1] How have they built themselves into the spaces available to them and what is represented in the "buildings"? I shall concentrate on the buildings themselves in the literal sense of the term but shall argue that these buildings cannot be completely understood without a larger sense of the

---

1. Editor's note: this article, published originally as *Fang Architectonics*, Working Papers in the Traditional Arts, No. 1 (Philadelphia: ISHI, Institute for Study of Human Issues, 1977), has been revised and abridged by the editor.

architectonics of Fang culture and Fang cultural history. By architectonics I mean the particular inter-relatedness in the quality of experience of mythical, cosmological, domestic, social, and personal space. A number of concepts appear thematically in the discussion: centrifugality, centripetality, decentering, microcosmic extensions, structural replications. Some of these terms have gained common use in anthropology. The concluding discussion will attempt to clarify their meaning in relation to the notion of "quality space."

Cosmology and Legend: Cosmic Space. I shall not detail but only point out certain features of Fang cosmology and legend relevant to this topic.[2] The earth was created by Sky Spider (*Dibobia-abo*) under the aegis of the creator god *Mebege*. *Abo* dropped an egg sack onto the ocean for the earth was nothing but water. The egg sack contained the souls of men (*minsisim*) and termites (*sigibim*) who, pulling up the earth from the bottom of the ocean, created land. The spirits of men, like the *sigibim*, belong to the earth. The great spirits belong to the sky. All living and dead things whose abode is in or on the earth must look to the sky to negotiate their fate. While in many aspects of the Fang ancestral cult the living negotiate with the dead without reference to the above, in the cosmological and final sense, creation and power come from above and spirits, when they are active, are active above. Living men endeavor not to rise too high or fall too low. Fang cosmology then gives one essential dimension of Fang quality space: height and depth.

The Fang migration legends give us the second dimension: upstream (*oswi kui*), downstream (*oswi nken*). Upstream and downstream are the cardinal directions among the Fang and subtend in their affairs an axis roughly northeast-southwest. The migration legend, which has some basis in history, situates the progenitors of the Fang far upstream by the margins of a great body of water and upon a savannah or a desert. Driven from their homeland by invaders and by hunger, they commence a long migration downstream through the savannah and into the rain forest. The hazards of their migration are many: the crossing of various rivers, pursuit by more powerful tribes or by a power described as a giant crocodile, and the entrance into the rain forest symbolized as a giant tree (*adzap mboga*) through which they must bore a hole. The final objective of this migration is often said to have been the ocean, variously described as the abode of the dead or the abode of the moon which rises there.

Values attach themselves symbolically to these directions. Upstream is said to be the male direction and downstream the female direction. This association is compounded from several facts. The sun, which is male, rises in the east, *oswi kui*, and the moon, which is female, rises in the west, *oswi nke*. Upstream are the forces which have dislodged the Fang from their original home and pursued them. Downstream is the abode of those peoples whom the Fang have readily conquered or displaced in their rapid migration into the forest and towards the sea. In general, within Fang territory, wives are sought from downstream clans and husbands welcomed from upstream clans. Upstream tribes of the Fang are esteemed as being more advanced. And indeed, in terms of the contact with the west, the Bulu and Ntumu have enjoyed progressive advantages over the Fang proper, the Okak and the Meke. In respect to the fissiparous character of Fang lineage dynamics it is the junior segments that have generally split away from their seniors and moved on downstream to re-establish themselves. Upstream is thus associated with seniority in both clan histories and migration legends; downstream has the subservience of junior status. For a combination of these reasons, upstream is the dominant direction and downstream the recessive direction. Informants still testify to a norm by which both the village as well as the house structure are aligned or should be aligned on the *oswi nkui - oswi nkeng* axis. One speaks thus of both up-river and down-river directions in the

---

2. Full accounts may be found in V. Largeau, *Encyclopédie Padouine* (Paris, 1901); H. Trilles, *Le Totemisme chez les Fang* (Munster, 1912); G. Tessman, *Die Pangwe*, 2 vols. (Berlin, 1913).

village and in the house itself. In actual construction this alignment is rarely correct with respect to real space or real river direction though villagers may still speak of the up-river part of the village or the up-river part of the house. This is the semantic of migration along the second dimension of our developing Euclidean space.

But the third dimension is less salient among the Fang. Informants speak of front and back or head and foot on the analogy of a man extending his right hand, the male hand, upstream and his left hand, the female hand, downstream. Here we see the body microcosm extended to organize macrocosmic space. There can be no doubt that the primary experience of the body and body image is fundamental to Fang spatial architectonics though varying use of this metaphor is made by informants. They are a highly egalitarian and undogmatic people in this and every respect.

Progress on the vertical dimension would seem to be circular. Spirits rise from the earth, become men, fashion their better selves out of the combined action of brains and heart against the gross visceral appetites of stomach, bowel, bladder and genitals, rise further to negotiate with the higher powers, and are fated finally to fall back to earth only to rise again as spirits are called to negotiate and reassume mortal shape.

Progress in the other horizontal dimension is linear and noncircular. There is no notion of a return to the original savannah homeland. One might believe that the sea as final destination represents a return to that original body of water beside which the Fang first dwelt. But I have no evidence of that return or the identification of the ocean with the ancestral sea. There is no eternal return in that sense but rather progressive transformation of nature and destiny.

Social Space and Domestic Zones. At a level of abstraction where anthropologists quite comfortably dwell, we can talk about Fang occupancy of social space: we can locate the Fang in his clan structure by examining the concepts with which that structure is erected. By now, and for a good many decades in the past, the concepts by which the clan universe has been constituted have been uncertainly understood. The corporate bonds of the group defined by these concepts have been weakened and in many cases are only vestigial. In a manner of speaking the structure has opened up and the individual has been released to make his way with his own resources. He has become subject to centrifugal influences.

The same centrifugal influences are at work in respect to space. For if the Fang have a very uncertain sense of their place in clan structure, so they have misgivings as to their place in space — and in particular in relation to that center space, once powerfully centripetal, of the Fang village.

Studies of Fang genealogies and the histories associated with them demonstrate how the Fang commonly remember between five and eight abandoned village sites previous to the site they are now occupying. They remember and locate their former villages according to the nearest stream or river. Every tributary has its name and since Fang country is an equatorial rain forest the watercourses are abundant and their cognitive map can be a very complex one. Younger men, when asked to draw maps of clan lands, almost always draw them by reference to the new road system. Whereas the rivers lead to the sea, these roadways have as their focus and destination towns and trading centers of the colonial and modern world.

While macrospace was traditionally organized by reference to rivers and the sea, and more recently by reference to the colonial arteries of commerce and administration, the microspace of village life was organized first by reference to the forest and the plantations and secondly in relation to the traditional structures: the women's dwellings or kitchens (*kisin*), the men's apartments (*nda* proper) where the ancestral shrines (*nsuk bieri*) were found, the men's council house (*aba*) and the central courtyard (*nsun*).

There is in the mind of every Fang an important affective contrast between the forest and the village. The former is cold yet it is the prime arena of male activity — of hunting, warfare, defense of frontiers. The latter is hot, yet it is the arena of women's work — the cooking of food, the raising of children. From the village to the forest, one passes through various life zones, each redolent of its particular set of associations according to the activities carried out in it. One begins in the central court of the village, passing through the wall of houses on either side and out the back door to the zone of small gardens and banana groves. At its fringes we find isolated stands of forest (*okan*) where the latrines are located and where ceremonial activities of the ancestor cult and the secret societies take place. Wild fruit trees are maintained there, and during their season the *okan* is the scene of much pleasurable activity. Beyond this zone are the plantations, the frontier between the forest and the village. Here the forest is defeated for the sake of village life. The men clear the area and the women cultivate it. The forest beyond is a foreign place which has not been defined by any building activities; what occurs there is always unexpected, adventurous. On its frontiers men do their battle slashing and burning of new fields, laying traps for its fauna and entering in for hunts. Deep within the forest a stream or a ridge makes the boundary with another clan-segment, a zone of potential hostility. But the forest itself, regardless of the societal frontier, quickens thought, for there men engage in the chase, and there shades of the troubled dead and other malevolent spirits wander.

The movement out from the village into the forest is not only an experience of succeeding zones with qualitatively different associations; it also marks the passage of a threshold, that of theredoubtable *olele-afan* interposed between the domain of the familiar and domestic activity — the village and its associated gardens and plantations, and the deep forest with its useful trees, game, and well stocked streams, but also with its alien uncertainties.

Although existing in sharp contrast to the forest, the village is yet constructed out of it, and to that extent the distinction between these two realms is transformed into a close association. Men circulating back and forth between the forest and the village create a unity where a set of contrasting spatial categories existed before. This synthesis is expressed in Fang architecture itself. Their homes are so much a part of the village yet so essentially of the forest.

In reality, patches of forest are likely to be everywhere and often press upon the village itself. On the other hand, our scheme does indicate both basic Fang spatial categories and the stages in that journey which the Fang experiences as he goes out to the forest and returns again to the village. It is a journey celebrated in a variety of ceremonial sojourns in some of the traditional cults. It is celebrated, as we shall see, in the new cult of Bwiti. It is also architecturally formulated there. But again this is a symbolic journey of the past. At present it is the comings and goings upon the roads and highways which excite the imagination of the young. The new frontiers are the trading centers and cities by the sea. One is decentered. It is hard to go home again and experience the synthesis which home traditionally provided.

The Village: Images. To an observer, the traditional Fang village with its two long rows of houses facing each other across the barren courtyard provokes the notion of opposition (fig. 1). This opposition corresponds in some respects to social structure, for men of a common (*ndebot*) minimal segment build side by side, while those of the medial segment (*mvogabot*) already subject to fissionary processes, build opposite where, it is said, they can shout insults across the court. Nevertheless, the village plan was traditionally conceived with defensive purposes in mind: it was a tight enclave which was easily protected against internecine strife by palisades and the strengthening of houses' outer walls. That a sense of opposition was also expressed in its layout is a structural replication of

1. Traditional Fang village.

the importance and vitality of oppositions, including segmentary oppositions, in many aspects of Fang life. The village itself in its very structure expresses these oppositions at the same time that it constitutes a self-contained enclave — a microcosm — very clearly defined against an outside world. Thus the village as a symbol — and it is a symbol to the Fang — condensed, not surprisingly, both meanings of opposition and fission and of solidarity.

Within the village the notion of oppositions evoked by rectangular patterning has also undergone change as, more and more, the men of the patrilineage have undertaken to build houses in the European fashion — multi-roomed dwellings with concrete floors, wattle and daub walls, and zinc roofs. Often called "cold houses" because unlike traditional dwellings no fires burn within, these houses gather their associated complex of women's kitchens and men's council house around them into a compound. This compounding effect has tended to break up the common plaza and has no doubt had an influence upon the unity provided by that plaza. In the old days the men's council houses could survey the whole village, but now the council houses are often found within the compounds and cut off from each other. This development is congruent to a developing familialism on the one hand and a centrifugality in village life on the other. I do not believe that the Fang are very comfortable in these cold houses. They are nevertheless a source of prestige; they are the consequence of the arduous laying up of funds and materials, and are universally desired. The traditional houses are still associated with all the major events in Fang life from birth to death. Often the cold houses are kept closed except for social occasions: they are not yet really lived in.

The heart of Fang microspace in the traditional village can be found in the relationship between the men's council house (*aba*) and the combination sleeping quarters and cook hut (*nda - kisin*).[3] It is the general feeling that the *nda-kisin* belong to the women and the *aba* to the men. An old tale is often cited to account for the difference:

> Man and wife built one house to live in together. But life became so
> unbearable that man abandoned woman to her house and built the
> *aba* in which he might dwell with other men. Men and women can

---

3. Before the construction of cold houses, men slept in another hut (*nda* proper) or in a portion of the kitchen partitioned off from the cooking and the women and children.

only live together by living apart. So to this day if a man's presence should bother a woman, she may always smoke up the fire and drive him out with eyes smarting. She says: "Go to your council house you bother me." The *kisin* is women's sanctuary and she has means to defend it.

The *Nda-Kisin* is largely inhabited by women and children. It is a compact world with practically every bit of space used for some purpose. A *kisin* of more than several years of age is so thoroughly sooty from the cooking fires that the interior is very obscure, lit only by the two doors — the one leading out into the plantations and the other opening upon the central court. This obscurity, combined with the constant smokiness, creates an atmosphere in striking contrast to the world outside. In this sense it is a world of its own. Once accustomed to the atmosphere of the *kisin* the visitor feels a palpable coziness. Men, when they are sick or dying, generally prefer to return to a bed in the *kisin*. They were born there after all, and brought up amidst its constant activity.

The specialness of the space delimited by the structure of the *nda-kisin* can be seen by reference to four rituals which occur in relation to this building and which express certain attitudes towards it.

In the case of difficult delivery, when labor is exhausting the mother, the expectant father is encouraged to climb upon the roof of the *kisin* and, by carefully poking about, to try to discover the spot precisely above the stomach of his wife. Thrusting a hollow banana stem through the thatch he then pours a medicinal water through the stem onto his wife's belly. This medicine is a mixture of leaves and barks from various plants grown in the inner gardens (*fala*) and may also contain a splinter from the lintel of the back doorway. The explanation of the plant items from *fala* is that the child is thus encouraged to be born into the human world of responsiblities, out of the village of the dead from which his spirit comes. The actual village of his birth is thus assimilated to the village of the dead, and the confines of the womb to the confines of the village. The use of a splinter from the lintel of the back door has the same general meaning but assimilates the doorway, it appears, to the cervix of the womb.

The ritual is called simply "roof medicine." It appears to assimilate the house to the womb as well. Having penetrated the womb to create the child, the father must "penetrate" it again in symbolic form to release the child. The ritual which I observed was witnessed by perhaps a dozen villagers. Their quiet amusement at the father's poking around on the roof — their sense of the ribald — confirms the interpretation I have put upon the act.

It was the custom to take the clothes, weapons, and personal gear of a recently deceased man and display them on the roof of his hut at the time of the mortuary ceremonies. This is said to show who had died and what his sister's son would inherit; but it is also true that as the man's spirit had departed his clothes so it had departed his hut.

Another ritual associated with birth reflects upon the meanings tied up with the *nda-kisin* and its assimilation to both the womb and the sacred space of the ancestors. The mother and newborn remain in the house for upwards of a month without going out except for the necessary bodily functions, as neither is supposedly strong enough to leave. Within the house they are protected from the evil and envy of social life by the ancestors who cannot protect as effectively in the public arena of village life. The interior of the house is in some sense their space. After a month's time or so the child is ""outdoored": brought to the men's council house where he is given a name, he comes to occupy a place in public social space. The Fang say that he is not given a name at once because it is not certain that he has really survived — that the ancestors have really given him up. During the woman's confinement with her infant in the *nda*, special attention is paid to returning herself and her womb to normal. She undergoes vaginal irrigation and is purified by being whipped briskly with branches dipped in boiling water. I interpret this to mean that the identification achieved between house and womb is shifted and that by flagellation she is being toughened and prepared for her move away from a preoccupation with the womb, with internal space, into public and social space.

A related ritual occurs when the child is not born in the home. Often a woman, if facing her first birth, will chose to return to her mother and her own clan or, as is common nowadays, will choose the hospital for delivery. On returning to her husband's home she lays the infant inside the threshold, steps over him, and takes him up again. Thus, it is said, he is properly made at home and will not be unhappy or sick in his own house. I should like to suggest that if this association between house and womb prevails at the moment of childbirth, it is inappropriate that the child precede his mother into her own "womb." Rather he should be welcomed by her into it. It may also be suggested that by stepping over him she symbolically gives birth to him again within his and her proper home.

If the *nda-kisin* is the scene of the Fang's most vital primary experiences, it is not surprising that it and its structure are assimilated to the corporeal arena of these experiences. The assimilation may seem farfetched to us because of our tendency to treat our dwellings as "Skinner boxes" which we change rapidly, which condition us rather than becoming identified with our bodies, and in which we choose neither to be born or to die. But it is a perfectly natural application of the penchant for analogic extensions which the Fang manifest and which give to their world a unity it could not otherwise possess, in the absence of their interest in abstraction.[4]

The *aba* was the most heavily armed structure and the center of defense during unsettled times when the villages were palisaded. Throughout the day and night men were on guard within it. It was the structure from which the whole village was surveyed. Since the suppression of warfare it has functioned as the center of judicial dispute, and though it is no longer so centrally placed as to survey the entire village, it still maintains its importance in social and cultural affairs. Although smaller than in former days, it can still provide sleeping quarters for men of the village or strangers. Young men and older boys will often sleep there. Custom still requires that strangers first be hospitably seated and received there while they are carefully scrutinized. As a center of major ceremonies it provides a place of concealment for the changing of costumes or for the examination of neophytes. The main supporting post of the entrance, the *akon aba*, is at the center of these ceremonies. All those who enter and leave ritually lay their hands on the post, thus giving it an accumulated power.

When the village is ritually cleansed, the *aba* is the last and most important place to undergo purification. It is a lounging place during the day, and most masculine activities such as netmaking, basketry, iron and brass founding, carving, and the weaving of raffia roofing sheets take place within it. At night it becomes an arena for the imagination and for the recreation of the past as the center of story-telling or of entertainment by travelling troubadours who recount the great legends and wonder tales of the Fang.

Various ceremonies confirm the *aba* as the center of the man's world. There the male infant must be ritually presented by his mother to his father's close relatives shortly after he is born. When he is married, his wife and mother-in-law must each cook a ritual meal and present it to him and his relatives gathered there. It is there that he undertakes the ritual prohibitions and preparations for the outstanding pursuits of manhood such as warfare and courtship. Serious concern begins to be

---

4. J.W. Fernandez, *Fang Representations under Accultation*, The SSRC-ACLS Conference: African Intellectual Reactions to the West.

entertained on his account when, in his old age, he can no longer make his way to the *aba*. And when he dies, his male friends and relatives must gather there in proper recognition of his death, and as a dramatic demonstration that the group has surmounted this loss.

The *aba* played and still plays a crucial role in the acculturation of the young. It is there that Fang boys and young men learn how to act and how to speak, for the *aba* is fundamentally the place of talk (*adzo*). It is expected that after years of respectful and attentive observation of the techniques of dispute a man already married and with children can take a strong position in the affairs of his family.

It must be made clear, however, that the *aba* is no longer the arena it once was. In conjunction with the construction of European-style houses for the use of the nuclear family head rather than for the extended family (*ndebot*), there has been a movement by the younger men who hold a primary school diploma to take their meals in these "cold houses" rather than in the *aba*. The threat of abandonment of such an arena of social and cultural affairs is naturally felt by the older men as a threat to the Fang way of life as a whole.

The Village: Plans. The Fang speak of the various plans in a man's head — *akomengeh, mekomengeh* (literally "preparations"). Among these is the plan to build a house — *akomengeh nda*. Traditionally a young person will have participated by his early teens in at least one shift of village and, by the age of puberty, will find himself in need of his own quarters where he and his brothers can entertain others free of the injunctions of his mother and father. He will also have participated in the pleasurable construction of those small houses — *ebem elik* — in which the Fang protect themselves when sojourning at old village sites or in the deep forest. He will also have come to appreciate the meaning — the interplay of images — of various architectures of Fang life.

There is thus a very positive feeling associated with the planning and bringing to completion of new structures. In respect to old structures which have outlived their vitality — their positive association with primary experience we might say — this planning and construction is revitalizing. Yet the Fang, in my experience, relish anticipation more than consummation, and houses will often stand in a state of partial incompletion for a long period of time.

The importance of leadership in the building of the *aba* reminds us how important this factor generally is in Fang society — a society highly egalitarian and individualist in impulse. Any visitor to Fang country remarks considerable variation in the aesthetic aspect of the villages.[5] Some are perfect replications of the ideal — with every house aligned and every house completed, with a common bark decoration throughout and the courtyard swept clean every morning of animal droppings and trash; while others seem in a perpetual state of half completion with trash strewn about and weeds growing in the central court. These great differences are directly traceable to the powers and talents of persuasion and sense of order of the lineage leaders.

In considering the building practices of the Fang, it should be pointed out that the verb for house construction — *along* — means "to weave," and is the same word for the construction of a basket. The materials used in house building — liane strips and raffia are virtually the same as those used in basketry, and so the common verb is appropriate.

It is important to point out the association between house building and basket making for several reasons. First, a frequent experience of young children is to be carried to the plantations by their

---

5. Tessman, *Die Pangwe*, p. 72.

mothers and to be left in a back basket (*nkweng*) to sleep and for protection against the elements.

Also, though we have been discussing Euclidean space in this paper and have referred to the varieties of rectangular and cubic forms, we must be cautious. Just as we have had difficulty in identifying the third dimension of Euclidean space among them, so we must also point out that while from the Euclidean view a round basket and a square house may be entirely different structures, much more of a homomorphism or topological equivalence may prevail in Fang thinking. This equivalence is expressed in the common verb and in other ways such as the fact that basket weaving and house weaving are felt to be male responsibilities.

In traditional house building women were involved only in the muddy work of preparing the foundation. In the more modern housing the Fang have adopted a Cameroon custom of using bamboo wattling, then filling the walls with four inches or more of mud. Making this mud wall, which is often finished with a cement crepissage, is a task which falls to women because of the traditional division of labor in which pottery making and other tasks involving mud and clay were their responsibility. But the consequence is that women now have an important role in house building, a fact which to some extent undermines the traditional distinction between men building the structures and women filling them with vital activity. The extension and replication involved here is that by which, in the creation of the infant, the red drop of female blood containing the homunculus is surrounded by the protective and fostering shell of white male semen. In the adult person the male element is the skeletal structure and tissues and tendons, all white, within which the sources of vitality, the blood and organs, carry on their primary activity.[6]

When we examine the migration stages associated with the genealogy, we note that Fang villagers rarely remain longer than fifteen years in the same location and the average is closer to eight to ten years. It is said that this is the time it takes the thatch on the roofs to rot twice over. This periodic decentering of the village had a powerful revitalizing effect, as testified to by the Fang themselves. Now that their villages have been regrouped and relatively fixed in place by government sanction, the Fang remember vividly the challenge of chopping a new home out of the forest, the construction of new dwellings, and the transfer of belongings from the old to the new. Often, of course, new villages were constructed because of bitter conflict within the *mvogabot*, but the act of establishing a *ndebot* anew within the forest affirmed the strength and independence of the family members involved — an independence that had often been brought into question in the *mvogabot* dispute.

Fang mental and material culture, it should be noted, was not so complex or recondite as to prevent an extended family from breaking away and re-establishing the Fang cultural universe virtually in its entirety elsewhere in the equatorial forests. The point to be made here is that these periodic decenterings were an affirmation of the group's powers in respect to their culture — their total containment of that culture, as it were. We see in Bwiti, the cult whose architectonics are examined below, this same confidence in recreating a universe. In both cases the consequences are revitalizing and in both cases an essential part of that revitalization is found in new construction itself.

The recent decentering caused by the attraction of towns, trading centers and coastal capitals is not similarly restorative, however. In most cases it is dispiriting. The villages, rather than being the centers of their universe, as they were in former times, are coming to seem backwaters. In the minds of many villagers now, to be really revitalized is to experience life in the towns. This is an important

---

6. J.W. Fernandez, "Principles of Opposition and Vitality in Fang Aesthetics," *The Journal of Aesthetics and Art Criticism*, XXV, 1, Fall 1966, pp. 53-64.

shift in the Fang sense of spatial location. While formerly they could revitalize by recreating their old culture with new buildings in new space, now as their villages open up, they are confronted by the necessity of meeting an alien culture in alien buildings and in alien space.

What has happened is that men's plans for construction have shifted to focus upon the "cold" houses: they are a suitable replacement, for by cost and size the bringing to fruition of such a plan is a much more lengthy and laborious process. It is not unusual for men to be at work for up to a decade trying to gather the resources to complete one. Instead of the periodic revitalization of entirely new construction we have the ebb and flow of revitalization as one or another addition or improvement is achieved in the same long planned construction.

The Aba Eboka: A Syncretic Religious Structure. It is appropriate to conclude this discussion of Fang architecture and architectonics with a discussion of the chapels built by the contemporary Fang syncretist cult of Bwiti.[7] These are called the *aba eboka*, "the council house of *eboka*" (from the alkaloid hallucinogen, *tabernenthes eboga*, taken in this cult).[8] In examining this structure, we see how many of the meaningful elements which are seen embodied in traditional structures are incorporated in new constellations. In the cult of the Bwiti, however, we find produced out of centrifugality, a return to centripetality by a harmony of progressive in-turning spirals in space.

We have pointed out that a centrifugality is replacing the centripetality of everyday village life — the endless circles out to the plantations and into the forest and back to the village again. These centripetal poses of Fang domestic life were strung on the deeper unilineal historic migration northeast to southwest. Gradually, by a process of involution, the circles grew too tight — "the obscure forest creeps in upon the village and overhangs it" in the claustrophobic idiom of the Fang (*bi amora jibi akal ndendang; afan du so mbu ase, da bo bia jibi*). The Fang villages moved out and onward in their progressive migrations to the sea. Transitional circumstances of colonialism and migration have changed all that. The villages have practically all been stabilized so that the drive to the sea is no longer possible. But at the same time the attractions of the cities, towns, and trading centers have decentered this stabilized village life. In respect to the traditional spatial harmonies, it is the worst of all possible worlds.

Another consequence of modernization is the increasing concentration of energies on the "cold houses," which cost so much in time and resources that they tend to deflect the meaning of Fang architecture away from the primary and vital experiences and male and female distinctions with which the *aba* and the *nda-kisin* were associated (and which infused their structure with content) directing that meaning instead to the materialist component. Moreover, as we have pointed out, the new houses tend to cluster their accessory structures, including the *aba*, in compounds about them and thus break down the essential "unities in oppositions" of the classic Fang village. Finally, the complementarity in the traditional sex roles — insofar as the *nda-kisin* was centered — where men built a structure for women to inhabit, is confused by the important contribution of both sexes to the construction of the cold houses. The *aba eboka*, a hot house, must be understood architectonically as a response to the various dissolutions, decenterings, and redistributions in the Fang spatial and social order.

---

7. See J.W. Fernandez, "Christian and Fang Witchcraft," *Cahiers d'Etudes Africaines*, Paris, II, 6, pp. 244-270; "Symbolic Consensus in a Fang Reformative Cult," *American Anthropologist*, Vol. 67, No. 4, Aug. 1965, pp. 902-927; "Unbelieving Subtle Words: Representation and Integration in the Sermons of an African Reformative Cult," *Journal of the History of Religions*, vol. 6, No. 1, Aug. 1966, pp. 43-69; *Fang Representations under Accultation*.

8. Harrison Pope, "Tabernenthes Eboga: An African Narcotic Plant of Social Importance," *Economic Botany*, Vol. 23,No.2, pp. 174-184.

In most Bwiti villages (rarely are all the inhabitants of any village members of the cult) the *aba eboka* occupies a central place at one end, the same place formerly occupied by the *aba*. This is one reason for its name, although the *aba eboka* is a good deal more dominating than any traditional *aba* and, moreover, opens out upon the village plaza as the *aba* rarely did. Many of its rituals extend out well into the central court, inviting the involvement of the entire village. The plaza is thus restored to its centrality of place and the *aba* to the surveillance, spiritual in this case, of the entire village.

Other reasons help to account for the choice of the name *aba* for the Bwiti chapel. Most relevant perhaps is the fact that the *aba* as the male building was the local seat of the patrilineage and of the clan. Chief among the objectives of the Bwiti cult is the re-establishment of contact with the ancestors too much abandoned under the influence of Christian evangelism. Since the *aba* was the structure where the living representatives of the patrilineage gathered to celebrate their communality of descent, it is appropriate that the religious arena in which the Fang are trying to reassert that communality be similarly named. Furthermore, those who participate in the *aba eboka* come to dwell, like those who participated in the myth of telling and legend singing of the *aba*, in other realms of being — in realms of the creative imagination.

By no means, however, is the *aba eboka* to be understood as an exclusively male world. Here we have an important syncretic integration. In former days women very rarely took part in men's rituals, just as it was exceptional that they should take any place in the *aba*. By contrast, in the *aba eboka*, they take virtually equal part and equal place. The *aba* itself is, in most Bwiti traditions, clearly divided into a male side and a female side, an opposition which attracts to it a whole set of binary oppositions in the minds of some Bwiti cosmologists.

Just as the oppositions which were salient in traditional villages were mediated by the round of social intercourse, so the basic oppositions of the chapel are mediated by the dance patterns which knit together in their circles the side of the sun and the side of the moon, the side of the male and the side of the female. In respect to the presence of both men and women in the ritual as well as to the circularity of these dance patterns, the members of Bwiti say that just as an infant cannot be created without the congress of men and women, so the religion of Bwiti cannot be created without men and women dancing together. The expression is particularly apt, for in their cult house and among themselves, the members of Bwiti are fashioning a spiritual body (*esamba*). It is apt in a further sense as well: in the decades preceding the 1960's, the Fang suffered a population decline which they recognized as infertility in their women. One of the often declared purposes of Bwiti in the 1940's and 1950's was to make the women fertile again.

Figure 2 indicates the circular configuration described by the Bwiti membership as they enter into the chapel, as they carry on their night long performance, and as they exit in the gray dawn. I would emphasize that the architectonic structure of the Bwiti chapel is not adequately apprehended without an understanding of the ways the rituals that proceed within and around it integrate its parts and give it content. This is the same point we made for the *nda-kisin* and the traditional *aba*. The essentials of the dances are: 1) the progressive circles of the entrance and exit dances as seen in our diagram, and 2) the circularity of most of the interior dances which begin at the altar, sweep around the sacred pillar — *akon aba* — and return to the altar. In the entrance dances (called collectively "dances of the *minkin*") we see a reasonably approximate reiteration of the Fang migration experience: the progression from the barren savannah into the equatorial rain forest and on to the sea. The dances proceed in progressive circles from out in the center of the *nsung*, to the small welcoming hut for the ancestors, around the sacred pillar in a tight and loose circle, and finally to the altar. The area behind the alter is called *mang* (sea) or *si ayat* (the land beyond). The entrance ritual is also a representation of the diachronic development of the Fang relationship to their total space.

The *akon aba* is highly important in this interpretation just as it is symbolically central in all Bwiti ritual. Like the *aba eboka* itself, the *akon aba* has its origins in a traditionally important feature of Fang architecture, the *akon* or entrance post of the men's council house upon which a gorilla head was often hung and which was touched for support and guidance by all men coming in and out. It thus expressed and "absorbed" the power of the male community and it is of interest that ceremonies of village cleansing were often staged around it.

The widespread general features of the *akon aba eboka* are the following: 1) the manufacture of the post out of the redwood of the *padouk* tree (*pterocarpus S.*) relating it to the red path of life and death (*zen ening ye awu*) which the soul of the adept must trod in passing over to the far land (*si avat*) 2) the carving of at least one and usually two holes running transverse to each other, labelled variously the birth of man (*abiale mot*) and the birth of the soul (*abiale nsisim*) or the entrance hole of the birth of man (*abiale mwan mot*) and the exit hole (the bottom hole) of the death of man (*awu mwan mot*) 3) the division of the column into three sections: a) *djop*: heaven, the above, the land of the spirits; b) *si ye ening*: the land of the life between the two holes; and c) *song*: the grave, the earth, the portion of the column below the death hole, descending into earth. The members of Bwiti say that the spirits of new men descend down the *akon aba* and pass through the birth hole into corporeal existence. They continue down through life on this earth, pass through the death hole and into the grave, from whence they arise again, in two transformations, back to spiritual life in the sky. Thus there is a circulation of spirits on this axis mundi both descending and ascending. Life is a descent and death an ascent.

The vertical axis is very important in the Euclidean space of the Bwiti chapel. Prayers are often made addressing the ceiling, for the spirits of the dead are said to cluster along the ridge pole as they come in out of the forest in response to their ritual invitations. The rafters are strung with raffia streamers, and a "telephone" line of liane strips is laid from the top of the *akon aba* to the altar. From it are suspended the sacred circles (*nkat*) which define the three focal spaces of sacred activity. Along this line the spiritual messages pass back and forth between altar and sacred pillar.

The pillar has a further important association with the mythical *adzap* tree of Fang legend which symbolizes Fang entrance from the savannah into the rain forest.[9] The progress of the Fang, *oswi nken*, in their migrations was blocked by this tree and with the help of the Pygmees they had to bore a hole through it in order to pass on. In this way the pierced column of the *akon aba* contributes to a significant reliving of the Fang past in the progressive spirals of the entrance dances.

The dances within the chapel, both those involving the cult leaders and those involving the entire membership,are circular and counter-clockwise, and of various tempos ranging from the vertiginous *obango*, the dance of the drums, to the very slow *esameh*, the dance of the candles. In reiteration of some of the most favorite traditional dances of the Fang a few begin with rows of men and of women facing each other on either side of the cult house, then dancing together and retreating, imitating various agricultural and housekeeping motions. The symbolic account of these dances by Bwiti leadership is often quite extensive, but the point here is that they are intended to bring together the various quadrants of the cult house in centripetal fashion. The dances culminate in the ritual compression of the entire membership into an ever tightening circle until they are one body or one heart (*nlem mvore*). Another objective is to enable the soul, *nsisim*, to escape the body and join the ancestor spirits on the roof of the chapel through the compounding harmonies of the dance. Hence these interior centripetal dances knit the structural parts of the *aba eboka* — both

---

9. See J. W. Fernandez, *Redistributive Accultation and Ritual Reintegration in Fang Culture*, unpub. Ph.D dissertation, Northwestern University, Evanstown, 1962.

vertical (the below with the above), and horizontal (the upstream and the downstream), both the *akon aba* and the *mang*.

The *aba eboka* is often complexly subdivided by Bwiti leaders. What follows is the topography of the chapel as conceived by Musingi Eko Obama of the Asumege Ening branch of Bwiti, Ayol, District of Medounu (fig. 2). The third dimension, so often missing in traditional accounts of Fang space, is here introduced as the dimension of binary oppositions which are integrated both in the progressive circles of the entrance dances and in the centripetal interior dances. We should be aware from our diagrams that the *aba eboka* includes *both* male and female chambers. These are robing chambers as well as the chambers for the private rituals of the male and female membership. Just as the ritual of cult ceremony integrates male and female contributions, so the *aba* itself syncretizes within its overall construction the male and female buildings which were, traditionally, separately distinguished.

The complexity of the Ayol chapel organization lies in the fact that it not only divides the chapel on the *akon aba*-altar axis upon which the male-female and associated binary sets are arranged, but it also has a right of chapel — left of chapel axis perpendicular to the former, which divides the arena

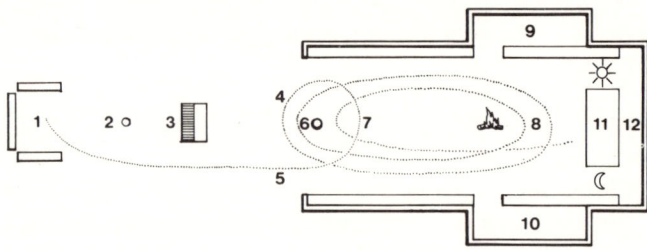

2. *Plan of the* aba eboka, *showing the circular configurations described by the Bwiti membership as they enter the chapel.*

1. Njimba *— creation spot 2.* Ku *— after-birth 3. Welcoming hut for the spirits 4. Death 5. Birth 6.* Akon aba *— entrance post 7.* Bunume *— this world 8.* Mbwol *— the other world 9. Men 10. Women 11. Altar 12.* Mang esi ayat *— the sea, or, the land beyond.*

of natural activity from the world of the beyond (*si ayat* or *mang*). Entering the chapel, one passes in through the left side of the *akon aba* (facing out). This is the female side, the side of birth. When exiting from the chapel one passes out the right side which is the male side, the side of death and cruelty and war. In the reversal of realities, which is a Bwiti objective, the people make their entrance in the evening on the birth side, being born into the world of the ancestors, while in the morning they pass out the right side and die back into the world of the living. The overall division of the ritual is between the *Zen Abiale*, the road of birth, which is sung and danced until midnight, and the *Zen Awu*, the road of death, which is sung after midnight until dawn. Thus in Bwiti ceremony there is the phase associated with entrance and the phase associated with exit.

A closer account of some ritual occurrences involved in entrance dances will, as in our discussion of the *nda-kisin*, give us a clearer idea of the primary experiences which are being extended into the chapel structure and assimilated in its content. We already recognize that the space within the chapel is a space of spiritual reality. But we must also consider the corporeality of the structure as suggested by the dances of entrance immediately following the *njimba* — the gathering of all the membership outside the chapel for preparation and personal prayer. At this point the men and women divide into two groups. During the preceding *minkin* they make their entrance dances all together into the chapel. Here, the women enter first. The three senior female members of the cult, *Yombo*, are clothed in white and precede the rest of the membership, which is clothed in regular red and white ritual garments. These women dance into the chapel, with candles in hand, bringing with them a small stone found in a clear sacred pool in the forest. This stone, sent to man by Nyingwan Mebege, the female principle of the universe, is the principle of creation, the stone of birth (*akok abiale*). The *Yombo* deposit it at the altar where its presence will enable the ritual inducement of fertility.

The assimilation of the chapel itself to a womb is seen not only in the placement of the "sacred homunculus" within it but also in the men's entrance dances which take place immediately after the women's. Arriving at the birth entrance of the chapel, the men stop. The leaders place their hands on the thatch or the lintel piece above them, then the entire group, in close formation, backs up and comes forward again, this time proceeding a short distance into the chapel. This process continues until the male group arrives entirely within the chapel to begin their circles around the *akok abiale*. These ritual actions at the birth entrance are predominantly explained as: 1) the difficult birth of men out of this life into the spiritual world of the ancestors, and 2) the entrance of the male organ into the female body. The first explanation confirms the assimilation of the chapel space to the spiritual world and the second explanation confirms the assimilation of the chapel to the female body in ways similar to the assimilation we have pointed out for the *nda-kisin*. The entrance dance represents sexual entrance, the dying out of this world and birth into the next.

Though the primary association of the chapel is with the female body — the structure also emerges as androgynous in the consequence of syncretism. From time to time informants speak of the chapel as representing a person on his back with the *akon aba* — whose female association has been discussed — in this case standing as well for the male member. Since Fang does not make gender distinctions, the English convention of "he" is not in the original which is rendered in the impersonal and neuter.

> The chapel is a person crucified. On the right hand the men's chamber on the left the women's chamber. He lies on his back. Behind him is his life and death the earth. Before him the future of his spirit. On the right the sun, on the left the moon. The head is the *sugu*, the area of mystery. In the center of the chapel is the fire which is the heart. The *akon aba* is sex organ. It is of the man and the woman.

> Outside the chapel are a fire and a hole *(ku)* in which the blood of the sacrificed chicken and the afterbirth of this person of the chapel are buried. So there we also put the afterbirth of each member of Bwiti who is born into the life of *Eboga*.

> The fire in the center of the chapel is directly opposite the entrance doors of the male and female chambers. It is the heart. It is also the sexual mingling of man and woman. It is the fire that burns at the center of the earth. The fire warns and protects the chapel against evil spirits but we replace it with a lantern when dancing begins in earnest. The fire is too strong for the spirits. It offends them. We replace it with a *douce lumière*.

One reason why the fire may offend arises from the fact that the spirit world is conceived of as without sexual distinction, and in the process of their rituals the Bwitis aspire to attain that state. Any kind of overt sexuality is censured in Bwiti although at the symbolic level reference may be made to sexuality in an attempt to restore fertility to the real world. In a similar way the chapel itself, while manifesting in its various parts male-female and other binary distinctions, moves toward androgyny. Overall, we may say that the assimilation of the female body to the chapel is dominant by reason of the rebirth and fertility themes in worship and the fact of Nyingwan Mebege as the chief object of worship. But we see as well that the traditional male association of the *aba* and indeed the overall complexity of Bwiti symbolism make any such unitary or reductionist interpretation of the architectonics of the cult house incomplete.

Within the structure of the *aba eboka*, many things are happening at many levels at once, but we may reemphasize the overall contribution that the Bwiti and its cult house makes in the face of the decentering and centrifugality and the materialistic individualism the Fang have experienced in recent years. By ritual process it reestablishes the content of structure, the interactive representation of body in building, and building in body. Its rituals relating to the topography of the cult house restate the progressive characteristics of traditional Fang mythological-legendary movement in space. The rituals of interior circulation, with their increasingly tighter knitting-together of opposites or contraries (male side - female side, spirit side - earth side) finally reduce all to that unity called oneheartedness (*nlem mvore*). Above all, in the face of the secularization (empirical reductionism) of modernization, the Bwiti chapel provides a sacred space in which troubled men can be reborn — a space away from the daily glare and oppression of the sun, a space of the more *douce lumiere* of the night, of the moon, of the Sister of God, of the imagination. At the same time, just as Bwiti and the *aba eboka* offer a syncretism of elements traditionally separated, and does not in that way simply attempt to return to the architectonics of the past, so the *aba eboka* itself is not simply a house of raffia and liane like the traditional woven houses. With its wattle and daub walls and in its membership's desire that it be roofed with zinc, it partakes instead of that modernity in house structure desired by the Fang. But even here it is compensatory in its modernity. While superficially a "cold" house, it is very much heated up with meaningful activity.

Conclusion: The Axiology of Quality Space — The Passion for Journeying Contained. I have tried to relate Fang buildings to the architectonics of Fang life which arise out of their myths and legends, their migration experiences, their kin and clan group experiences, their relationships within the village and between the village and the plantations and the forest, even out of their relationships with their women and with their peers in dance and song. Ritual actions in relationship to particular structures are helpful in our understanding of the part these structures play in the overall architectonics of the culture. Where rapid transition and acculturation break down the associations and extensions between these personal spaces and this larger architectonic, men begin to concentrate on structure itself — in the Fang case they concentrate on the material rather than on the aesthetic aspects of structure. The cult house of a Fang religious movement consciously sets about (through ritual action in relation to cult house topography) reestablishing the relationship of personal space to cultural architectonics.

The colonial situation has been an unsettling, decentering experience for Fang. The blandishments, the activities, and the material attractions of colonial life all preyed upon the Fang passion for journeying, and many ended up alienated from their world in colonial towns and colonial enterprises. The Bwiti cult chapel provides a locale where the passion for journeying — at least symbolic journeying — could be satisfied within and about a vital center where centrifugality (decentering) could be experienced in a centripetal way.

I have directed the discussion toward the notion of "quality space" with several thoughts in mind. First, in space defined by architectural structure a special quality arises partially as a consequence of the constraints of that structure but more importantly as a consequence of the activities that take place within that space. Secondly, that space must contain both an extension of personal body images and an intension of mythical and cosmic images if it is to have quality. I have tried to show how this is the case. Thirdly, I would speculate that any organization of architectural space must locate those who live in that space in an optimum position in respect to their own bodies and in relation to the cosmos. Though there should be some caution involved in extending a Euclidean three-attribute space to the Fang, nevertheless the Bwiti chapel and its topography achieves quality in space because it locates the membership in respect to: 1) downriver progression (*mfa oswi nkeng*); 2) counter clockwise centripetal involution resulting in a drawing in of vectors toward a central point (*nlem mvore*) in the horizontal cross-village, cross-chapel plane; 3) spiritual ascent and descent in the vertical plane clearly framed in the *akon aba*.

But more than locating the membership in this space, the intent of worship is to move the membership beyond life and death over to the other side (*mfa avat*). The final qualitative achievement of the cult house and its ritual is to enable the membership to escape its confinements.

Sermon in Stone

Robert Maxwell

Dean Robert Maxwell was interested in discovering "readings which were relevant to the recent discourse on ritual," and this led to a search through the indices of his favorite books, a process that became in his own words —"a skit on me as a teacher." He explained, "there is skepticism in the face of propaganda, if you like. I wanted to explore ideas... arouse curiosity... with a theatrical quality. In a piece this short, for teaching purposes, it's not as important to cover a field as to stimulate the student." The article takes the form of a dialogue between Man and Woman, yet it is "hardly a Socratic dialogue — more like the alternation of male and female voices on a French radio station." When asked whether he thought the act of writing itself had become a ritual activity, he replied, "as a shadow of an idea."

Q: What can this elusiveness of meaning suggest?
A: Exactly that it is elusive.

■   ■   ■

IN A SMALL ART GALLERY in Manhattan it is no surprise to encounter an easy-chair, an occasional table, a television set, all made of stone. After soft sculpture, hard. These objects are not made for relaxation, but for recreation. We know this. We accept it. We collaborate with it. Yet there is some surprise, when we press the button marked participation, to be made party to a conversation. By a knowing trick of the display, the voices appear to emanate from the television, whose stony screen maintains an inhospitable blankness. There is nothing for it but to listen for the moment, always expecting to give up at a certain point ....

Woman: Ritual is a communal form of magic.[1]

Man: Connected at first with the prolongation of magic in myth; then as history speeds up, with the prolongation of myth in religion, of religion in art, of art in life. Today the most commonplace object has its aura of magic, to which its price in the marketplace is not unrelated.

Woman: To us the most essential point about magic and religious ritual is that it steps in only where knowledge fails. Supernaturally founded ceremonial grows out of life, but it never stultifies the practical efforts of man.[2]

Man: There is always a point where knowledge fails. In science, the known stretches to the edge of the unknown. Nothing, therefore, is fully known. What remains unknown is framed within the known, but the unknown also frames the known.

The practical efforts of man constitute a sphere of activity which, like the earth's own biosphere, is extended between unknown heights and depths. It is both tenuous and hollow. This sphere is

---

1. Langer: *Philosophy in a New Key.*
2. Malinowski: *The Foundations of Faith and Morals.*

maintained as much by artifice as by common sense.

Woman: A constant component of poetic significance is that the poem's language looks as much like a ritual or a game...or pure artifice, as it does like a means of conveying sense.[3]

Man: Games and rituals are sustained as much by artifice as by common-sense. They both exist to perpetuate a myth, to prolong it efficacy, to extend its hold on life.

Woman: Regardless of whether the myth or the ritual is the original, they replicate each other; the myth exists on the conceptual level and the ritual on the level of action.[4]

Man: In the football game, the level of action is constantly interrupted by the intervention of the rules; the match cannot for instance be allowed to degenerate into a brawl. The rule structure is sacrosanct, it defines the nature of the game; thus the rules of the game are repeatedly brought to our liminal consciousness, although we believe that what we see is at the level of action. By exposing its rule-structure as a fragile creation of the mind, the game returns us to ritual solidarity, to the will to perpetuate it.

Woman: All games are defined by a set of rules which in practice allow the playing of any number of matches. Ritual, which is also "played," is on the other hand like a favored instance of a game, remembered from among the possible ones because it is only one which results in a particular type of equilibrium between the sides. The transposition is readily seen in the case of the Gahuku-Gama of New Guinea, who have learnt football but who will play several days running, as many matches as are necessary for both sides to reach the same score. This is treating a game as a ritual.[5]

Man: In the modern game the ritual is implicit. We like to think that we read newspapers only for information. To the extent that we protect our rituals, our rituals protect us. In good health, we forget how much we depend on ritual.

Woman: While other diseases de-socialize, tuberculosis project[s] you into a minor ethnographic society, part tribe, part monastery, part phalanstery; rites, constraints, protections.[6]

Man: It is in the minor ethnographic society that the power of ritual is most energetically affirmed — the perpetuation of solidarity requires it.

Woman: There are perhaps no other external traits which are so typical of the secret society, and so sharply distinguish it from the open society, than the high valuation of usages, formulas, and rites, and their peculiar preponderance over the purposive contents of the group, if not their contrast with them. At times, in fact, the contents are less anxiously guarded than the secret of the ritual.[7]

Man: We have heard of the rites of learned discourse, another instance of implicit values. However, if we cease to protect our rituals from life, they will no longer have the power to protect us: like stories, like art, they depend on a willing suspension of disbelief.

---

3. Riffaterre: *The Semiotics of Poetry.*
4. Levi-Strauss: *Structural Anthropology*
5. Levi-Strauss: *The Savage Mind.*
6. Barthes: *Roland Barthes on Roland Barthes.*
7. Simmel: *The Secret Society.*

Woman: Ritual...is primarily an *articulation* of feeling. The ultimate product of such articulation is not a simple emotion, but a complex, permanent *attitude*.... A rite regularly performed is the constant reiteration of sentiments toward "first and last things": it is not a free expression of emotions, but a disciplined rehearsal of "right attitudes."[8]

Man: With the loss of belief comes the loss of power. Ritual is a fragile form; it constitutes a discipline and exacts good form in behavior. It cannot survive doubt. Outside of tribal loyalties, outside of the monastery, outside of the Unité d'Habitation, doubt is endemic.

Woman: Life can express itself and realize its freedom only through forms: yet forms must also necessarily suffocate life and obstruct freedom.[9]

Man: So long as good form governs behavior, so long as belief persists, forms render objective and universal all that which, at its origin in feelings and urges, is confused and inarticulate. So long as belief persists, forms enable us to see ourselves in relation to others. When belief fails, we suffer an unremitting urge to re-establish belief at another level: new form, new art, new ritual. Is not new ritual a contradiction?

Woman: The forms in which life manifests itself and by means of which it acquires an objective form signify both a resistance to life and an indispensable support. If they present obstacles to it, it is obstacles through which it becomes conscious of its power and learns to use that power.[10]

Man: To be constructive, then, we have first to destroy; but that also implies that in order to be properly, fully destructive, we have to construct.

Woman: Life can manifest itself only in particular forms: yet, owing to its essential restlessness, life constantly struggles against its own products, which have become fixed and do not move along with it. This process manifests itself as the displacement of an old form by a new one. This constant change in the content of culture, even of whole cultural styles, is the sign of the infinite fruitfulness of life. At the same time, it marks the deep contradiction between life's eternal flux and the objective validity and authenticity of the forms through which it proceeds. It moves constantly between death and resurrection--between resurrection and death.[11]

Man: There is something paradoxical in that. Although it is possible to distinguish, correctly it seems, between the objective forms of art and the subjective states of mind which both produce it and are reproduced by it, that formulation does not seem to allow for the intensity of the struggle between art and life, as I myself experience it.

Woman: The work of art leads its life beyond reality. To be sure, the work of art draws its content from reality; but from visions of reality, it builds a sovereign realm.[12]

Man: That realm is itself magical, in that it will resolve for me only what it has resolved for itself. To participate in that resolution I have to give myself to it. To enter that sovereign realm demands that I be abject — a loss of my own sovereignty. By contrast, ritual is less demanding. Through ritual even a simple object of common utility can draw me into magic, without leaving the every-day.

---

8. Langer: *Philosophy in a New Key.*
9. Simmel: *The Conflict in Modern Culture.*
10. Cassirer: *The Philosophy of Symbolic Forms.*
11. Simmel: *The Conflict in Modern Culture.*
12. Simmel: *The Handle.*

Woman: A spinning machine is perhaps the most impressive manifestation of a functional idea, and an "abstract" painting is perhaps the most expressive manifestation of pure form, but both have a minimum of content.[13]

Man: It would seem then that there is nothing made by man which does not have both form and content. Form is indispensable, but obtrudes itself between our desire and its fulfillment. We long for form to be transparent, but the longer we gaze, the more it becomes opaque... the way the photograph of someone we love turns into an enigma.

Woman: The Photograph belongs to that class of laminated objects whose two leaves cannot be separated...[14]

Man: But an enigma whose ...

Woman: The Photograph belongs to that class of laminated objects whose two leaves cannot be separated without destroying them both.

Man: It's hard to see how disbelief can affect a photograph. Its loss of power is more a loss of stimulus--it reveals less and less of what we first thought we knew. Of all objects, the photograph is among the flattest. Yet it is this minimal quality which allows it to function as an object of common utility, to be carried in the wallet, shown to friends unexpectedly, found in due course on our dead body, listed among our effects. What started as an actuality has hardened into a replica, lived on as an emblem, died as a relic, been resuscitated as a symbol.

Woman: Symbolic liaisons can be included among the liaisons of coexistence; these exist between the symbol and what it evokes and are characterized by the relation of participation. They are set in a mythic or speculative vision of a whole in which symbol and thing symbolized are equal parts.[15]

The tape comes to an end. Our curiosity aroused, we look keenly around the gallery. It is empty. The custodians are looking at us strangely. It is time to go. From the door, we look back at the stone television. Its screen is still completely blank, although fleetingly we have the impression of an image. Something, or some idea of something ....

13. Panofsky: *Meaning in the Visual Arts.*
14. Barthes: *Camera Lucida.*
15. Perelman: *The Realm of Rhetoric.*

1. Duchamp: "Hidden Noise."

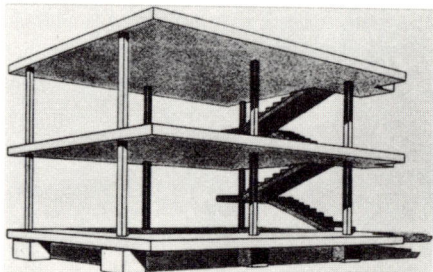

2. Le Corbusier: The Domino Diagram.

Georgica and LeBrun Houses [1]

*Diana Agrest
and Mario Gandelsonas*

IN OUR HOUSES, ritualistic elements of the city are transformed and used at a smaller scale. The clash of incorporating the public into the private domain — of transforming the basilica type, the piazza, large public stairs, into domestic forms — always creates the potential for rituals to occur. The houses frame sequences of particular places and experiences, with specific architectural elements allowing the transition from one situation to another. One always has the indication that there is something beyond, something to look at or someone to look to. This is related both to film, where meaning is generated through a sequence of frames, and to theatre, where meaning is created in a symbolic performance. Different spaces are created for possible rituals, whether they be an elaborate ball in a gallery or the theatrical descent of a stair.

In our architecture, meaning is derived from the relationship between objects rather than from a single object. Sometimes two conflicting *partis* are overlapped and generate new situations in their effect on one another. For example, the Georgica House can be read as the transformation of two bars into four towers by the intersection of the gallery. The axis of symmetry is shifted from the front public edge to the rear water edge through a basilica-type spatial sequence, generating a fifth tower and a new symmetry. From the water, the house becomes a backdrop for the sequence of towers and galleries.

1. Georgica House. Leonardo Zylberberg, Kathy Kling, Kevin Kennon, Karen Ludlow, and Jon Stark, *Assistants*.
LeBrun House. Kathy Kling, Leonardo Zylberberg, Karen Ludlow, Michael Stanton, and Jon Stark, *Assistants*.

1. Georgica House, East Hampton, New York, 1981-82. View from east.

2. Georgica House. Front elevation.

3. Georgica House. Rear elevation.

4. Georgica House. View from entry drive.

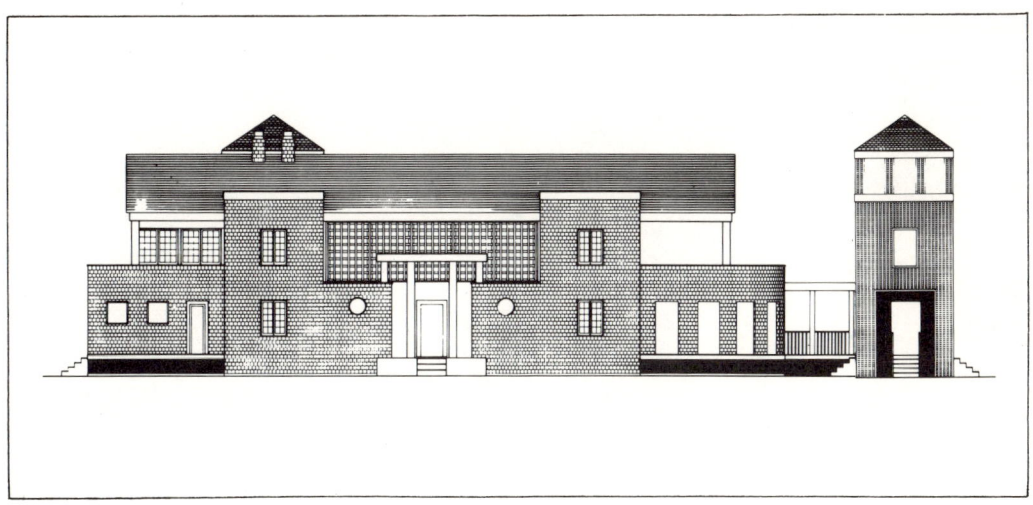

5. Georgica House. Front elevation.

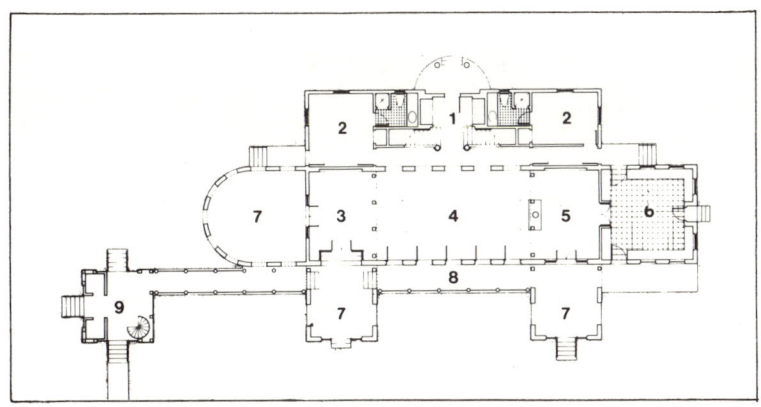

6. Georgica House. First floor plan.

1. Foyer 2. Bedroom 3. Library 4. Living room 5. Dining room 6. Kitchen 7. Porch 8. Gallery 9. Pool house 10. Balcony 11. Living room below 12. Master bath 13. Dressing room 14. Master bedroom 15. Bedroom 16. Porch

7. Georgica House. Second floor plan.

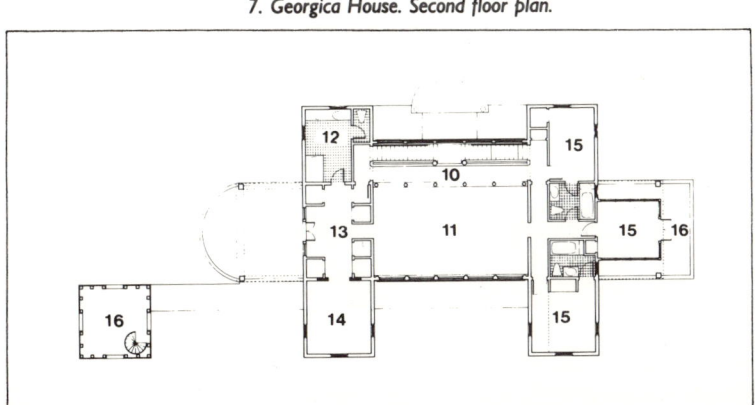

8. LeBrun House, Scarsdale, New York, 1982-83. Front elevation.

9. LeBrun House. Rear elevation.

10. LeBrun House. Section.

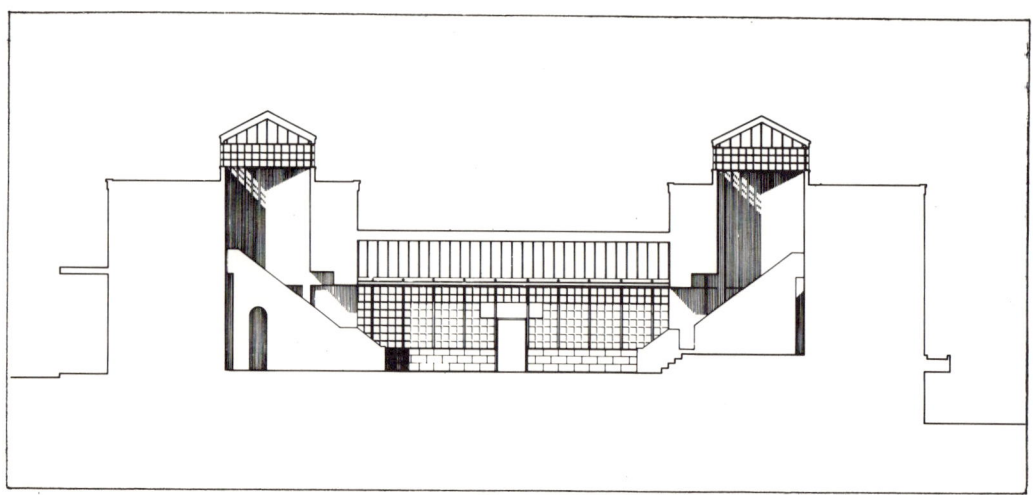

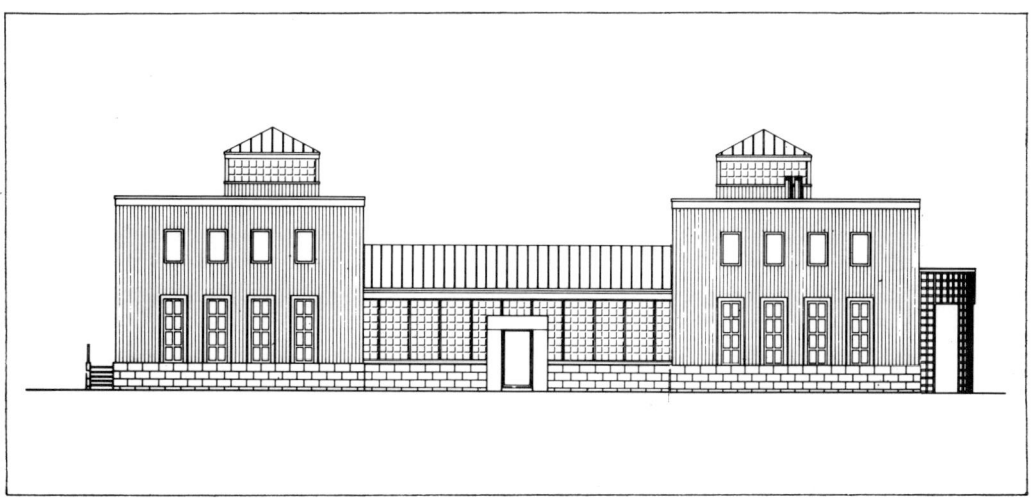

11. LeBrun House. Front elevation.

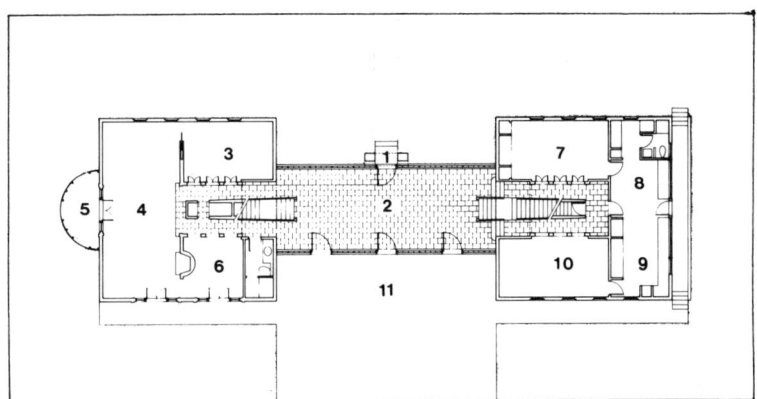

12. LeBrun House. First floor plan.

1. Entry 2. Gallery 3. Library/guest room 4. Living room 5. Porch 6. Den 7. Family room 8. Breakfast room 9. Kitchen 10. Dining room 11. Terrace 12. Dressing room 13. Sitting room 14. Master bedroom 15. Master bath 16. Bedroom

13. LeBrun House. Second floor plan.

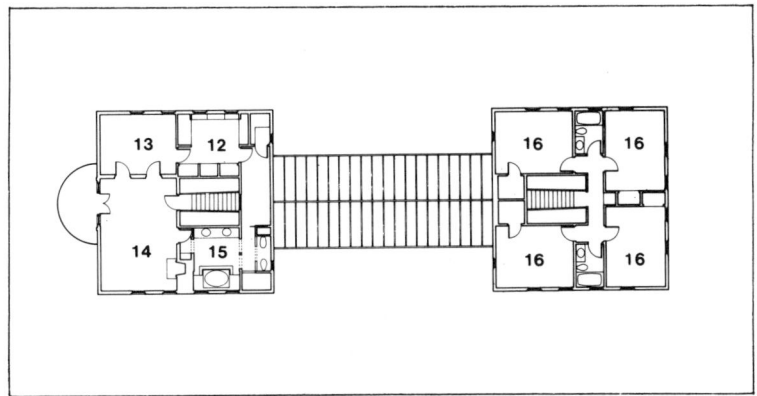

The Georgica House is designed for the rituals of summer and of leisure, with the towers looking to the pool, the ocean, and the sunset. In the end, specific domestic rituals are involved, in contrast to our earlier House for the Musician (Les Echelles) which is designed entirely around rituals of music and theater. In the latter case, the use of an external stair makes the house an immediately ritualistic public object.

The Lebrun House becomes two houses, one for the parents and one for the children. The common element is the gallery which allows one to pass from the front to the garden without touching either house. Varying degrees of outside and inside space are marked by the gallery: the front door occurs as a solid within a translucent wall, and the three glass garden doors are transparent within the rear translucent wall. The public space is articulated both externally and internally in the extension of the glass block gallery vertically to the lanterns on the pavilion roofs which light the two staircases below. Internally, this places the drama in the most public space of the house. A ritual of passage and entry is ultimately established in the separation of the two houses, each of them having their own door from the connecting gallery. As in other ritualistic structures, one has to go through several doors to get to the most sacred or intimate domain.

■   ■   ■

The Georgica and LeBrun houses by Agrest and Gandelsonas deny the existence of fixed domestic rituals. Instead, they suggest possibilities through which private activities might achieve the status of ritual. This potential is created by the formal organization of the houses. In both projects the center is occupied by a large non-specialized space. Surrounded by interior façades, behind which are smaller specialized rooms, these central spaces display the attributes of a stage. Integral with this centering operation is the use of multiple entries and frontalizations, seen most explicitly in the glazed loggia of the LeBrun house and in the central hall of the Georgica house. And it is in this respect that the concerns of the Agrest and Gandelsonas projects intersect with the domestic work of Tadao Ando. Ando's houses also emphasize the designation of the dwelling as a "kind of stage" which people inhabit. But whereas Ando relies on Japanese tradition, which maintains some relatively fixed modes of behavior, thus permitting his architecture to be integrated with predictable daily ceremonies, Agrest and Gandelsonas have a different attitude towards ritual altogether. Ritual for them is clearly not the universal cultural force it once was. It exists, but in a form that is atomized and scaled down. It occurs on a private, individual level, consciously brought into being by the inhabitant. Possibilities are exploited, paths established, and meanings imposed. Because ritual in their projects does not perform its traditional western role, that of legitimizing power and conveying ideology, it is free to realize a new possibility, that of shaping the act of mental representation itself.

Passages into the City

The Interpretive Function of the Roman Triumph

Alan Plattus

When in the eighteenth century Winckelmann denigrated Rome in favor of Rome's Greek heritage, he offered a subtle and rhetorically convincing argument against Roman originality in the arts, an argument which has exerted an indirect yet powerful influence on the sensibility of modern historians of art. Roman art and architecture are underappreciated partly because they are so often considered formalistically — thus functional ornamentation appears fustian and proud, monuments sound the note of the worst sort of imperialism, and sculptures become the pale copy of Greek originals.

In writing about the triumph and the triumphal arch, Alan Plattus redresses this imbalance by showing the importance of historical context to our understanding of an artifact. Although recent criticism has been increasingly generous to Roman achievements, even such an enthusiast for Roman culture as Mortimer Wheeler claims that triumphal arches are "idle contrivances of grand but nonsensical irrelevance." This is partly accurate. Augustus, the first great builder of arches, had one of his inscribed celeberrimo loco: it seems to be just a glorious monument adorning a busy public place. But Wheeler also claims that the arches were symptomatic of "personality-cults"[1] — and it is in stopping here that positions like his are most inadequate. A Roman arch is fundamentally unlike, say, The Square of the Great Heavenly Peace in Peking (which contains a big white neoclassical temple built in memory of Chairman Mao), just as it is unlike the arches of the City Beautiful Movement in America and the Arc de Triomphe in Paris. The Roman arch was never conceived solely as a memorial or even as a focal point for an area of land.

Triumphal arches represent one of the single most important advances in Roman design.[2] The stories of victory carved and monumentalized on the arches were matched by the pattern of the triumphal march itself. Thus the arches formed a network which organized and gave meaning to a sprawling city. The bas-relief was unlocked into life.

In the fifteen hundred years that passed between the collapse of the Roman empire and the founding of a unified Italian state, the triumph was forgotten. During Garibaldi's and Mazzini's fight for independence the English poet

---

1. Mortimer Wheeler, Roman Art and Architecture (New York: Oxford University Press, 1979), p.152ff.
2. See, e.g., Luigi Crema, "Significato della architettura romana nei suoi sviluppi e nella sua posizione nella storia dell' arte antica," in Bollettino del Centro di studi per la storia dell' architettura, No. 15 (Rome, 1960); and Ranuccio Bianchi Bandinelli, Rome, the Centre of Power, 500 B.C. to A.D. 200 (London: Thames, 1970).

Arthur Hugh Clough could write:

> Rome, believe me, my friend, is like its own Monte Testaceo,
> Merely a marvellous mass of broken and castaway wine-pots.
> ...What do I want with this rubbish of ages departed,
> Things that nature abhors, the experiments that she has failed in?
> What do I find in the Forum? An archway and two or three pillars.

Modern Roman city planners have tried to compensate for Rome's lack of focus (a continuing problem at least since Napoleon's imprisonment of Pius VII at Fontainebleu, the end for any hope of the Vatican providing a unifying force) with the Vittorio Emanuele Monument, which sits along a triumphal route that includes the Arch of Titus. Yet there is no feeling of procession; the structure itself blocks off a view of the rear half of the Forum. Romans ridicule it as the "typewriter" and the "wedding-cake." As an architectural centering device, it fails lugubriously.

Plattus ends his essay with an echo of The Waste Land, "mixing memory and desire, stirring dull roots with spring rain." Eliot had attempted to reinsert ritual and totemism into modern poetry. Fraser's Golden Bough and Weston's From Ritual to Romance were combined with the peace which passeth understanding, and were meant to contrast with the hollowness of contemporary belief. But his readers rejected the ritual elements of The Waste Land — they admired fragmentation and the forms of ruin, but refused their synthesis. Datta Dayadhvam Damyata shantih shantih shantih intoned at the end of the poem could not undo all the weight of Eliot's despairing private language. So too attempts to reify the purpose of the triumph into a single building, to remedy diasparaction with one bold stroke, have appeared alternately anachronistic and hilarious. The Eiffel Tower is the unique instance of a modern monument which anchors an entire city. Ancient Rome furnishes an example which contrasts with that of Paris. In Rome a triumphal march through widely separated arches concentrated in the minds of its audience the spectacle of the imperial city-state and the glory of its urban landscape. It took the seals off all pulses and replaced them with the systole and diastole of an empire.

■ ■ ■

When something worth seeing is taking place on level ground and everybody crowds forward to look, those in the rear find various ways of raising themselves to see over the heads of those in front: some stand on benches, some roll up barrels, some bring carts on which they lay planks crosswise, some occupy a neighboring hill. In this way in no time they form a crater. Should the spectacle be often repeated in the same spot, makeshift stands are put up for those who can pay, and the rest manage as best they can. To satisfy this universal need is the architect's task. By his art he creates as plain a crater as possible and the public itself supplies its decoration. Crowded together, its members are astonished at themselves. They are accustomed at other times to seeing each other running hither and thither in confusion, bustling about without order or discipline. Now this many-headed, many-minded, fickle, blundering monster suddenly sees itself united as one noble assembly, welded into one mass, a single body animated by a single spirit.

Goethe, Italian Journey, 1786[1]

---

1. Johann Wolfgang von Goethe, *Italian Journey* (1786-1788), translated by W. H. Auden and Elizabeth Mayer (San Francisco, 1982), p. 35.

It is tempting to read Goethe's meditation on the Roman amphitheater at Verona ("the first great monument of the ancient world I have seen") as a dramatist's and theatrical producer's version of the myth of the origins of architecture. As such, it would provide a striking contrast to so many other versions of the myth, which proliferated throughout the eighteenth century. In its characteristic form, the myth sponsored various tendentious reconstructions of the Vitruvian primitive hut, "designed" to ground, and ultimately to sanctify, the preferred treatment of ornamented structure through an appeal to the "natural" origins of architecture.[2] Goethe, on the other hand, suggests an emphasis on the social and performative origins of architecture, according to which the architect imitates not nature, but life. Furthermore, he suggests that this mimesis is not merely a passive reflection, but rather is founded upon a more subtle and symbiotic relationship between monument and collective behavior in which the architect plays an active role, abstracting and ordering, as well as transcribing, the traces of his heterogeneous raw material. In this way, the barely perceived patterns of ordinary experience are raised to a level of reflective self-consciousness that is fundamental to the function of the monument as Goethe understands it, providing "society" with both a point of reference and a vantage from which to see itself as a "society" with both a point of reference and a vantage from which to see itself as a potentially coherent entity.

Thus the monumental typology of the city and its "assembled" inhabitants define and complete each other, as in the elaborate ballet of courtship and mating between the Eiffel Tower and the city of Paris described so poignantly by Roland Barthes. In Barthes' account, the tower becomes a paradigmatic example of the reflexive monument, participating in "both sexes of sight": "an object when we look at it, it becomes a lookout in its turn when we visit it, and now constitutes as an object simultaneously extended and collected beneath it, that Paris which just now was looking at it. The tower is an object which sees, a glance which is seen...."[3] The Tower focuses and summarizes the entire city, while displaying the city to itself as a suddenly revealed panorama. In the same way, the amphitheater had allowed the urban mob to "suddenly see itself united as one noble assembly."

Upon his arrival at the ultimate goal of his pilgrimage, the city of Rome — and in particular the ruins of ancient Rome — Goethe found himself in need of just such a panoramic point of view. Plunging, however, into the midst of the living city without an overview of an Eiffel Tower, Goethe found the task described by Barthes as "decipherment" to be "a difficult and melancholy business." "Only in Rome can one educate oneself for Rome," but so hopelessly entangled are the "traces both of magnificence and of devastation" that the work of distinguishing ancient and modern Rome and of "grasp[ing] not only how Modern Rome follows on Ancient, but also how, within both, one epoch follows upon another," seems to defy conventional methods of interpretation. ("One would need a thousand styluses to write with. What can one do with a single pen?")[4] It is, then, revealing to see how Goethe, on his second visit to Rome over a year later, constructs his own "Roman amphitheater" from which he can at least view the modern city. He does this by means of a systematic description of the Roman carnival, which is "not really a festival given *for* the people

---

2. Goethe was not above this polemical strategy, and in his youthful attack on the Abbé Laugier and doctrinaire classicism, he invokes a version of the "Gothic" primitive hut, only to conclude that although it was "a far more basic invention,... you could not even extract [from it] a principle for your pig-sty." "On German Architecture, D. M. Ervini a Steinbach," in *Goethe on Art*, edited and translated by John Gage (Berkeley, 1980), p. 106.
3. Roland Barthes, *The Eiffel Tower and Other Mythologies*, translated by Richard Howard (New York, 1979), pp. 4-5. One might add, among other *apercus* of this kind, Henry James' brilliant account of Venice, which hinges upon the identification of "that universal privilege of Venetian objects which consists of being both the picture and the point of view." Cited in *Italian Hours* (New York, 1979), p. 34.
4. Goethe, *Italian Journey*, pp. 120-121.

1. The Triumph of Marcus Aurelius. Panel relief from a lost triumphal arch, ca. 175 A.D., now in the Museo dei Conservatori, Rome.

but one that the people give themselves."[5] The reflexive synthesis of a complex city and its life is now provided, not by a singular monument, but by an elaborate ritual event. The key was of course to populate the city, which, like the amphitheater, "ought not to be seen empty but packed with human beings," since "such an amphitheatre, in fact, is properly designed to impress the people with itself...."[6]

In supplementing archaeology with ethnography, or perhaps actually conflating the two, Goethe reenacts his discovery of the complementary roles of monument and ritual. Now at the scale of the city, ritual, like the monument and in overt conspiracy with it, performs what Clifford Geertz has identified as an interpretive function: for the Romans it is indeed "a story they tell themselves about themselves."[7] And Goethe, in good anthropological fashion as a participant-observer, can begin to read the story himself. Might one then suggest that it is this sort of ritual vantage point that Goethe needed in his initial and bewildered confrontation with the *disjecta membra* of ancient Rome? Having populated in the mind's eye, and thus "understood," the amphitheater at Verona, and having studied contemporary Roman society in ritual motion, Goethe might have short-circuited the process of learning the ancient city by rote, by means of a reconstructive mnemonic such as the spectacular ritual procession of the Roman triumph. That quintessential Roman

---

5. Ibid., pp. 445-496. One of the many issues this essay neglects is the problematic distinction between high and low ("popular") festival culture. Carnival and the Roman triumph might initially seem to fall on opposite sides of this distinction, but neither in ancient nor in eighteenth century Rome is the distinction absolute. For one version of this issue in general see Mikhail Bakhtin, *Rabelais and His World*, translated by Helene Iswolsky (Cambridge, Mass., 1968), which includes a discussion of Goethe's account of Carnival and its relation to his work in general (pp. 244-257).
6. Goethe, *Italian Journey*, p. 35.
7. Clifford Geertz, "Deep Play: Notes on the Balinese Cockfight," in *The Interpretation of Cultures* (New York, 1973), p. 448. Geertz says of the cockfight what Goethe, had he been a modern social scientist, might have said of the amphitheater: that "it provides a metasocial commentary upon the whole matter of assorting human beings into fixed hierarchical ranks and then organizing the major part of collective existence around that assortment."

performance wound its way through the dense fabric of the ancient city, identifying and collating monument and place in an ostentatious idealization as ruthlessly purposeful as any Michelin itinerary. The triumph was to become, after all, for the archaeologists and ideologists of the humanist culture to which Goethe belonged, a significant vehicle not only for the reconstruction of ancient Rome, but also for its imaginative transferal and continuation in the more ambitious cities of early modern Europe.[8] Its ability to sustain such excavation and transformation points to what Goethe would have recognized as the vitality of its function in ancient Roman culture, as an interpretation of Rome to itself.

• • •

In taking the Roman triumph as a brief case study in the interpretive function of urban ritual, one should not discount its inherent heterogeneity — both functional and formal — as a historical phenomenon developing over a period of perhaps a millenium.[9] As such, it provides an index to, and is a primary participant in, the elaborate and often subtle mutations of Roman culture and society as they respond to internal pressures and external events. This account aims to suggest how that flexibility might have been possible within the framework of a particular ritual. That is to say, it is less concerned with the specification of a particular meaning at a particular moment than with the operation of a general mechanism of meaning.[10] To anticipate conclusions, one might already predict that if the triumph was in fact an "effective" urban ritual, in the sense suggested by Geertz and proposed here as an appendix to Goethe, then it must have been capable of interpreting the city to itself as the city's aspirations, roles, and form changed over time. This cannot only be a question of time as *la longue durée*, but also of the immediate time of political and social "events" and of the ceremony itself, which must find the triumph available as an instrument of both long-term "structure" and short-term "strategy."[11] As an interpretive practice, the triumph had not only to identify, but also to reconstitute, its object of study at each new ceremonial manifestation, and this involved, as we shall see, what Goethe had already perceived as the complementary strategies of repetition — of the same event in the same place; and transformation — from ordinary experience to extraordinary ritual occasion to generalized and multivalent urban monument, and back again.

• • •

However early we date its origins as a distinctive urban ritual, the Roman triumph would have found itself at work upon an urban text of considerable mythic and formal sophistication.[12] In the

---

8. Goethe himself was to write in some detail about one of the most important of these reconstructions, Mantegna's depiction of the Triumph of Caesar in *Goethe on Art*, op. cit., pp. 150-165).
9. Most treatments of the Roman triumph have been analytical, rather than historical, in structure and focus. For the general historical development and context of the triumph see the very broad survey in Robert Payne, *The Roman Triumph* (London, 1962), and for the period of the Empire, Concetta Barini, *Triumphalia. Imprese ed Onore Militari durante l'Impero Romano* (Torino, 1952), as well as the more specific and technical studies cited below.
10. The point is that the triumph continued to effectively interpret the city and its monument form in relation to structures of political power in spite of enormous changes in those structures. Thus I am not only unconcerned with the question of a late imperial "decline" of urban ritual, but am generally skeptical of the question. That is not to say that the representational mechanism itself is impervious to change, but rather that one must distinguish between a specific change in emphasis or role, by means of which the ritual interprets an event or development, and a more general displacement or eclipse of the interpretive function on the order of Victor Hugo's "ceci tuera cela." In general, I am inclined to agree with Richard Sennett, who suggests in *The Fall of Public Man* (New York, 1974), that the definitive crisis of urban ritual is a phenomenon of recent centuries. For a sophisticated account of the "decadence" of late Roman ritual, see Johann Huizinga, *Homo Ludens. A Study of the Play Element in Culture* (Boston, 1955), pp. 173-179; but cf. also note 38 below.
11. The distinction between an objectivized structure with its *rules* and a concrete practice with its *strategies* is developed by Pierre Bourdieu, *Outline of a Theory of Practice*, translated by Richard Nice (Cambridge, 1977).
12. Both Livy and Plutarch, among others, credit Romulus with the first "Roman" triumph soon after he founded the city. But as in the case of so many Roman traditions, the Romans themselves eventually referred their own triumphs to Etruscan precedent. The name itself seems to derive from a Greek victory hymn, the refrain of which repeated the formula *Io triumphe*.

fundamentally civic world of the Roman citizen, this accumulated significance was in fact dated, and indeed derived, *ab urbe condita* ("from the founding of the city"). As Joseph Rykwert has shown, the various rituals associated with the act of foundation — as performed, remembered, and repeated — sought to constitute the urban object not only physically, but symbolically.[13] Among those foundation rituals, the actual delimitation and definition of urban space through the laying out of boundaries was one of the most important. One may turn to Plutarch's "Life of Romulus" for the traditional legend of the Romulan foundation, according to which the founder-hero, having participated in the appropriate divinatory rites, marked out the boundary (*pomerium*) of the aboriginal city by plowing the first furrow (*sulcus primigenius*) with the ritual bronze plowshare. Naturally the *pomerium*, and eventually the walls that roughly followed its initiatory circuit, were, Plutarch tells us elsewhere, "sacred and inviolable," as indicated by the custom of interrupting the furrow at the location of the gates (which were "profane" passages across a sacred line), and as brother Remus learned the hard way when he mockingly leaped over what no doubt seemed to him a mere ditch.[14]

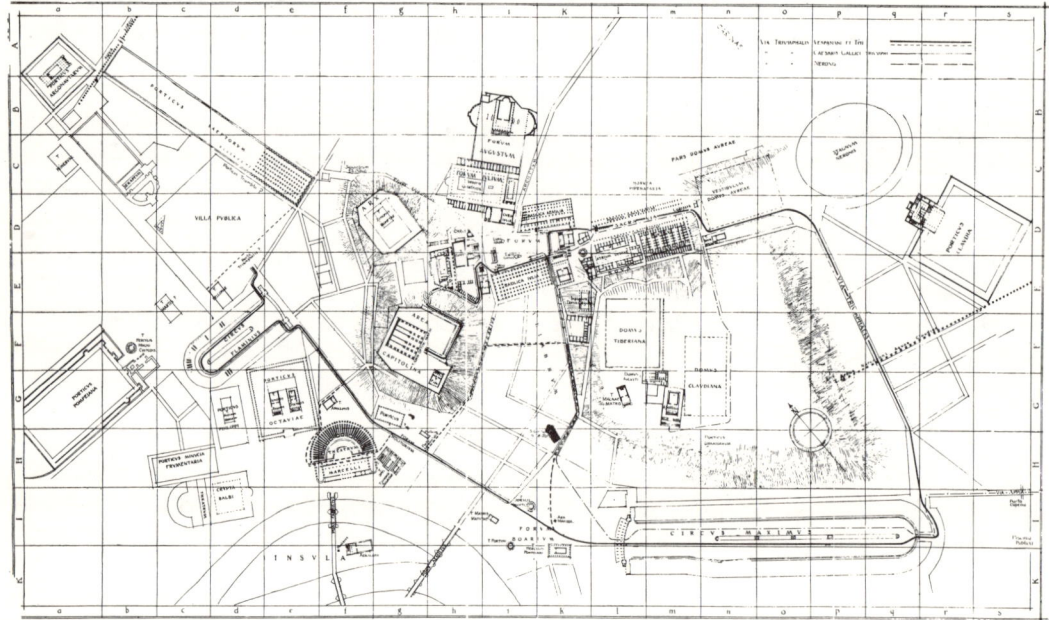

2. *The triumphal route of Titus and Vespasian.*

Presumably the Romans would at first have had a direct and powerful monumental index of these foundation rituals in the walls and gates of their city. As the city grew along with its empire, both walls and *pomerium* were extended and could become physically quite dissociated, but they remained ritually concentric, as the citizens were reminded periodically, and even seasonally, of the original foundation through rituals which invoked, and sometimes re-enacted, the archetypal event. Although seldom as literal as the somewhat scandalous behavior of one emperor who, in his *hubris*, replowed the *pomerium* and re-named the city after himself, festivals such as the wild and

---

13. Joseph Rykwert, *The Idea of a Town. The Anthropology of Urban Form in Rome, Italy and the Ancient World* (Princeton, 1976). Rykwert's emphasis on the non-contradiction or, more strongly, the interdependence of pragmatic and mythic thought in ancient urbanism is crucial. Ritual, in the ancient city, is seldom merely an ideological mask for technological or political "rationality;" rather, it both effects and reveals the coexistence of the everyday (pragmatic) city and the symbolic or mythic city.
14. Cf., Ibid., pp. 27-29, 65, 91-94, for a discussion of the story as told in Plutarch and in other sources.

wooly *Lupercalia* seem to have involved the tracing of the legendary Romulan city.[15] This sort of ritualized re-dedication and purification of an urban territory survived in Western culture well into the modern period, and Samuel Johnson, for example, remembered his father presiding over the ceremonial "Riding" of the boundaries of his native Lichfield in the early eighteenth century.[16] Thus the city is formulated and persists not only through its changing monumental structure, but in the tenacity of spatial and topographic memory reinforced by ritual.

If then the city was from its beginnings "for the Romans... the centre of life, charged with an especial holiness and separated from the rest of the outside world by a magic line, the *pomerium*, the ritual boundary within which no one could be buried," it stands to reason that the violation of that boundary must either be punished severely, as indeed it was from Remus on, or celebrated as a special ritual occasion.[17] One notable example of the latter was the suspension of the burial prohibition for the founder of the city, and various other heroes.[18] Yet another, not unrelated in its significance, was the temporary suspension, on the occasion of a triumphal entry, of the law forbidding a general to retain his command (and to appear at the head of his army) within the *pomerium*. Thus on the day of his ceremonial entry, the *triumphator*, be he victorious republican general or campaigning emperor, was allowed to conquer — symbolically — the city. The ritual suspension of the normal precautions, which excluded the active exercise of military command within the city for sound practical reasons, called attention to this exceptional "conquest" and its highly theatrical, but potentially very real, violence.[19] The city, however, was quite willing to sanction its own violation in this case because the *triumphator* was seen, like the founder of the city, as one favored by the gods, and perhaps even a god himself, at least for the duration of his triumph. He brought to the city not only the actual spoils of his victory, but the even more important symbolic capital of his own "good fortune" (*felicitas*) which was, along with the tangible riches won in battle, to be incorporated into the urban treasury.[20] The triumph thus represented a double responsibility — owed by the city to the victor and by the victor to his urban sponsor. It was, literally, a two-edged sword. If the *triumphator* seemed to perpetrate a ritual conquest of the city, he was also in turn *captured* by the city, which re-confirmed, and at the same time enhanced, its own identity and mythic stock of good fortune.

This sense of reciprocal conquest and capture would have been most dramatic at that point along the triumphal route where the city of Rome asserted most powerfully its spatial and symbolic identity: the point at which the procession crossed what was in fact, or according to tradition, the sacred urban boundary. The act of entry and the so-called *Porta Triumphalis*, the structure which both effected and eventually represented the entry ceremony, is thus an appropriate place to begin an investigation of the various aspects of the triumph. Indeed, many of the surviving ancient depictions of the triumph employ a condensed imagery in which the juxtaposition of *triumphator*

---

15. For the *Lupercalia*, see W. Warde Fowler, *The Roman Festivals of the Period of the Republic* (London, 1899), pp. 310-321; and Rykwert, op. cit., pp. 93-97.
16. For a general and cross-cultural account of boundary lore and ritual see Nigel Penninck, *The Ancient Science of Geomancy* (London, 1979), esp. Chap. 4.
17. Richard Brilliant, *Roman Art from the Republic to Constantine* (London, 1974), p. 58.
18. Cf., Rykwert, op. cit., pp. 34-36.
19. The relationship between ritual and violence is yet another important topic which this essay mentions only in passing. Certainly ancient Rome, like other cultures, affords numerous cases of ritualized violence, violence erupting from an overwrought or "failed" ritual occasion, and violent events—e.g., real conquests—perceived, or actually cast, in ritual form. Since a primary function of ritual is to control, order, or "re-integrate" sources of conflict and crisis, the potential for violence seems to be inherent in many ritual forms, especially those analyzed by Victor Turner, following van Gennep (cf. note 22 below), as transitional or "liminal" rituals. See, e.g., Victor Turner, "Social Dramas and Ritual Metaphors," in *Dramas, Fields, and Metaphors. Symbolic Action in Human Society* (Ithaca, 1974), pp. 23-59.
20. This interpretation of the *triumphator* is developed by H. S. Versnel, *Triumphus. An Inquiry into the Origin, Development and Meaning of the Roman Triumph* (Leiden, 1970), pp. 371-397.

3. The adventus *(or triumph) of Domitian: Domitian being met outside the city, prior to his entry by "Roma" and by the Senate and people of Rome. Panel relief from the Palazzo della Cancellaria, Rome.*

and gate stands for the entire ceremony, with the addition of the processional goal, the Temple of Jupiter Optimum Maximus on the Capitoline Hill, sometimes rounding out the metonymic representation of the city (fig. 1).[21] In much the same way, many of the interpretations of the triumph that have been advanced focus on the act of entry and the role of the *triumphator* to the exclusion of other triumphal manifestations. In doing so, they demonstrate the impact not only of the available visual evidence, but also of the interpretive framework suggested by the anthropologist Arnold van Gennep, who briefly analyzed the Roman triumph in terms of the three-part schema which he proposed as the generic structure of all "rites of passage":

I propose to call the rites of separation from a previous world *preliminal rites*, those executed during the transitional stage *liminal* (or *threshold*) rites, and the ceremonies of incorporation into the new world post-liminal rites.

Thus in the case of the Roman Triumph:

The victor was first required to separate himself from the enemy world through a series of rites, in order to be able to return to the Roman world by passing through the arch. The rite of incorporation in this case was a sacrifice to Jupiter Capitoline and to the deities protecting the city.[22]

The dominant traditional interpretation of the triumph emphasized and often conflated the first two parts of van Gennep's schema, identifying the function of separation from the enemy world with the threshold articulated by the *Porta Triumphalis*. In this account the triumph is seen as a rite of purification, in which the *triumphator* and his army, having been "contaminated" by the dangerous power (*mana*) picked up by contact (*contagio*) with an alien and impure enemy, must be cleansed by passage through, or "contact" with, a sort of magic portal which drains or rubs off the blood (*mana*) of the enemy world lest it infect the city.[23] Significantly, this interpretation casts the city, represented by the *Porta Triumphalis*, in a rather passive role. By contrast, the most comprehensive recent study of the triumph, by H.S. Versnel, emphasizes the latter two parts of

---

21. See Inez Scott Ryberg, *Rites of the State Religion in Roman Art*, Memoirs of the American Academy in Rome, Vol. XXII (Rome, 1955), pp. 141-162; and on the Marcus Aurelius panel in particular, Ryberg, *Panel Reliefs of Marcus Aurelius* (New York, 1967), pp. 15-20; and Per Gustaf Hamberg, *Studies in Roman Imperial Art, with Special Reference to the Roman State Reliefs of the Second Century* (Uppsala, 1945), pp. 78-99. 22. Arnold van Gennep, *The Rites of Passage*, translated by Monika Vizedom and Gabrielle Caffee (Chicago, 1960), p. 21.
22. Arnold van Gennep, *The Rites of Passage*, translated by Monika Vizedom and Gabrielle Caffee (Chicago, 1960), p.21.
23. The *Porta Triumphalis* is presented in the context of the triumph as a straightforward "purification rite" in Ferdinand Noack, "Triumph und Triumphbogen," *Vortrage der Bibliothek Warburg* (1925-26), pp. 151-154. This argument is criticized in a review by C. Weickert, *Gnomon* 5 (1929), pp. 24ff., who asks, rhetorically, why a victorious army was more in need of purification than one that had been defeated. H. Wagenvoort, *Roman Dynamism. Studies in ancient Roman thought, language and custom* (Oxford, 1947), replies to Weickert in the context of a general discussion of the concepts of *contagio* and *mana* (pp. 164-168), arguing that it was precisely because they were victorious, and therefore contaminated with the blood of their slain enemies, that the victors required purification. But there are many examples of similar rites of passage applied to defeated warriors; cf., e.g., Louise Adams Holland, *Janus and the Bridge*, Papers and Monographs of the American Academy in Rome, XXI (Rome, 1961), pp. 88-89.

van Gennep's schema, connecting the *Porta Triumphalis* with the function of incorporation, and thus suggesting an active role for the city in the capture and incorporation of the *triumphator* as "the bearer of good fortune."[24]

The connection of the *Porta Triumphalis* with the role of the city in the transaction portrayed by the triumph is crucial, and Versnel begins his "new interpretation" of the *Porta Triumphalis* with a reminder of the apparently obvious fact that this structure was, as its name suggests, a special kind of city gate (*porta*). Like an ordinary city gate, and unlike such fundamentally free-standing monuments as the *arcus* or *fornix*, the *Porta Triumphalis*, wherever it actually stood and however detached it might be from its implied physical context in the city walls, would have embodied distinctions of "outside" and "inside" and the possibility of passage between those conditions, controlled by the qualifying distinctions of "open" and "closed." This is not, as it might seem, to belabor the phenomenologically obvious. The *arcus* (or triumphal arch, in its most elaborate form), while it may initially have derived from the gate and eventually influenced gate design (including perhaps the imperial version of the *Porta Triumphalis*), was originally a free-standing commemorative monument, which did not necessarily relate to a directional passage.[25] The rich conflation of the iconography of the city gate, the triumphal arch, and the *Porta Triumphalis*, was a product of ritual and historical time, a subject to which we shall return. But the specific function, and therefore the possible meanings, of the *Porta Triumphalis* derive from its general characteristics as a marker and a modulator of passage.

That specificity of function is hinted at by Cicero in his oration "Against Piso" in a remark — one of the few pieces of solid information available concerning the elusive gate — that suggests that the *Porta Triumphalis* may only have been opened on the occasion of a triumph.[26] Extrapolating from this clue, it might be assumed that the "special" status of the triumphal gate would have been further enhanced if it did not fall, like "ordinary" gates, at a break in the *pomerium*, where the plow have been carried over the profane ground marked for daily passage of goods and people, but rather actively *broke* the *pomerium* on those significant occasions when it was used. This hypothesis cannot be substantiated, but we know from Suetonius' account of Nero's triumph in 68 A.D. that the Romans were familiar with the Greek tradition of allowing victors in the Olympic and other games to enter their native cities through an actual breach in the city walls, a section of which was torn down for the occasion and then rebuilt.[27] Versnel's interpretation invokes that Greek tradition:

...The victor enters the town, not via an existing gate — which is used by everyone and continues to function in this way — but via a gap in the wall that did not exist before, and which, *after the entry will disappear again*. In other words: the town makes it impossible for its valuable honorary citizen and bringer of good luck to disappear again, removing all traces of the passage through which he entered.[28]

From this point it is a short but significant step to a parallel interpretation of the *Porta Triumphalis* in operation as a figurative representation of what must otherwise have become, given the frequency

---

24. Versnel, op. cit., pp. 371-397.
25. Cf., Brilliant, op. cit., p. 119. Versnel, op. cit., pp. 152-153, emphasizes this distinction: "the name *porta* indicates that concretely or symbolically, it must have given admittance to the city or city area." Both authors call attention to the Etruscan origin of the *porta*. For a speculative discussion of the form and iconography of the Imperial *Porta Triumphalis*, in relation to the city gates and triumphal arches, see E. Baldwin Smith, *Architectural Symbolism of Imperial Rome and the Middle Ages* (Princeton, 1956), pp. 25-27.
26. Cicero, "Against Piso," XXIII, 55. Cf., Holland, op. cit., p. 90, n. 61, which compares the *Porta Triumphalis* to the Jubilee Door of Saint Peter's, which is closed and walled up between the Jubilee Years, which fall every twenty-five years.
27. Suetonius, *The Lives of the Caesars*, Book VI, "Nero," XXV. Nero made similar breached-wall entries into Naples, Antium, and Albanum on his way to Rome, where he radically rearranged the triumphal route, entering near the Porta Capena and ending at the Temple of Apollo on the Palatine, having also knocked down an arch in the Circus Maximus. Needless to say, this was not a traditional triumph.
28. Versnel, op. cit., p.159.

of triumphs, a rather costly and time-consuming process of dismantling and rebuilding city walls. With the symbolic economy of a stage prop, the *Porta Triumphalis* could thus have supported the theme of simultaneous conquest and capture which is emerging as characteristic of the reflexive function of the triumph.

Given the lack of textual evidence, and the uncertainly of archaeological evidence, it is not surprising that the *Porta Triumphalis* has become a kind of free variable in the various formulae which purport to give the "meaning" of the triumph, and as one scholar has put it, "there are advocates for every possible form and location of the *Porta Triumphalis*."[29] Although it would be helpful to be able to answer definitively the question of the gate's precise form and location, it is more important in the context of this discussion to have suggested the way in which it may have worked within the performance of the triumph as a ritual whole. Whether or not it was originally one of several gates in a section of the old Servian walls, as was once proposed, and whether it marked a particular historical location of the *pomerium*, which was after all a zone (not a "line"), the *Porta Triumphalis* would have indicated the point of symbolic and ritual entry into the city on the special occasion of the triumph.[30] What would have eventually "fixed" the *Porta Triumphalis* in the midst of an expanding city is in fact ritual usage, and the memories it invoked. It was the repetitive relation of gate and ritual over time which would have sustained what one knows to have been a continuous elaboration and variation in the form of the ritual, and what one suspects would have been a corresponding elaboration in the form of the monument. If it began as a simple freestanding, and even temporary structure, it was nevertheless capable of absorbing the accumulation of iconographic and formal articulation developed in a variety of both related and independent contexts. We shall see this process at work in the case of the triumphal arch, and by the same process, the *Porta Triumphalis* could, *a fortiori*, become in its actual monumental form what it already was in its ritual function: an urban focus to which would accrue and "adhere" the imagery of collective civic identity, imperial or divine presence, and urban prosperity of *felicitas*.[31] Its ritual function was to represent this ramified image of the city in relation to its sacred *pomerium* (wherever the juridical *pomerium* might lie at a particular moment), just as other rituals represented and "remembered" the original foundation of Rome.[32] The *Porta Triumphalis* was thus a real gate into an ideal, or at least ritually idealized city.

• • •

What "activated" the *Porta Triumphalis* and brought the ideal city of the triumph temporarily into being was of course the passage of the *triumphator*. It should therefore be clear by now that the triumph was from the outset based upon an elaborate structure of ritual dialogue between two active parties, the city and the conquering hero. Both have roles to play in what turns out to be very much like those ritualized events described by the anthropologist Victor Turner as "social dramas," and it is misleading to cast the city, even in late imperial times, in the role of a passive spectator.[33] Certainly the elaborate makeup, costume, and props of the *triumphator* have tended to focus attention on his role. With his purple tunic, gold-starred gown, gilded shoes, a sceptre in his left hand, a laurel branch in his right, his head crowned with a laurel wreath, and his face painted

---

29. Holland, op. cit., p. 89. n. 56. See also H. Petrikovits, "Die Porta Triumphalis," *Jahreshefte des Oesterreichischen Archaologischen Instituts in Wien*, 28 (1933), pp. 187-195; and the discussions cited in note 42 below. The extreme case is the theory of a temporary and movable *Porta Triumphalis*, advanced by Morpurgo, *Bolletino Communale*, XXXVI (1908), pp. 109ff., which is based on extravagant imperial variations on the triumph, such as Nero's.
30. For an illustration of the Servian Wall location, see Rodolfo Lanciani, *Ruins and Excavations of Ancient Rome* (New York, 1967; first published 1897), fig. 24, p. 59. On the *pomerium* as a zone, cf., Rykwert, op. cit., p. 136, and in general, pp. 129-137
31. For a discussion of this imagery in relation to its various architectural transformations, see Smith, op. cit.
32. Cf., Rykwert, p. 132: "In Rome, though the sanctity of the *pomerium* was regarded as an anachronism by the end of the republic, that part of the foundation ceremony by which it was established retained its importance...."
33. Turner, op. cit., pp. 37-42.

bright red, he has seemed to some to be the god Jupiter, to others a king-for-a-day based on an Etruscan model, and finally to others a gory warrior returning from battle steeped in blood and spoils.³⁴ But whatever his precise status, one must remember that it was conferred upon (and would be taken from him by) the *Senatus Populusque Romanorum*. In fact, the ritual dialogue began long before the actual triumph itself, and what might be called the preliminary negotiations culminated with a special petition from the candidate for triumph to the Roman Senate.

Livy, in his account of the double triumph of Marcus Livius Salinator and Gaius Claudius Nero in 207 B.C., gives what may have been the standard formula for this petition:

In the Senate after the manner of all commanders-in-chief they stated their achievements and demanded that for a brave and successful conduct of the war honour should be paid to the immortal gods; likewise that they themselves should be permitted to enter the city in triumph.³⁵

It is known from numerous accounts that this request was not, at least at first, an empty formality, that the prerequisites for the celebration of a triumph were specific and significant, and that the Senate could and did refuse the triumphal honors when the prerequisites were not fulfilled. The criteria included not only the obvious one of victory on the battlefield (which may actually have been determined in the purely quantitative terms of a body count), but also the prior possession by the candidate of a special status conferred upon him before setting out from Rome by virtue of participation in divinatory religious rites (*auspicium*) on the Capitoline Hills, the taking of a special vow, and the granting of supreme military command (*imperium*).³⁶ These prior conditions summarized in the recurring formula *imperious auspiciumque*, made the triumph, when granted and performed, an organic and apparently intransitive whole: beginning on the Capitol with the assumption of the *imperium militiae*, exercising the command successfully, returning to and entering the city with that power intact, displaying its fruits, and finally relinquishing the *imperium* and dedicating the spoils upon return to the Capitol. Any slip along the way could compromise the *ius triumphandi* (the right of triumphing), for like any full-blooded ritual, the triumph depended for its complete and effective significance upon the performance of specified acts in a prescribed form and order. Any departure or innovation, however radical, acquired its significance in the context of what was perceived as a structure of precedent and expectation. Thus the lesser honors granted a victor who had fallen short in some respect could be differentiated from the triumph by the absence or denial of certain essential elements, as in the case of the *triumphus in monte Albano*, in which the *pomerium* was never crossed, or the *ovatio*, which withheld the *currus* (the triumphal chariot), the *ornatus triumphalis* (the triumphal attire), the sceptre, and the laurel wreath.³⁷

The high degree of subtlety and precision of which this ritual dialogue seems to be capable, is clearly dependent upon the active role of all the parties concerned and of the entire triumphal apparatus. It should be apparent, for example, that the precise implications of what must be seen as the political, as well as religious, status of the *triumphator* depends in large measure on the role that the city chooses for itself, and this will be the case even after the emperor has usurped for himself the exclusive *ius triumphandi*. If, in the Republican times, the granting or withholding of a triumph was an index of the power of the Senate and its sensitivity to the various power groups (including

---

34. The Jupiter theory is advanced by J. G. Frazer, among others, in *The Golden Bough. A Study of Magic and Religion* (New York, 1963), pp. 171-172, and is attacked by W. Warde Fowler, "Iuppiter and the Triumphator," *The Classical Review*, 30 (1916), pp. 153ff. and others, including Wagenvoort, op. cit., who emphasizes the early (Etruscan?) origin of the triumph, and suggests that the image of Jupiter was copied from the *triumphator*. Versnel judiciously advances a composite theory of the *triumphator* as both "Iuppiter and Rex," op. cit., pp. 55-93.
35. Livy, *From the Founding of the City*, translated by F. G. Moore, Loeb Classical Library, Vol. III (Cambridge, Mass., 1949), XVIII, 7-8, p. 39.
36. For these criteria and their terminology, see Versnel, op. cit., pp. 164-195.
37. Ibid., pp. 165-171; and Payne, op. cit., p. 63.

the *vox populi*), then the triumph remains, under the Empire, however exotic, perverted, or subject to imperial whim, a critical occasion for civic self-definition and representation in relation to an emperor who might present himself as a god, as a protector of old republican ideals, or as a raving madman.[38] What is consistent throughout is a dialectical structure of reciprocal interpretation that provides a transcript of both continuities and transformations. And insofar as this dialogue between *triumphator* and city exploits all the means at its disposal, and takes the entire city as its stage set, it informs not only the inital casting of the spectacle, but also provides an essential point of reference for the entire ritual in its various dramatic and monumental manifestations. To focus exclusively on the triumph as a costumed ceremony is to ignore what surviving accounts make abundantly clear: that the transaction which seems to center around the *Porta Triumphalis* was in fact elaborately extended in urban space and time.

•   •   •

The fifth-century historian Orosius informs us that from the founding of Rome until the reign of the emperor Vespasian, Rome witnessed at least 320 triumphs.[39] Thus there was a considerable body of ritual experience upon which to draw by the time another historian, Josephus, wrote what was probably an eyewitness account of the triumph celebrated jointly by Vespasian and his heir apparent, Titus, in honor of their victories in Judaea and the final conquest and sacking of Jerusalem by Titus in 70 A.D. As it is one of the most complete and vivid accounts of the ceremony, it is worth quoting at length, beginning with Titus' return to Rome:

After a voyage as favourable as he could have desired, Rome gave him such a reception and welcome as it had given to his father.... Before many days had elapsed they decided to celebrate their achievements by one triumph in common, though the Senate had declared a separate triumph to each. Previous notice having been given of the day on which the pageant of victory would take place, not a soul among the countless host in the city was left at home: all issued forth and occupied every position where it was but possible to stand, leaving only room for the necessary passage of those upon whom they were to gaze.

The military, while night still reigned, had all marched out in companies and divisions, under their commanders, and been drawn up, not round the doors off the upper palace but near the temple of Isis; for there the emperors reposed that night. At the break of dawn, Vespasian and Titus issued forth, crowned with laurel and clad in the traditional purple robes, and proceeded to the Octavian walks; for here the Senate and the chief magistrates and those of the equestrian rank were awaiting their coming. A tribunal had been erected in front of the porticoes, with chairs of ivory placed for them upon it; to these they mounted and took their seats. Instantly acclamations rose from the troops.... After the prayers, Vespasian, having briefly addressed the assembled company, dismissed the soldiers to the customary breakfast provided for them by the emperors, and himself withdrew to the gate which, in consequence of the triumphal processions always passing through it has thence derived its name. Here the princes first partook of refreshment, and then, having donned their triumphal robes and sacrificed to the gods whose statues stood beside the gate, they sent the pageant on its way, driving off through the theatres, in order to give the crowds an easier view.

It is impossible adequately to describe the multitude of those spectacles and their munificence.... Silver and gold and ivory in masses, wrought into all manner of forms, might be seen, not as if carried in procession, but flowing, so to speak, like a river; here were tapestries borne along,... transparent gems, some set in golden crowns, some in other fashions, swept by in such profusion as to correct our erroneous supposition that any of them was rare. Then, too, there were carried images of their gods.... Beasts of many species were led along all caparisoned with appropriate trappings... moreover, even among the captives, none was seen to be unadorned....

But nothing in the procession excited so much astonishment as the structures of the moving stages;... many of them being three or four stories high.... For many were enveloped in tapestries interwoven with gold, and all had a framework of gold and wrought ivory. The war was shown by numerous representations, in separate sections, affording a very vivid picture of

---

38. This point is developed in an impressive study of late imperial rhetoric and ritual by Sabine G. MacCormack, *Art and Ceremony in Late Antiquity* (Berkeley, 1981), cf. , esp. pp. 17-89, where MacCormack, in analyzing the *adventus* ceremony, which became a late imperial (and early Christian) cognate of the triumph in various cities throughout the empire, argues that far from representing a decline into empty rhetoric and merely formulaic ritual, "the twin elements of consent and the transaction of business conveyed in the ceremony of the *adventus* made this ceremony one of the most characteristic expressions of late antique public life, the means whereby a population formulated its corporate identity, in both good times and ill."

39. Barini, op. cit., pp. 201-204, provides a list of triumphal celebrations for the entire imperial period. The important point is the apparently high frequency of triumphs, in spite of several long interludes (especially in the earlier centuries). Very few Roman citizens would have failed to see at least several triumphs during their lifetime.

its episodes. Here was to be seen a prosperous country devastated, there whole batallions of the enemy slaughtered; here a party in flight, there others led into captivity; walls of surpassing compass demolished by engines, strong fortresses overpowered.... and the art and magnificent workmanship of these structures now portrayed the incidents to those who had not witnessed them, as though they were happening before their eyes. On each of the stages was stationed the general of one of the captured cities in the attitude in which he was taken. A number of ships also followed.

The spoils in general were borne in promiscuous heaps; but conspicuous above all stood out those captured in Jerusalem. These consisted of a golden table, many talents in weight, and lampstand, likewise made of gold.... After these, and last of all the spoils was carried a copy of the Jewish law. Then followed a large party carrying images of victory, all made of ivory and gold. Behind them drove Vespasian, followed by Titus....

The triumphal procession ended at the temple of Jupiter Capitolinus, on reaching which they halted; for it was a time-honoured custom to wait there until the execution of the enemy's general was announced.... After the announcement... the princes began the sacrifices, which having been offered with the customary prayers, they withdrew to the palace.... For the city of Rome kept festival that day for her victory in the campaign against her enemies, for the termination of civil dissensions, and for her dawning hopes of felicity.

The triumphal ceremonies being concluded and the empire of the Romans established on the firmest foundation, Vespasian decided to erect a temple of peace.[40]

The first thing one notices about Josephus' ceremonial *ekphrasis* is that it devotes very little attention or rhetorical energy to those aspects of the triumph that have preoccupied most scholars, the role of the *triumphator* and the entry ceremony at the *Porta Triumphalis*. Admittedly, the entry ceremony might eventually have been taken for granted. It was, along with the the concluding act at the Temple of Jupiter, no doubt the most conventionalized part of the ritual, while the procession was, as we shall see, inherently flexible, and its contents must have changed according to the particular foe conquered. Thus it is certainly important to understand that more obscure, but repetitively constant initiatory performance. To conclude however, that "the triumph is essentially an entrance ceremony," is to close the book too soon.[41] Such a bias in favor of invariant ritual structures tends to relegate a considerable portion of the performance to the status of mere *panem et circenses*. One must take the textual evidence at face value that the extended procession, which seems to become longer and more elaborate throughout its life, was an important vehicle of the Roman aesthetic of "ostentatious display" and as such the principal means by which the city described to itself its growing accession of good fortune.

Josephus reminds us that there was, in fact, considerable ceremonial activity well before the procession formed up and approached the gate. These "preliminal rites" are presented as a semi-autonomous event, taking place "outside" the city in an area of the Campus Martius that was soon to be extensively rebuilt by Titus' successor, Domitian (fig. 2).[42] The key elements of the setting described by Josephus were, however, probably retained, changing in form and perhaps in location, but playing the same basic role in the ritual. Vespasian and his son had spent the night before their triumph "near the temple of Isis" in the Campus Martius, presumably in a sort of state-operated suburban palace which was known as the *Villa Publica*. Like the papal Villa Madama in Renaissance

---

40. Josephus, *The Jewish War*, translated by H. St. J. Thackery, Loeb Classical Library, Vol. III (New York, 1928), VII, 119-158, pp. 540-551.
41. This is Versnel's conclusion, op. cit., p. 389, admittedly in oversimplified form. Even in the late imperial and medieval *adventus* ritual, of which one might legitimately say that it was essentially an entry ceremony, the survival, and sometimes (especially in the Renaissance) the more or less literal recreation, of aspects of the triumph extended the entry itself in urban space in a highly significant way.
42. On the urban geography of the triumph, see the reconstruction based on Josephus' text by Ena Makin, "The Triumphal Route, with Particular Reference to the Flavian Triumph," *The Journal of Roman Studies*, XI (1921), pp. 25-36; and A. von Domaszewski, "Die Triumphstrasse auf dem Marsfelde," *Archive fur Religionsiddenchafft*, XII (1909), pp. 60-82, which posits a connection between the lustrational or purification function of the triumph and the sacred stream of the Petronilla, which crossed the Campus Martius just beyond the presumptive site of the *Porta Triumphalis*. Smith, op. cit., p. 25, develops this suggestion in his discussion of Domitian's building projects in the area and their relation to the architectural apparatus of the Triumph. Holland, op. cit., pp. 50-73, explores the idea, suggested by many ancient sources, of a primitive "natural" boundary of the ancient city based upon water courses and presided over by Janus. According to her account the Janus/water boundary was supplanted by the Etruscan idea of the *pomerium*, but would have retained some fragmentary ritual significance.

Rome, it was used by the city for a variety of ceremonial purposes, such as the reception of foreign ambassadors and the lodging of the *triumphator* prior to his official entry. Upon arising, Vespasian and Titus were met by the army and moved on to what Josephus calls "the Octavian walks," elsewhere referred to in generic terms as the *Porticus Triumphi*, where the *triumphator* would receive the members of the distinguished civic delegation which had gone out to meet him. This was an important enough moment in the ritual to be frequently depicted, usually in a symbolically condensed portrayal which included figures representing the Senate and People of Rome, and the city of Rome "herself" (fig. 3).[43] In this case, the civic representatives would have confronted Vespasian and Titus enthroned upon what was apparently a temporary grandstand, establishing a dramatic relationship which would shortly be reversed as the procession moved through the streets and theaters of the city. Indeed, it is characteristic of the entire ritual that the see-and-be-seen equation is seldom stable for long, and that the roles of performer and audience oscillate as the city presents itself and the *triumphator* is presented to the city.

After a short intermission for refreshment, which suggests that the preliminal ceremony was not as brief as it sounded and probably included some long-winded speech-making in addition to Vespasian's address, the participants approached the *Porta Triumphalis*.[44] In this context it would be, like the *Villa Publica* and the *Porticus Triumphi*, another architectural component of the structured dialogue between *triumphator* and city that was already well underway. Most importantly, this particular gate would have admitted and captured the bearer of military power and good fortune intact. Thus one is able to "send the pageant on its way" through the city with the *triumphator* still in possession of his potency, and able to hold up his end of the dialogue which would continue to be the ordering principle of what was the most conspicuous part of the ritual.

Most conspicuous, as far as Josephus was concerned, were the "promiscuous heaps" of spoils which he diligently catalogued in his somewhat breathless description of the procession. This is the concrete and highly visible evidence of the captured good-fortune of the *triumphator* himself, and the manner of display suggested by the text implies that the city, on its part, was not merely to bear witness, but actually to participate. The moving stages which so impressed Josephus were not simply display cases, but painted and apparently populated *tableaux vivants* re-enacting the circumstances of the victory for "those who had not witnessed them, as though they were happening before their eyes." It is indeed as if the war was still being fought, now for the benefit of the throngs crowding the streets, porticoes, theaters, circuses, and probably the surrounding hills of Rome itself. In fact, if the triumph at its most general level was, like the temple of Janus, a symbolic passage between war and peace, then that passage has been extended by the procession to include the entire city in the liminal stage of transition, in which the *triumphator* is still, in effect, a symbolic warrior.[45] The conquest-capture thematics of the entry are thus reinforced by the construction of the processional performance as a ritual re-enactment and prolongation of "battle." This battle will finally conclude only with the symbolic — and perhaps cathartic — *coup de grâce* of the execution of the enemy general on the Capitoline, after which the *triumphator*

---

43. On the reliefs representing Domitian's *adventus* (or triumph) at Rome, see *I Rilievi Flavi Del Palazzo Della Cancellerim* (Rome, 1945); and Hamberg, op. cit., pp. 50-56.
44. For the elaborate panegyrics which traditionally accompanied the late imperial *adventus*, see MacCormack, op. cit., pp. 1-14. However different the specific content, this sort of speech-making was based on a tradition which flourished in the late republican and early imperial periods, and the civic leaders who greeted Titus and Vespasian would certainly have agreed in principle with the late second century orator cited by MacCormack (p. 20): "This task falls on you on behalf of everyone, and just as some law and obligation obtains as is as the dignitary enters the first gate, as the saying goes, namely that the cities should in common acclaim the entry, so it is right that one of the best men according to education and culture should make an address, and speak with an official voice, and in a speech made on behalf of all."
45. Cf. Rykwert, op. cit., pp. 141-142; also Huizinga, op. cit., p. 177, where the triumph is described as "far more than a solemn celebration of military success; it is a rite through which the state recuperates from the strains of war and re-experiences its well being."

4. The triumph of Romulus. Detail of a Pompeian fresco.

would dedicate the spoils, lay down his still active *imperium militiae*, and complete his reincorporation into the civil (peacetime) society of Rome. The processional display is thus an integral part, and a significant unifying agent, in the "ritual process," and not some sort of sideshow or *intermezzo*. There are many further details that could be brought to bear in support of this line of argument, none more important than the ritual function of the spoils as the primary ingredients of the procession. However promiscuous the heaps may have seemed to Josephus, they are often as precise in their message as the theatrical *tableaux* and as traditionally founded in their legendary origins as the triumph itself.

According to Plutarch, Romulus, after his victory over Acron, the chieftain of Caenina, celebrated the first Roman triumph in the following manner:

Romulus, after considering how he might perform his vow in a manner most acceptable to Jupiter and accompany the performance with a spectacle most pleasing to the citizens, cut down a monstrous oak that grew in the camp, hewed it into the shape of a trophy, and fitted and fastened to it the armour of Acron, each piece in its due order. Then he himself girding his raiment about him and wreathing his flowing locks with laurel, set the trophy on his right shoulder where it was held erect, and began a triumphal march, leading off in a paean of victory which his army sang as it followed him under arms, and being received by the citizens with joyful amazement. This procession was the origin and model of all subsequent triumphs.[46]

Thus what poses as the archetypal enactment of the triumph, invented by the "inventor" of the city itself, is fundamentally preoccupied with symbolic display — to an audience of Jupiter and the "citizens." Having dispatched the enemy general on the field of battle, rather than in the city, Romulus made a model of him, which became the prototypical triumphal artifact, or "trophy" (fig. 4), and as such was the "type" of an important class of Roman (and Renaissance) monuments assembled from the (representations of) spoils taken from a vanquished foe. As any reader of the *Iliad* will recognize, the armor of the enemy had a special status among the spoils of war, and was especially worth the risking of one's life. However, "unlike the Greeks... the Romans shrank from the enemy armour they had captured. It was, loaded as it was with enemy power, dangerous and not to be brought within the walls of Rome."[47] It was, therefore, burnt on the battlefield; all except the armor of the enemy commander — the *spolia opima* — which only the victor — the holder of the *imperium auspiciumque*, the potential *triumphator* — could by virtue of his victory — his superior *mana* — possess and bring back with him as a trophy to be dedicated to Jupiter and the city. Here again one finds the active principle of a ritual transaction between the *triumpha-*

---

46. Plutarch, *Lives*, translated by Bernadotte Perin, Loeb Classical Library, Vol. I (New York, 1918), "Life of Romulus," XVI, 5-6, p. 137.

47. Versnel, op. cit., p. 309.

tor and the city, based on the conviction that "these *spolia opima* possessed the energy which might be useful to the possessor, i.e., Jupiter Feretrius and through him Rome itself."[48] While this transaction may initially have been mediated through the agency of the gods, it was also extended in urban space by the procession, which eventually supplemented the basic Romulan trophy with an array of appropriate representations, such as the small-scale three-dimensional models of the conquered cities which were sometimes included among the "real spoils."[49] These models suggest that Rome was to benefit not only from the good fortune of the *triumphator* as represented by the *spolia opima*, but also from the *urban-mana* of the subjected territories absorbed by the conquest. Thus in the processional reenactment of his good fortune in war, the *triumphator* seems to lustrate, or anoint, and ultimately to endow the city with those emblems of his *felicitas*.[50]

5.   6.   7.

5-16. *The triumph of Julius Caesar. Series of woodcuts by Jacopo da Strasbourg, 1503.*

As in the case of the liminal passage of the *triumphator* from war to peace, this process of display and endowment was fundamentally spatial in its articulation. The character of this extended performance is perhaps best conveyed by Renaissance reconstructions of the triumph, based on written accounts such as Josephus'; the most dramatic being Mantegna's paintings of the Triumph of Caesar and Jacopo da Strasbourg's woodcuts of the same event (figs. 5-16). In these panoramic

11.   12.   13.

sequences attention is focused on the spoils as they are deployed across the urban landscape. While the captured good fortune of the *triumphator* was assumed to persist spiritually, the physical evidence of his passage often left quite literal traces along the trajectory through the city. These might include the spoils piled along the *spina* of the Circus Maximus, or the beaks of the enemy ships from the battle of Actium attached by Augustus to the Rostra Julia in the Roman Forum, or

---

48. Ibid., p. 311.
49. Josephus does not mention such structures in his account (presumably the paintings, which are also depicted in the Jacopo da Strasbourg woodcuts, served a somewhat similar purpose), but they figure prominently in texts such as Addian's description of the triumph of Scipio in 201 B.C., where there were both "towers representing the conquered cities, and pictures of the principle episodes of the war." (*Punic Wars*, LXVI).
50. For a detailed analysis of the trophy, its origins and development in Roman history and art, as a symbol of *felicitas* and of the *charisme* of the victor, see Albert Charles Picard, *Les Trophées Romains. Contribution a l'Histoire de la Religion et de l'Art Triumphale de Rome* (Paris, 1957), esp. pp. 167-170; cf. also Versnel, op. cit., pp. 360-371.

even the undocumented temporary structures erected for the triumph itself. Many of these traces were eventually monumentalized as permanent structures — *in situ,* or as part of independent assemblages — and in time, the accumulation of the "remains," and the repetition of the ritual, must have conspired to make the city *seem* to be permanently *en fête*: an urban stage set almost too intense for the conduct of ordinary life. This image of the city as the product of a genuinely Piranesian *bricolage*, sponsored by the triumph, is not at all fanciful. The collection and architectural assembly of spoils provides a material analogue to the syncretic process by which Rome collected and assembled its civic institutions, its religion, indeed its entire culture, from the "spoils" of its contacts and conquests. So it is significant that at the same time a countervailing process of abstraction and typification was at work, casting those triumphal representations in the form of

8.

9.

10.

generalized urban types susceptible to independent architectural manipulation, available for use both on and off stage.

A case in point is the triumphal arch. These monuments were among the most conspicuously spectacular of the various sedimentary deposits associated with the triumph. They were first set up in the Roman Forum, and eventually throughout the city and the Empire, as free-standing

14.

15.

16.

commemorative monuments beginning as early as the second century B.C., when they were probably semi-permanent wooden structures for the display of statues and trophies. Although the triumphal arch had from the outset what one scholar has described as "a topical relationship to the triumph that engendered it," it also had a typological life of its own in its architectural development as a matrix for the deployment of elaborate iconographic programs.[51] Furthermore, each arch, while following and developing a recognizable pattern, seems to have established its own particular topographic and genealogical relationship to the triumph, so that while some arches seem to have straddled the triumphal route, others stood like highway signs to one side and others were apparently unrelated to the actual route. By the same token, a number of arches were erected in celebratory commemoration of a particular triumph, others were apparently wishful thinking

51. Brilliant, op. cit., p. 119.

about an unconsummated triumph, and others, especially in the later diffusion of the type, were incorporated as an appropriate articulation of various formally and functionally discrete types or as generally available urban decor.

Thus the precise nature of the relationship of the triumphal arch to the ritual from which it derives at least its name has been the subject of considerable debate. One theory is that the arch as we know it was a more or less direct descendant of the *Porta Triumphalis*, but as in the case of that monument, the familiar name is both a mask and a hieroglyph.[52] As a hieroglyph, the name *arcus triumphalis* suggests a picture of what now seems to have been the initially autonomous development of the *arcus* as an abstraction from the physically and functionally engaged arcuated portals of Etruscan and Hellenistic towns and palaces.[53] "Triumphal" thus denotes the adjectival modification of the *arcus* by the attachment and typological regulation of the "promiscuous heaps" of triumphal paraphernalia and ritual iconography. In any case, by the time the *arcus* had become definitively triumphal in the first century, the "topical relationship" was well enough established to set up a fruitful play of triumphal iconography and architectural vocabulary that probably conditioned the rebuilding of the *Porta Triumphalis* itself, that certainly conditioned the form and meaning of city gates throughout the Empire as indices of an imperial *adventus* or icons of the imperial presence, and that would continue to provide a repertoire of formal and symbolic permutations for as long as the classical tradition had any genuine ideological resonance.[54]

One might then characterize the structural relationship of the arch to the triumph as metalinguistic. Having been proposed and qualified as an appropriate filing station for the representational traces of the triumph, the arch "returned" as an established type in the corpus of urban monuments to comment upon, and in fact interpret, the same ritual. The full potential of this relationship is, however, explicitly activated only by the spatial and temporal strategy of the triumph *as performed*, when *it* "returns" to rediscover and collect its own traces, finding that they have become a veritable hall of magnifying and refracting mirrors. As the ever more elaborately "triumphal" arches proliferated along the processional route, they reflected back to each successive pageant the accumulated tradition of the ritual and the reiterated diagram of the ritually established relationship between the act of entry (as embodied in the form of the arch), the display of spoils (as depicted in the decorative iconography), and the urban apotheosis of the *triumphator*, monumentally mounted in his *quadriga* atop the arch. This diagram might even include an explicit reference to the symbolic passage from war to peace, as in the case of the Arch of Constantine, which displays battle scenes on one face, the triumphal procession in the interior of its arched opening, and scenes of Constantine and his subjects enjoying peace and prosperity on the other face. Thus the passage of the procession through the city would include its juxtaposition to a series of monuments which served to recapitulate and, in a certain sense, to reenact the full ritual significance of the act of entry, not only for the members of the calvacade, but for the citizens crowded along the way. The triumph was, in this way, ruthlessly opportunistic, and probably exploited such possibilities for self-mimetic repetition and aggrandizement as the old gates in the Servian Wall (before their destruction) and the portals in the various public monuments through which the procession passed.[55] To suggest a very crude analogy, this process was something like

---

52. Cf. Noack, op. cit., who develops van Gennep's suggestion (op. cit., p. 21) that the "evolution from magic portal [*porta triumphalis*] to the monument seems also to have occured in the case of the Roman arch of triumph." The "also" refers to a parallel drawn with the temple portals of the far east.
53. Cf. Brilliant, op. cit., p. 119; and Smith, op. cit., p. 24, who is mainly concerned to assimilate, rather than distinguish the city gate and the triumphal arch.
54. Smith, op. cit., provides the best general survey of gate iconography in relation to the late imperial, byzantine, medieval, and near eastern traditions.
55. My own sense of the procession is that it not only must, by topographical logic, have passed *through* several of the many arches which once cluttered the Via Sacra in the Roman Forum, but also would have detoured to pass through, or at least

17. "Triumphal" sequence of Roman monuments, as depicted on the tomb of Haterii. The Lateran Museum, Rome.

contemporary Presidential signing ceremonies, in which the full signature is produced by a dozen or so different pens, each of which having participated in the inscription of a part, then becomes a token of the whole ceremony for the various participants among whom they are distributed.

The propensity of the triumph for self-mimesis in the appropriation of monuments such as the *arcus*, which would portray the intransitivity of a ritual endlessly picking up its own pieces, is balanced by an equally ambitious and acquisitive precision in the identification and spatial incorporation of a wide range of independent urban monuments. The purposeful meandering of the procession to include monuments which represented the distinct typological articulation of other aspects of urban experience, documents the transitive function of the triumph as an ongoing interpretation of a changing civic landscape. The city was not a stage for ritual until it was taken as such. The available monuments, buried as they were in the sediment of daily life, would remain as spatially and chronologically heterogeneous as they seemed to Goethe, until they were ritually "excavated" and laced together in an urban order that had been, previously, only latent. So the triumph took the city as it found it — as Romulus and his successors had founded and built it — and interpreted the city as it existed, as well as proposing its transformation.

When Josephus says that the procession was sent off "on its way, driving off through the theaters," we may take him to mean that the procession passed along a traditional route that would have included the Circus Flaminius and the Circus Maximus, but might also by the first century have modified its itinerary to include the more recently completed Theater of Marcellus (13 A.D.), where some 20,000 additional, and no doubt privileged, ticket-holders could have ring-side seats (Figure 2).[56] In this way the intention to maximize display — to maximize the range of the dialogue between city and *triumphator* — would have coincided with the interpretive function of identifying and ordering the significant monuments of the city, old and new (and not yet built), in an idealized ritual framework. It is perhaps this sense of the triumph, as a carefully edited selection from the urban transcript, that forms the array of monuments depicted in the reliefs from Haterii tomb (Figure 17).[57] If this interpretation is correct, then one is presented with a significant image of the city as summarized in that set of monumental representations linked by the processional

---

paused to confront, the most significant monuments. Versnel, op. cit., pp. 135-137, exaggerates the strict independence of triumph and triumphal arch, mainly because he focuses on the singular act of entry to the exclusion of the re-iteration and elaboration of that act in the procession.

56. Cf. Makin, op. cit., pp. 33-34.

57. Smith, op. cit., suggests this interpretation of the Haterii tomb reliefs. For a survey of the various interpretations of the reliefs, see F. Castagnoli, "Gli Edifici Representati in un Relievo del Sepolcro Degli Haterii," *Bolletino Della Commissione Archeologica Del Governatorato Di Roma*, Anno LXIX, (1941, XIX-XX), pp. 59-69. 58. I have discussed such images of the Renaissance city in which the depiction of an ordered selection of pageant decorations in relation to a procession represents the city as an idealized project, in "Emblems of the City: Civic Pageantry and the Rhetoric of Urbanism," *Artforum* (September, 1981), pp. 48-52.

structure of the triumph.[58] Josephus' plural and very real "theaters" are thus fused in an image of Goethe's unified and noble assembly: a singular and imaginary urban theater within which the city may reflect upon itself, upon its increasingly oppressive burden of acquired and monumentalized "good fortune," and upon the emerging relationship between its history, its everyday existence, and its ritual projection as potentially "a single body animated by a single spirit."

●   ●   ●

And so, on to the Forum and the Capitoline Hill where "the triumphal procession being concluded and the empire of the Romans established on the firmest foundations, Vespasian decided

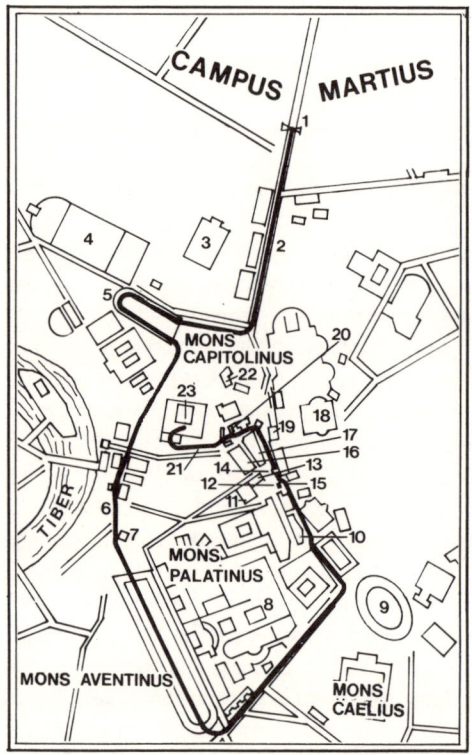

18. The Roman Forum and the Imperial Fora, Rome.

1. Porta Triumphalis 2. Via Lata 3. Baths of Agrippa 4. Theatre of Pompey 5. Circus Flaminius 6. Forum Boarium (Cattle Market) 7. Altar of Hercules 8. Palace of Augustus 9. Flavian Amphitheatre 10. House of Vestals 11. Temple of Augustus 12. Regia 13. Temple of Castor and Pollux 14. Arch of Augustus 15. Via Sacra 16. Basilica Julia 17. Forum Romanum 18. Forum of Augustus Caesar 19. Forum of Julius Caesar 20. Mamertine Prison 21. Steps to Capitol 22. Arx 23. Temple of Jupiter Capitolinus

to erect a temple of peace" (fig. 18). Josephus' conclusion is, of course, too good to be true, both in terms of the illusory, or at least ephemeral, sense of reconciliation and integration effected by the ritual, and in terms of the foreshortening of history suggested. But for the purposes of this discussion, the juxtaposition of the ritualized termination of war and the ritually informed constructive pursuits of peace is irresistibly convenient. It is entirely appropriate that a powerful ritual interpretation of the city and its monuments should be presented as leading to an ambitious

---

58. I have discussed such images of the Renaissance city in which the depiction of an ordered selection of pageant decorations in relation to a procession represents the city as an idealized project, in "Emblems of the City: Civic Pageantry and the Rhetoric of Urbanism," *Artforum* (September, 1981), pp. 48-52.

spatially ordered urban ensemble such as Vespasian's *Templum Pacis*. It is equally significant that the implied accession of good fortune (not to mention the actual accession of real wealth) acquired in battle, and confirmed and celebrated in the triumph, should be juxtaposed to the "real" expansion and embellishment of the city through the realization of "public works." Urbanism, Josephus seems to suggest, is the moral equivalent of war.[59]

The ideological connection between victory in war and prosperity in peace, as embodied in the monuments of the Imperial Fora including the *Templum Pacis*, is the basis of Josephus' *rhetorical* connection. In this sense, one might well conclude that the rhetoric of the triumph is fundamentally the rhetoric of Roman urbanism in its monumental manifestations. However the extent to which one might literally connect the spatial form of Roman ritual with the spatial composition of the Imperial Fora, or any other monumental urban project, in more than a loose and generalized way, remains an open question. Frank Brown has identified the very essence of all Roman architecture as the direct spatial embodiment of ritual form, and Richard Brilliant has taken this proposition a convincing step further by relating the processional form of the triumph to a kind of planning which he calls "nodular":

The articulation of the processional way, adapted for activities including the parade of the triumphator, affected the extension of the Via Sacra at Rome, which passed from the Circus Maximus over the Velia into the Roman Forum, then up the Capitoline Hill to the Temple of Jupiter. Although this path had a natural origin in the primitive history of Rome, it evolved programmatically but without consistent planning over the centuries. Yet the Via Sacra itself was studded, at points of juncture where direction and elevation changed, with many different monuments; these became nodes of affirmative action (*celebratio*) and arrest, while the intervals were spaces for passage. This kind of organization, although apparently casual, was closely tied to the Roman concept of the ostentatious public monument and greatly influenced the development of Roman urbanism, while it also informed the character of architectural planning.[60]

Let it be noted, however, that this is not the kind of planning that Brilliant identifies with the formalized axiality of the Imperial Fora. And yet the Fora seem, in some respects, even apart from Josephus' broad hint, to be more intriguing as a monumental urban correlative to the spatial character of the triumphal ritual as described by Brilliant, than any literal and direct translation of the procession into architectural form. That is, one might suggest, because the Imperial Fora embody not the phenomenological reality of the procession, but rather what is here taken to be its implied ambition to interpret the actual city as a potentially ordered and continuously coordinated entity. Ritual works with, and upon, the existing city, as Brilliant's account of the Roman Forum shows, but as interpretation it works also upon civic self-consciousness. When it comes time to build a "new" forum, in Rome or in a provincial city, the collaboration of ritual and independent architectural research produces an image not of the actual space of the Roman Forum — which is the "raw" space of ritual experience — but of that space *as interpreted*. Through the essential mediation of abstraction and generalization, the triumph derives not merely a plan of its specific configuration within the existing city, but rather a set of intensified spatial and semantic relationships: between forum and temple, temple and gate, gate and city, city and *triumphator*, and so on. These relationships are then available for future interpretation.

Thus to cast the configuration of a specific ritual in concrete would be both to suffocate the city — which must be "renewed" not only when meaning is lost, but also when it becomes too particular — and to strangle continuous ritual interpretation. The interpretive function of ritual depends upon its *difference* from the material discourse of architecture. It can comment, provoke, and transform only when it is neither identical to, nor wholly detached from, the object of its

---

59. On the iconography of the "imperial peace" in triumphal monuments, see Brilliant, op. cit., p. 128. Significant in this context is the fact that, by law, the *pomerium* could only be extended when the limits of Roman rule where extended, thus linking urban growth to imperial victory.

60. Brilliant, op. cit., p. 56.

interpretation. Indeed, if the architecture of the city was simply "an art of shaping space around ritual" in the literal sense of a soap bubble, if it directly embodied a specific ritual to the extent that "it required it, it prompted it, enforced, it," and in fact all but performed it, then architecture and ritual would cancel each other in an orgy of mutual redundancy.[61] That such a claustrophobic utopia was never fully realized in Rome is demonstrated by the continuous vitality of the triumph, in its subsequent transformation, as a tool of urban interpretation. One example, the entry of Charles V in 1536, may perhaps suffice as a suggestion of the possibilities explored by all the numerous papal "triumphs," by the real and imaginary efforts at imperial *renovatio* cast in triumphal form by characters as diverse as Frederick II and Cola di Rienzo, and by the endless "arrivals" of more of less important visitors.[62]

The Holy Roman Emperor, Charles V, was of course seen by Pope Paul III as a particularly important visitor. It is not immediately clear whether Charles was a "bearer of good fortune" to Rome in the spring of 1536. His troops had, after all, sacked the city just nine years before, and the papacy continued to occupy an ambiguous position in the peninsular wars between Charles and Francis I of France. And yet he was the Holy Roman Emperor, and it was his propagandists who incessantly invoked the themes of imperial *renovatio* and Christian crusade which had so often in the past tempted the Romans and even a wary papacy. More concretely he was, if not the bearer of good fortune, at least the bearer of potential for both destruction and positive coexistence, and as such was clearly to be placated and gently instructed.[63]

Charles' entry was accordingly a masterpiece of strategic ambivalence. The urban decor was appropriately imperial; temporary triumphal arches constructed by the leading Roman architects complemented the partially disinterred remains of ancient Rome. They served to mask the more glaring medievalisms of the modern city and attempted to fill the gaps between the genuine artifacts, while articulating a triumphal route that was very far from being a faithful reconstruction of the original.[64] Indeed, the route followed by Charles, his troops, and his hosts, differed significantly from that of both the ancient triumph and the medieval imperial processions. Approaching the city from the south along the recently restored Via Appia, Charles moved towards the base of the Palatine Hill, from which point he temporarily rode alongside the ancient *triumphator*, through the Arch of Constantine and into the Forum via the Arch of Titus. Here, as elsewhere, the entry had been the occasion for extensive urban renewal and restoration so that the city might be more effectively presented to Charles *all'antica*. But there were limits to the illusion, for at the Arch of Septimus Severus, where the *triumphator* had begun his ascent of the Capitoline Hill, Charles turned aside, skirting the hill and moving into the Piazza San Marco, now with modern papal Rome stretching out in front of him. So while the classical goal of the triumphant emperor would have been the Capitoline, Charles, traversing the Campo Marzio, concluded his entry at St. Peter's. The ostensible reason for avoiding even a short visit to the Campidoglio was its ruinous state, but keeping in mind the extensive work done elsewhere in 1536 and the fact that in 1513 it had been the setting for an elaborate festival theater, one is tempted to guess that the planners of the entry preferred not to let the imperial associations go too far. One historian has suggested that the entry was to be seen as safely "architectural tourism."[65]

---

61. Frank Brown, *Roman Architecture* (New York, 1971), pp. 9-10. 62. Payne, op. cit., discusses a number of these triumphal survivals and revivals.
62. Payne, op. cit., discusses a number of these triumphal survivals and revivals.
63. For the political context of Charles' entry, see Peter Partner, *Renaissance Rome 1500-1559* (Berkeley, 1976), pp. 197-199; and for the broader ideological context, see Francis Yates, "Charles V and the Idea of Empire," in *Astraem. The Imperial Theme in the Sixteenth Century* (London, 1975), pp. 1-28.
64. The route and decoration for the entry are described and illustrated by Maria Luisa Madonna, "L'Ingresso di Carlo V a Roma," in *La Citta Effimera e l'Universo Artificiale del Giardino*, Marchello Fagiolo, editor (Rome, 1980), pp. 63-68.
65. Partner, op. cit., p. 197.

Furthermore, the displacement of the ceremonial focus of Rome from the Capitol to the Vatican had begun very early. Already in 312, Constantine may have refused to make the traditional sacrifice at the center of pagan Rome at the end of his "triumph," and the balancing act between classical and Christian traditions would certainly have been part of the 1536 events. In any case, the detour around the Campidoglio was symptomatic, either of an explicit dissociation from imperial pretensions or pagan cults, or of an incomplete renewal of the urban structure. In its particular transformation of the triumph in relation to the ancient and medieval conventions, and in the service of a specific dialogue between an emperor and the city, the 1536 interpretation had revealed at least one rather significant "silence" in the urban discourse. And when that problem was addressed, beginning in 1537, perhaps as a direct result of the events of the preceding year, Michelangelo's "reconstruction" of the Capitoline palaces turned its back on ancient Rome and, with Marcus Aurelius as a guide, directed its perspectively focused gaze towards the heart of Renaissance Rome and St. Peter's beyond.[66]

•   •   •

At the very end of his *Italian Journey* Goethe describes what are, in effect, parting visits to the Capitol and the panoramic view afforded by that vantage. His reflections on the city are by then calmer, if no less melancholy. The view from the Capitol still included the cacophony of fragments, ancient and modern, which might inspire Romantic meditation, but apparently defy rational order. And yet the same view might also have encompassed the procession of Titus and Vespasian approaching from the south and the cortege of Charles V moving away to the north, traversing the parallel city constructed by the interpretive work of ritual, in which, Goethe suggests, "the world as lived and the world as imagined, fused under the agency of a single set of symbolic forms, turn out to be the same world."[67] It is that fusion, with its sense of simultaneous perception, which another student of the palimpsest of ancient and modern Rome, Sigmund Freud, found to be lacking in the city as a model of mental life. Rationalist that he was, in method if not in results, Freud concluded that since "the same space cannot have two different contents," Rome, however densely layered it might be, could not be like the mind, "an entity... in which nothing that has come into existence will have passed away and all the earlier phases of development continue to exist alongside the latest one."[68] Ritual, however, will not so quickly accept these limitations and attempts periodically to overcome them in an interpretive fusion of past and present, of "ethos and world view," of memory and desire.

66. Cf. James Ackerman, *The Architecture of Michelangelo* (Baltimore, 1971), pp. 139-173; and Fritz Saxl, "The Capitol During the Renaissance: A Symbol of the Imperial Idea," *Lectures* (London, 1961), pp. 200-214.
67. Geertz, "Religion as a Cultural System," in op. cit., p. 112.
68. Sigmund Freud, *Civilization and its Discontents*, translated by James Strachey (New York, 1961), pp. 16-18.

The Return to the Origins

Rituals of Initiation in Late Eighteenth Century France

Anthony Vidler

In "The Architecture of the Lodges: Ritual Form and Associational Life in the Late Enlightenment" (Oppositions 5), Anthony Vidler argued that:

The concentration of historians on the "history of utopias" or the fantastic nature of "visions" separated from their conditions of production has hitherto obscured their real functionality. It is clear, however, that whether the idealizations refer to a primal past and the restoration of an archaic order, or to a projected future, a promised land that will come with time..., they stand, at the beginning of our era, as the purveyors of interests inseparable from those of their bourgeois makers.

Enlightenment man was considered to be a tabula rasa on which the architectural environment could inscribe lessons. Assuming that man's nature tended towards a single ideal form, truths conveyed by the institutions, ceremonies, and rituals of the Greeks and Egyptians were considered equally valid for the eighteenth century Parisian. The architecture of the Lodges, then, not only embodied ancient truths, but was actually the physical conveyance by which those truths could be imprinted on man's character. The one-to-one correspondence between truth in an object and moral development not only allowed for ritual's reification but demanded it as well.

That we no longer function under such ethical and epistemological suppositions is obvious. The ramifications of this change with regard to reification are poignantly elaborated by George Lukàcs in his Theory of the Novel. In contrast to a pre-industrial world where objects "are clearly human products, the result of preordained ritual," the modern world "is inhabited by chairs, motorcycles, food, houses, and revolvers [that] are no longer felt as the result of human activity [and] inhabit the world like so much dead furniture." Consequently, modern man "has developed ... elaborate methods of symbolism in the express hope of giving meaning to such stubbornly resistent things;" the symbol's presence "stands as an indication that the immediate meaning of objects has disappeared."[1] The symbolic language of ritual has lost what was once its distiguishing feature, the diaphonous relation between Interpretant, Sign, and Object (to use C.S. Peirce's terms). A given object's ability to convey meaning — particularly ritualistic meaning — no longer results from a direct relationship between user and object, but rather from the application of a non-intrinsic symbolic significance. Ritual has more often served as an apology for things as they are than as a brief for how they can be; and now utopian architectural visions no longer function easily as justifications for a particular aspect of the base-superstructure relationship of a society. Even given this qualified sense, then, the modern architect has an exceptionally difficult task in making the landscape of his imagination the terrain of the common man.

1. Frederic Jameson, Marxism and Form (Princeton: Princeton University Press, 1971).

■   ■   ■

Point de ville qui n'eût des confréries d'artisans, de bourgeois, de femmes: les plus extravagantes cérémonies y étaient érigées en mystéres sacrés; est c'est de lá que vient la société des francs-macons, échappés au temps, qui a détruit toutes les autres?

Voltaire, Essai sur les Moeurs[1]

It is not entirely clear by what stages the original masonic craft guilds ("operative masons") were, toward the end of the seventeenth century, gradually superseded by the societies of bourgeois and aristocratic association. Certainly in mid-seventeenth century England operative masons began to receive non-practicing members ("speculative masons") into their ranks, and a number of these societies, from the London tavern societies to the gentlemen's discussion clubs of the provinces, began to constitute themselves as wholly "speculative" circles. The group of philosophers and scientists involved in the establishment of the Royal Society, including Elias Ashmole and Robert Morey, were among the earliest recorded non-operative masons. By the turn of the century the operative form was more or less extinct, and the Grand Lodge of London was established in 1717 to regulate the constitutions of the various societies already in existence. The book of *Constitutions,* collated by James Anderson, was published in 1723, and marked this stage of unification by bringing together the heterogeneous rules, mythologies, and histories of masonry, some dating from the mid-fourteenth century, that had served the different lodges.[2]

Freemasonic Architects: Paris 1750-1789. Imported into France after 1725 as a wholly fashionable society, freemasonry was connected at its inception in Paris (where the first known lodge was of 1726) to a group of aristocratic Jacobite *emigrés,* led by Charles Radclyffe, the future Lord Derwentwater. The order rapidly became popular with aristocrats, bourgeois, and intellectuals — Montesquieu was recorded as having been initiated in London in 1730 — and attracted the attention of the Paris police from 1737 on. The Church of Rome issued its first Bull of condemnation in 1738. The period between 1737 and 1755 was one of considerable growth under the loose regulation of the early Grand Masters, the duc d'Antin and the Comte de Clermont. Police harassment continued until 1745; a second Papal Bull was issued in 1751. Nevertheless the order flourished, first under the Grand Lodge (from 1743) then the Grand Orient (from 1773). By 1778 there were at least eighty-two lodges active in Paris. The Grand Orient counted some eight-and-a-half-thousand members in the capital between its foundation and the Revolution, and beyond these there were the schismatics of the Grand Lodge, the women's lodges (called Lodges of "Adoption"), together with hundreds of breakaway and autonomous sects.[3]

Over one-hundred-twenty architects belonged to lodges in Paris affiliated with the Grand Orient between 1774 and 1789; of these, a considerable number are well known in the development of neo-classicism as the authors of influential texts or of important designs.[4] It seems that varying degrees of commitment to the ideals and the social life of freemasonry may be distinguished. J.B. Puisieux, chief architect of Sainte Geneviève under Soufflot, was a mason from 1727 to 1773 and a

---

1. Voltaire, *Essai sur les Moeurs, Oeuvres Complètes,* vol. 12, pp. 64-65.
2. *The Constitutions of the Free-Masons,* ed. James Anderson, revised edition 1738 (London, 1723) pp. 1-48. This masonic "history of architecture" was in fact a compilation of accounts of the history of the craft from manuscripts dating from around 1360. These are discussed in D. Knoop, "Pure Ancient Masonry," *Ars Quatuor Coronatorum* (1940), LIII, p. 4, et. seq., and republished in Knoop, Jones and Hamer, *Early Masonic Catechisms* (1943). The 1723 *Constitutions* was first translated into French in 1736 (Jean Kuenen, The Hague) and again in 1742 (de la Tierce, Frankfurt). The successive transformations in these historical accounts according to the development of architectural theory in general is particularly revealing as a way of understanding the specific relationship of architects to the Order. At times, indeed, the influence may have expanded from freemasonry into architecture; the discourse on the "primitive type" for architecture — the hut or the temple — must have been at least supported by the masonic affiliations of, for example, the abbé Lauquier or Quatremère de Quincy.
3. This account of the formation of the early Parisian lodges is largely drawn from Pierre Chevallier, *Les Ducs sous l'Acacia, ou Les premiers pas de la Franc-Maçonnerie française 1725-1743* (Paris, 1964), chapters 1,2, and 3.
4. This estimate is based on the lists published by Alain le Bihan, *Francs-Maçons Parisiens du Grand Orient de France* (Paris: Bibliothèque Nationale, 1966), supplemented by archival sources in the Bibliothèque Nationale.

high officer of his lodge; his treatise on geometry reflected his intense belief in guild masonic doctrine.[5] On the other hand, Jean-Jacques Lequeu, alienated, a pornographer, and probably half-mad, used the imagery and quasi-occultist concerns of his Lodges in Rouen and Paris in a highly eclectic and often satirical manner. In between were a large body of professionals who considered masonry to be either a simple extension of the social life of the salons — a ready-made patronage circle — or a theoretical doctrine, even if they did not use symbolic masonic themes directly in their designs. This latter group included official architects like Moreau-Desproux, architect of the City of Paris, and theoreticians and scholars like Quatremère de Quincy.

Of course, not all architects entered into any active relation with their brotherhood; few established themselves so firmly as de Puisieux, dean of all the venerables of Paris, or Poncet who designed the headquarters of the Grand Orient. Many were content to derive a convivial social life and a comfortable patronage from their membership in this bourgeois club *par excellence*. Some, however, and especially those concerned with the development of architectural theory, found in the analogical terms of the masonic doctrine — the terms by which society was referred to by architectural metaphor — a particularly redolent and evocative discourse. The Abbé Laugier, perhaps himself a freemason, seems to have merged his interests in the primitive type of architecture with those espoused by masonry. Certainly Quatremère de Quincy in his theoretical work before the Revolution exhibited all the characteristics of one who was influenced by his masonic affiliation — the emphasis on idealist typology, and the interest in Egyptian architecture well before Napoleon's expedition to Egypt, may be regarded as legitimately "masonic" concerns. Some architects went even further and took seriously implications of the masonic "analogous theory" of architecture as a means by which to join their work (in theory at least) to more utopian ends.

The Myth of Foundation: Architecture as Described in Masonic Texts. The architect was commonly held to be the paradigm of the mason himself: writing in 1784, Louis de Beyerlé argued that the wide range of knowledge required of the architect, his special facility in interpreting the foundation myths, constituted him as the very "type of Free-Mason,"[6] for whom the form of the lodge was of particular importance; it not only gave institutional confirmation to the new society, but was also the immediate extension of their adopted terms of discourse and the representation of the forms of ritual. Reviving the terminology of the old "operative" masonic guilds, the aristocratic and middle-class fraternity of the mid-eighteenth century still talked of "building the Temple," of "constructing the social edifice." In this exercise the Freemasons utilized the form and content of the old operative masonic "charges" as collected by the English lodges in their *Constitutions* of 1723. Their translation into French represented an important stage in the transformation of primitivism in architectural and social theory, joining the tradition of Freemasonry to the philosophic preoccupation with a narrative of "origins."

The *Constitutions* described architectural history as an active metaphor for social development; the pure and natural origins of architecture were both emblematic of, and in some way participants in the order of natural society. There was no need for the mason to construct any artificial philosophic system to unite paradigms in architecture with those in society, for his mythology proposed that one was integrally bound up with the other, that the original art of geometry was an allegory for the original social structure.

It was through the rebuilding of Solomon's Temple that this society re-established the original proportions of the "moral edifice," completing the first stage of regeneration. The mid-century

---

5. J.B. Puisieux, *Eléments et traité de géometrie* (Paris, 1765).
6. Jean-Pierre Louis Beyerlé (1738-?), Counsellor to the Parliament of Nancy, *Essai sur la Franc-Maçonnerie* (à "La tomopolis," 1784)

masonic writer, Couret de Villeneuve, refers to the Temple, built by Solomon's architect Hiram Abif, in his discussion of a primary "model": "Artisans de notre bonheur travaillôns sur des Plans tracés par la nature et compassés par la raison, à reconstruire un Edifice moral, dont le modèle éxecuté dans les premiers âges du monde, nous est conservé par l'idée universelle de l'Ordre."[7] The task of the freemason was to "reintegrate" the elements of this edifice, mutilated by time, to "reestablish" its original proportions in their "primitive purity" and to bring all the ornaments into accord with the whole.

The relation of the idea of the Temple to society was well understood. Willermoz, the masonic mystic of Lyons wrote,

la fΔ-mΔ fundamentale n'a pas essentiellement d'autre but que la connaissance de l'homme et de la nature: étant fondée sur le Temple de Solomon, elle ne peut pas être étrangère à la science de l'homme, puisque tous les sages qui ont existé depuis sa fondation ont reconnu que ce fameux Temple n'a existé lui-même dans l'univers que pour être le type universel de l'homme général dans ses états passés, présents et futurs, et le tableau figuré de sa propre histoire.[8]

Elsewhere the same writer spoke of the Temple of Jerusalem, the universal type of the science of man, as having been substituted, "because of its perfection, for all the types of symbols that have preceded it."[9] The proportions of the temple provided specifications for the Lodge building, and the endeavors of scholars from Perrault to Newton to reconstruct the Temple contributed to the establishment of this form as the type of masonic building.[10] Moreover, the apocryphal hierarchy established by the architect Hiram Abif between master, colleague, and apprentice, became allegorical for masonic degrees.

But the terms used by Villeneuve seem to imply a more fundamental origin, a design first delineated by nature, and only subsequently encompassed by the architect's rational geometry. The allusions are to Edenist primitivism, not to the luxury of Solomon's developed type. The changing character of this primitivist model may be seen in the changes made between the first and second editions of the *Constitutions* of 1723 and 1738. In the first edition the pre-history of the Temple from Adam through to Solomon is roughly and very quickly sketched. Adam, "created after the image of the great architect," is represented as having taught his sons geometry, and one of them, Cain, built a city with this knowledge; from thence to Noah, the building of the Ark, and the construction of the Tower of Babel, the translation of architectural knowledge to Egypt after its fall and the instruction of the tribes of Israel during the captivity. There is no mention in this account of Adam as more than the simple transmitter of geometrical wisdom. By the second edition, however, Adam's role is reconsidered: he is shown observing the principles of geometry as contained in the first hut, built for him by the Supreme Architect in the garden of Eden, side by side with the first Temple, also constructed by the Almighty Geometer. This primitive, original hut was "a well- proportioned and convenient place of shelter from Heat, and of retirement, rest and repast after his wholesome labor in cultivating his Garden of Delights," while the Temple, or place of worship, was "agreeable to his original, perfect, and innocent state." The knowledge thus gained by observing the perfect type was retained on his expulsion; forced to live for a time in "the most

---

7. Martin Couret de Villeneuve, *L'École des Francs-Maçons*, (à "Jerusalem," 1748), p. 13. In the "Discourse on Friendship," the analogy was made clear: "Elévons sur leurs modèles des Edifices qui surprennent par leur magnificence, que tous les ordres d'Architecture y brillent: c'est-à-dire, formons nos coeurs à toutes les vertus; mais que tout rende à la solidité de l'Edifice? N'est-ce pas dire encore, posons pour fondement l'union intime et l'amour social," [*ibid.*, p. 32].
8. Jean-Baptiste Willermoz, Letter to the duc de Brunswick (1780), quoted in Gustave Bord, *La Franc-Maçonnerie en France des origines a 1815* (Paris, 1908) I., p. 40. Willermoz (1730-1824) was continuously developing masonic mysticisms throughout his life; his theories, half occultist, half alchemical, were linked to the "Templar" movement.
9. *Op. cit.*
10. C.f., Wolfgang Herrmann, "Unknown Designs for the 'Temple of Jerusalem' by Claude Perrault," *Essays in the History of Architecture presented to Rudolf Wittkower*, ed. Fraser, Hibbard, and Lewine (London, 1967), and Frank E. Manuel, *Isaac Newton, Historian* (Cambridge, Mass., 1963), pp. 161-65.

convenient natural abodes of the land of Eden" to shelter from "Colds and Heats, from Winds, Rains, and Tempests, and from Wild Beasts," he was able finally to teach his sons the use of geometry in Architecture as they grew up to form the first lodge. Without this instruction from Adam, "the children of men must have lived like brutes in woods, dens and caves, etc., or at best in poor huts of mud or arbors made of branches of trees." Adam is not yet depicted as a builder, but only as the receiver of original knowledge; it is significant that both the House and the Temple were artifacts built in the first instance not by man but by God.

However in Couret de Villeneuve's text of 1748 Adam was finally given a primary constructive role: despite his fall, he had not lost the knowledge received from the Grand Architect, and "applied his science to the needs of human life." Leaving the "lieu de délices," he set to work to guard himself against the injuries of the air:

la retraite qu'il se fit devoit naturellement avoir les proportions géométriques; cette science faisoir partie de ses connaissances: c'est ainsi que le premier homme fut le primier Maçon.[11]

In the gradual fusion of the anthropological and religious models of origins, Adam has become identified with the natural, primitive man, just as Rousseau would describe two years later.

The legends of Adam, and those of Noah and Babel, were of fundamental interest to an architectural theory preoccupied since the publication of the Abbé Laugier's *Essay* with the return to origins. The mason, then, immediately connected such a paradigm or type of original architecture to one of a new social order, an association only implicit in Laugier. These narratives of "origin" were reinforced by a number of parallel narratives associated with the rituals of Freemasonic initiation. Even as architecture was envisaged as the primitive germ, so to speak, of a renewed society, so the "routes" by which a member of the Lodge achieved full incorporation, withdrew, that is, from the corrupted, "lay" world into a state of receptivity to the moral and social idealism of the new masonic world, were seen in spatial terms. And for the Egyptomanic masons of the 1760's and 1770's, Orpheus in the Underworld was the paradigmatic ritual; the quasi-philosophical novel *Séthos* published by the Abbé Terrasson in 1731, describing the adventures of Séthos as he followed Orpheus into the secret realm of subterranean Egypt, became the inspiration not only for the establishment of Egyptian rites within masonry in the 1770's but for their architectural translation into ideal environments of initiation by Jean Jacques Lequeu as well.

Hermetic Eclecticism: Lequeu's Lodge. In a series of related plates incorporated in the folios now in the Bibliothèque Nationale, Lequeu depicted with considerable fantasy the sequence of environments encountered by Séthos en route to and through the underworld. Lequeu's images, however, differ significantly from their literary model; whereas Terrasson described the initiatory route as a carefully ordered sequence of spaces within and below the great pyramid of Memphis, Lequeu takes this same sequence and unites it in a *building* separately dedicated to the rite. He was evidently concerned to design a Lodge building that represented the original route, as opposed to simply illustrating the adventures of Séthos in pictorial form. In this transformation we are seeing the final emergence of architecture as the art over all others that shapes, controls, and forms the route of initiation, and engenders the states of mind of the eventual initiate.

Lequeu's Lodge, designed probably for the Egyptian Rite founded by Cagliostro in 1781 and immediately adopted into Scottish masonry, consisted of four major spaces. The first, corresponding to the well down which Séthos climbed beneath the pyramid, was a vertical shaft and led immediately to a complicated system of gates that opened into the space of the first test or the ordeal by Fire.

---

11. Couret de Villeneuve, *op. cit.*, p.3.

This took the form of a huge vaulted room simulating a furnace, with smoke and flames generated under the floor. Séthos had been forced to walk over an iron grating of red hot bars; Lequeu's aspirant was directed across a floor covered with burning coals. The second trial, that by Water, involved Séthos in swimming across a wide stream, the Cocytus, keeping to a narrow path in order

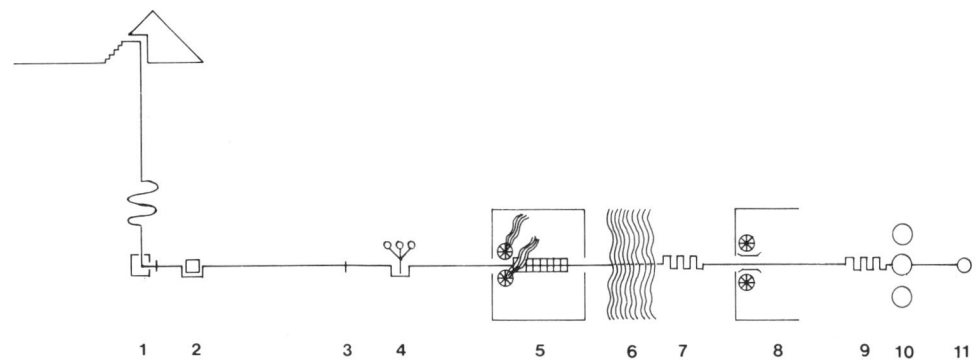

1. Initiation of Séthos into the Egyptian Mysteries, following the steps Orpheus in the Underworld. From Séthos, a hermetic romance, by Abbé Terrasson, 1731. This novel was used by the occultist sects as a "book of ritual." It was the model for Lequeu's "Gothic House" and infernal landscapes, and was used by Schikaneder for the libretto of the Magic Flute, Mozart's masonic opera.

1. Pyramid and shaft. 2. Warning tablet 3. Iron grill 4. Cerberus, the three-headed dog 5. Initiation by fire 6. Initiation by water 7. Steps 8. Initiation by air (drawbridge and wheels) 9. Steps 10. Statue of Isis 11. Cup of Lethe and Mnemosyne

to escape being swept away by the current. Lequeu's stream similarly passed through the third space with iron gratings defining the path. The final test, the ordeal by Air, was achieved by Séthos' negotiating a system of wheels and drawbridges that carried him up and through the last passage into the inner sanctuary of the Egyptian Temple. Both Séthos and Lequeu's initiate ended their trials as they emerged below the statue of Isis herself, behind the altar of the temple. Once within, they were received by the priests, who handed them first the cup of Lethe to enable them to forget the past, and then a cup of Memory in preparation for the mental initiation that would follow. On the Altar in Lequeu's drawing these two cups stood as marking the end of the ritual enactment. Beneath these initiatory spaces, Lequeu provided a subterranean passage for the use of the members of the brotherhood as they stage-managed the rites. This design is perhaps the most complete speculative vision of an ideal lodge in the late eighteenth century.

Whether this Lodge was ever built, whether its function was specified by an actual sect, or whether it remained a projection of Lequeu's imagination, the role of visionary architecture was clear, and this role was envisaged as much more than a simple representation of images referring to a mysterious past in order to educate the aspiring adept. In Lequeu's design the fire, the water, and the drawbridges were real; the atmosphere engendered within the spaces by all the mechanical artifices of theater was calculated to produce an extreme impression of terror and awe. This was no *architecture parlante* in a passive sense; all the resources of form were brought to bear as the supporting and confirming structures to the ritual.

The Route of Architectural Progress: Ledoux's Lodge. There exists an account, by a potential convert himself involved in magical experimentation, of a visit to such a lodge, a lodge also designed by one of the visionary architects, Ledoux. It is an account that explains in graphic detail the ritual and its architecture, and the particular status of the architect initiate. The story was recounted by the English writer and mystic, William Beckford, who was in Paris in the spring of 1784 and moving at the center of its high society. From the salons of Madame Necker to the fair of Saint Germain, in the hotels of the Farmers General and the pleasure gardens of Versailles, he savored with romantic delight the extremes of Parisian luxury and licentiousness.[12] Fascinated by the myriad cults and their magical experimentation, Beckford sought the company of those whose practices were informed

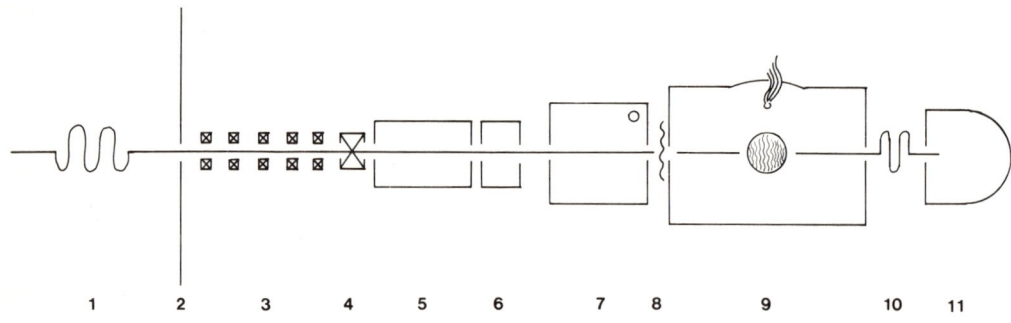

2. Ledoux's Lodge: described by William Beckford, 1785.

1. Route from Paris 2. Wall of the estate 3. Wood-piles 4. Pyramidal entrance 5. "Barnish hall" 6. Cottage and garden 7. Cube-room with white cockatoo 8. Curtain 9. Main salon with laver and fire 10. Grand stair 11. Chapel and tribune

by their knowledge of the occult and its philosophical derivations. He visited the architect Claude-Nicolas Ledoux, whose preoccupation with the visionary was common knowledge and soon to be publicly displayed in the monumental forms of the barrières. The visit described by Beckford in his letters not only confirmed this dimension of Ledoux's work but gave it a specific character and significance.[13]

Beckford first encountered the architect in his own house, "one of the strangest mock-palaces you ever saw," and spent some time leafing through the renderings of Ledoux's public and private works: hotels, follies, projects for the Ideal City of Chaux, designs for the toll-gates. By accident, one particularly elaborate drawing fell from the pile, "a beautiful drawing of a ceiling in colors heightened with gold." To Beckford's surprise Ledoux was disconcerted and reluctant to discuss its nature:

He put on a look of mysterious gravity, and replied in an altered tone of voice, "This is the ceiling of the most sumptuous apartment I ever erected — it belongs to a revered friend of mine whose thoughts, words and actions are not of the common world. His habits, his appearance, his garb are peculiar, very peculiar, so much so indeed that he never wishes to manifest himself, unless to persons born under peculiar influences."[14]

Persuaded that Beckford possessed certain hermetic powers Ledoux agreed to ask whether they might visit the house in question, cautioning the writer that he would have to submit to the rules of the secret visit — no questions, a closed carriage and so on. The next day, accordingly, they entered a covered fiacre, and set forth just before dusk. For over an hour they twisted and turned

---

12. C.f. Émile Lesueur, *La Franc-Maconnerie Artésienne au XVIII siecle* (Paris, 1914), op. cit., p. 127.
13. *Livre d'Architecture de la RΔLΔ de l'Amitié*, quoted in Lesueur, op. cit., p. 176.
14. Beyerlé, op. cit., ii., p. 178, "Concerning the locale of the Lodge." He divided his subject into Distribution and Decoration, and described as a type form, with much elaboration of the organization of the Archives, the plan generally in use from the 1740s.

through Paris, and alighted in front of a long greyish, moss-eaten stone wall "like the wall of a burying ground;"

The gates opening I found myself in a vast space entirely occupied by wood-piles, some of enormous dimensions and very lofty, others with thatched roofs acutely pointed resembling views I have seen of Tartarian villages.[15]

These wood piles formed apparently endless avenues, but the entire landscape was silent — save for the chirping of sparrows wheeling in clouds over the cold clear sky. The two visitors passed down one of the long alleys in the shadow of the piles, and came to a hall before the largest of them all. Over the low door were placed a few rough boards. Ledoux, Beckford's "conductor," knocked twice, and the door sprang open with a sharp whistle. They entered into a gloomy vestibule "more like a barn than a Hall," lit only by leaded casements in the roof. Groping their way through this hall they came to another low door, knocked again, and were admitted into a small plain room, "like the chamber of a cottage with its deal table and straw- bottomed chairs overlooking a little garden surrounded by well-clipped hedges." The gate of this small rustic cottage led into a better furnished apartment. Ledoux no longer made conversation, "nor did he smile — all his courtly blandishments seemed to have forsaken him." Advancing into a high square room decorated with marble pilasters and lit from above, Beckford noted a large white cockatoo on a high gilded perch in one corner. The two passed through into the major apartment. Through the open grand door, its tapestry curtains drawn back, they perceived the salon: Beckford recognised "the coved ceiling, richly painted with mythological subjects." Under a highly decorated chimneypiece a fire blazed, giving off exotic spicy scents. In front of this aromatic fire a formal looking old man of small stature but imposing presence sat on a strangely shaped, elaborately worked chair. The patron of this extremely sophisticated private lodge cannot be identified — Beckford posits that the old man he met was the same illumine who, it was rumored, led Phillipe Egalite to side with the Revolution.

He was habited in an antiquated court suit of changeable colored silk — his severe, forbidding countenance was overspread with the livid paleness of a dead body, but his eyes were as the eyes of the living — most vivid and most piercing.

With no acknowledgement of their greeting, lips incessantly quivering, the old man bade them examine the room and its decorations. Every recess was ornamented with elaborate armories of brass and tortoise shell. Beckford focused his attention on an enormous bronze urn raised up on green porphyry with large handles shaped in the forms of tritons and nereids and filled to the brim with transparent liquid. The red setting sun played over its surface. As the old man approached,

the water, becoming agitated, rose up in waves. Upon the gleaming surface of the undulating fluid, flitted by a succession of ghastly shadows somewhat resembling the human form in the last agonies of dissolution.

These horrible visions passed before Beckford's eyes; terrified, he exclaimed, not without a little English sangfroid, "This is most frightfully extraordinary." The old man turned on him with a chilling voice, and Ledoux, shaking his head, refused to answer his questions. When he turned back to the laver, the water had subsided. At once the sound of deep voices chanting in harmony rose up from beyond the salon. The old man motioned for Beckford to pass through the doors, which opened "sympathetically as it were." Ledoux encouraged him, speaking of "a staircase of my design and construction of which I am very proud," and the visitor moved toward the sound, followed by the old man and the "Architect" (now given the importance of an adept in Beckford's text). Beckford passed into a tribune from which he looked down into a large chapel: "Day was closing in, and darkness beginning to prevail when suddenly a stream of light shone forth." The sonorous voices chanted psalms, including passages referring to the fall of the mighty and the exalta-

---

15. Beyerlé, *op. cit.*, says that a lodge room 28' wide should be 54' long; that of *Amitié* in Arras was 21' wide and 33' long; the Grand Orient was divided into two parts, 21' by 51', and 21' by 27'; the Grand Lodge of London (1776) was 43' by 100'.

tion of the meek. Beckford knelt on the cushions of the gallery, head in hands and lost in mournful revery. The memory of the terrifying visions of the great urn were too much however and he suddenly found himself reciting the Lord's Prayer. This broke the chain of events. At once the old man vanished. Ledoux was troubled and serious, evidently disappointed that Beckford had been unable to complete his initiation: "You have lost an opportunity of gaining knowledge which may never return. Had you undergone a slight ceremony we were on the point of proposing you might have asked any question — you would not only have heard but seen things ineffable." They retraced their steps; the fire had dimmed, the bronze vase had disappeared and with it the old man's chair and the white bird. In the open air they were met by a servant with a lantern who led them through "the dreary labyrinth of wood piles" to the gate and their carriage.

The sequence of spaces constructed by Ledoux for the performance of this secret ritual bore an obvious relation to the routes already described.[16] But the architect-adept added another specific level of meaning to an established initiatory passage. From the dead landscape of woodpiles to the final space of the chapel Beckford moved through the entire history of civilization, each stage marked by its characteristic architecture. The woodpiles, "like some deserted Tartarian village," were evidently symbolic of the abandoned huts of primitive man; from there the entrance to the sequence was marked by a hut-pyramid, the archetypal reification of the primitive. The middle ages, indicated by the "Barnish Hall," led to a cottage of Rousseauvian simplicity — the eighteenth century home of rustic morality. The white bird stood at the beginning of the rite proper which was conducted in an opulent setting, within the most richly decorated apartments that civilization could conceive. The end was beyond civilization, in a spiritual realm formed by the individual, the initiated group, darkness, and a single ray of light. Architecture and its history was now brought into play to inform the stadial progression toward the new society.

• • •

With the tale of Beckford we are in the presence of fully developed romanticism; the edges of fantasy and reality are blurred, the spaces of the lodge take on an almost living character as they participate in the state of mind of their neophyte. Without the appearance of Ledoux, and the introduction of specific historical references, the story might form an indistinguishable part of the same author's *Vathek*, an oriental mystical romance first published in French two years later.[17] Beckford himself was willing to believe that Ledoux in his role as conductor was indeed a master of some occult magic. And even if the entire tale were fabricated, a product of Beckford's wayward and fantastic imagination, the discourse that would join the author and the architect, the object of his speculation, would finally be identical. For it was in the very nature of the cults themselves to merge the facts of everyday life with their mystical extensions into feeling and the heights of sensibility. The idea of an aesthetic of sensation was first and foremost tied to the creation of a trompe-l'oeil for the feelings. Few believed wholeheartedly in the mysteries, yet few were prepared to deny the possibility of witnessing the unseeable; here the boundaries between stage effects and their apparent reality, between the artifice that stimulated and the sense that recognized, were alike unclear.

This point where everyday life and a utopian vision of what might be were confused was the very point of the eighteenth century associational experience. Therein lay the peculiar ability of an apparently materialist century to live, and to project from life, the aspirations and ideals of a more perfect social order. It was by no means coincidence that the notion of the festival and the banquet

---

16. GΔOΔ de France, *Planche à tracer générale de l'Installation*, (June [sic], 1773); Pierre Chevallier has established the date of the installation as 22 October 1773.

17. William Beckford, *Valthek*, ed. with an introduction by Roger Lonsdale (London: O. U.P., 1970)

pervaded both the real social existence and utopian romance in the second half of the century. The festival was, after all, the instant of daily life where normal routines, even normal mores, were for a moment suspended.[18] In the life of the masonic societies, withdrawn from the world, the festive life could be lived to an even greater extreme. In a very real sense, the life of the associations was "lived utopia."

18. See the evocative article by B. Baczko, "Lumieres et Utopie," *Annales*, E. S. C.

Interview with Ando Tadao

Conducted and translated by Toshio Okumura

One hesitates before the architecture of Tadao Ando as before an empty landscape. His buildings evoke the austere beauty of a rocky plain, or of a cliff of chiselled stone thrown into relief by the harsh afternoon sun. His vocabulary of simple geometric forms, blank walls, and tiered concrete stairs remains mute and mysterious. Yet his spaces, especially the interiors, are nonetheless inviting.

In a recent interview with Toshio Okumura, Ando revealed that concern for human habitation motivates his designs. He hopes to temper the conceptual clarity of his initial schemes (the rational configuration of spaces) with what he calls the expressive element. Ando feels that the architect must evoke the habits and customs of the future inhabitants; he must produce an environment which is functionally and aesthetically conducive to the daily life of his clients.

This concern for lifestyle has restricted Ando to designing Japanese residences, for this is the culture he feels he best understands. But the two issues addressed in his designs have a broader application. Specifically, Ando concerns himself with two rituals of confrontation. First, he hopes to facilitate the meeting of man and his world. Sunlight becomes a way of bringing the sky down into a dwelling; courtyard gardens allow for a framing of nature. Secondly, Ando concentrates on the bringing together of man and man. His stairways and corridors become crucial elements, for they are the joints of his compositions, the sites where people emerge from private spaces and encounter one another.

Thus, while Ando's designs may seem austere and even formidable, they provide a ground on which the individual can carry on the irregular patterns of daily existence, while pausing to reflect upon his relation to nature and to society. Ando has understood that man's fundamental rituals are inseparable from the phenomena of daily living.

■   ■   ■

Okumura: Your work generally uses very strong forms. What is the relationship between those forms and your ideas about architecture?

Ando: Traditional Japanese architecture is based on an additive process: to take a well known example, the Katsura detached palace is composed of rooms one added to the next (fig. 1). A completely different approach is to use one simple plan based on the use of reason, a plan which incorporates one's ideas of the world. However, architecture cannot be made by rationality — by that simple plan — alone. Working against it is the world with which man is directly concerned, involv-

---

1. Interviewer's note: The idea of additive architecture refers to the asymmetrical, picturesque compositions of later Japanese palaces, in contrast to the formalized, symmetrical, geometrical compositions of earlier palaces following Chinese prototypes.

1. Katsura Imperial Palace.

ing considerations like eating, sleeping, and the reactions of one's senses and emotions. A system like "additivism" is appropriate in accommodating such an empirical world, but the use of that system by itself makes it difficult for the architect to express his rational side.

Okumura: What do you mean by the "architect's rational side"?

Ando: There are two worlds: the architect's rational world, which includes his creativity and his ideals, and the real world, which is actually a kind of tool for living. These two worlds must be formed into a unified whole. One way of doing this is in the use of a simple plan combined with the sensibilities [*nioi*, literally "smell"], which I as a human being have acquired throughout my life. Those sensibilities include such things as sense of proportion, method of selecting materials, and sense of color and handcrafting, all of which express my own human qualities. In my work I seek the point of contact between the continually developing world of my human qualities, and the world of my imagination. Take, for example, Tadao Ando: if, in his architecture, the characteristics and the disposition of that person are not revealed, the flavor [*nioi*] of the architecture will be missing. By flavor I mean expressiveness, sensibility, or emotion. If you detach that kind of world from architecture, the building is no longer necessary; all you need is the concept. But in order to actually make architecture you need both the conceptual and the expressive aspects. I try to combine reason with expressive human qualities using an "additive" architecture.

If you consider the rational type of architecture visually, in photographs, for example, the plan appears in all views, and is therefore very strongly expressed in form. The picture will give you one impression of the building, but you will experience a very different world if you actually live in it. I try to take this second world and combine it with the first to make a unified architecture. The problem then becomes the expression of the simple plan on the exterior.

Okumura: One gets a sense of those two worlds in the way your buildings are generally expressed in two parts.[2] In the Koshino house (fig. 2) the bedrooms are contained in a distinct volume, and connected by a corridor to the rest of the house. Given this separation, the corridor seems very

---

2. Interviewer's note: Ando drew diagrams as the interview proceeded. It was interesting to see that the tension or opposition between the two types of architecture — the two worlds he wishes to combine — were drawn as a relationship of two opposing squares similar to the formal composition of a number of his buildings.

important. Is its significance related to traditional Japanese architecture?

Ando: My architecture does not use any traditional architectural elements, yet I want to evoke the feeling of traditional space. The same concrete, steel, and glass, and the same construction methods are used throughout the world; therefore you can make essentially the same building anywhere. But the people living in those buildings are all different, whether they be American, European, or Japanese. The most important problem is how the people living in those buildings use them. If the people are different, one would expect fundamental differences in their architecture. In Japan, traditional architecture uses wood construction, which implies a particular concept of space. I have been considering the problem of how one can continue this tradition using the methods of modern architecture. About twenty years ago there was a controversy over the use of tradition, at which time it was asked whether traditional Japanese architecture could be carried over into modern architecture. However, the architects focused merely on such formal elements as roofs and coffered ceilings. Disregarding these elements, the buildings remained standardized and typically modern. In contrast, I would like to continue tradition using what I feel is a typically Japanese emotional sensitivity to daily life.

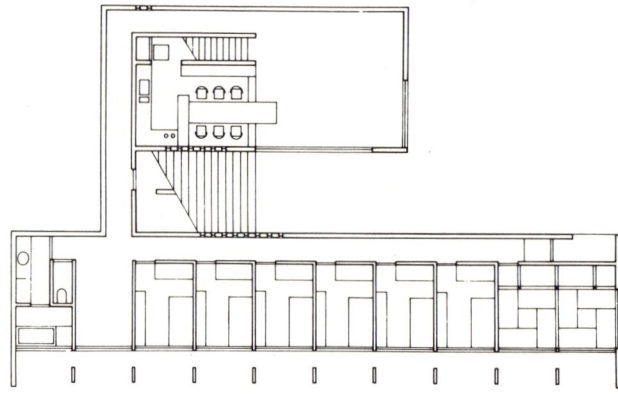

2. *Koshino Residence. 1981. First floor plan.*

Traditional Japanese architecture is, as I mentioned earlier, composed of parts: for example, A, B, C. The point of interest is the joint: the space created there is very rich. My buildings are generally in the form of A and B, with C being very rare. In the space between, I try to capture not the traditional form, but the traditional Japanese feeling for space. Furthermore, you can look at these objects A and B as having a human relationship: if A and B are facing away from each other, relationship is impossible. The space is there in order to *support* interaction.

While I think this is understood in modern architecture, the so-called post-modernists generally take the A-B relationship to mean only the forms A and B. If they could go beyond simple formal problems to include the human relation between A and B, they might overcome form and begin to possess meaning. However, because these considerations are ignored, post-modernism remains at the level of dealing with man *versus* form. Since the problem of A and B in architecture is the same as the problem of A and B for people, I think that one must make architecture which also addresses human relationship. By not permitting the form to express itself too strongly, one can encourage people to interact with one another.

Okumura: In the issue of *Space Design* magazine devoted to your work (SD 8106) you said, "it is important to consider the continuity of form and the scale and rhythm of space," and, "one must

3. Koshino Residence. Corridor.

make fundamental divisions of space according to the qualities of the light." How do these statements relate to your ideas about human relationships?

Ando: The meaning of a space can change simply by controlling the amount of light. Rhythms are created by alternating spaces having large amounts of light with spaces having less. In both cases, the form does not come to the foreground. An artist of the Meiji period, Okakura Tenshin, wrote in *The Book of Tea* that the meaning of architecture is not in the floor, walls, or ceiling, but in the world contained inside. In exactly the same way, I feel that the space contained is the primary concern, and not the walls, floor and ceiling which bound it.

The relationships of person to person and person to space are the basic determinants of a successful building. Given a building with a simple, regular form, I feel that you should not be able to perceive the plan's actual configuration when you enter the space. While the form is clear if you are above the work, that is, if you look at it in plan or in isometric, it should not be obvious if you live inside.

Okumura: How do you achieve this?

4. Koshino Residence. Stair.

5. Koshino Residence. Livingroom.

Ando: What we got from modern architecture was a sense that people were overwhelmed by vast spaces [*horikomu*, literally, "to bury"]. One must envelop them instead in a gentle environment, and in order to do this I think that more study of people is necessary.

Starting around age 15, I often went out to study old rural houses [*Minka*] and other examples of traditional Japanese architecture, in order to impress upon myself the image of traditional Japanese space. This is not expressed directly in forms, but rather in the sensitivity I use when I design something.

Okumura: Could you give some examples of how you have applied what you learned about traditional Japanese houses? In the Bansho house for instance, light defines the character of the rooms and you have suggested that it actually becomes a focus much as a fireplace would in a traditional home.

Ando: In the Bansho house, light only enters from above on one side. In the morning it shines on the dining room table, and reflects into the living room as well as into the second floor bedroom. Then it gradually spreads out, and as it moves, the rooms change in character. One can make completely different spaces depending on whether light is direct or reflected, and whether or not it comes in from one direction. With light coming in from one direction, I try to create different spaces depending upon the way it is received This method is found in traditional Japanese architecture — in tea rooms for example, or in houses built in the style of tea rooms [*sukiya*].

Okumura: You make use of light in two ways: one is to give character to the rooms, as you have just explained, and the other is a more sculptural use, as in the living room of the Koshino Residence.

Ando: In the Koshino Residence, the light behaves in a sculptural way for only twenty or thirty minutes when the sun shines directly in from the west (fig. 5). Light can be used as an object, but a more gentle light is generally necessary for everyday life. There is the artistic problem of using light sculpturally, and then there is the problem of gently manipulating light to facilitate daily activities, to make the environment more comfortable, or to provide a pleasant atmosphere. For example, light entering from a low window is very gentle; but because it is diffuse it does not photograph well. Light entering from the top, though, can be very beautiful. Simply by manipulating light in these different ways, the space can be made sufficiently rich. This method was not used by modern architects since they were concerned more with economic problems, with building in large quantities,

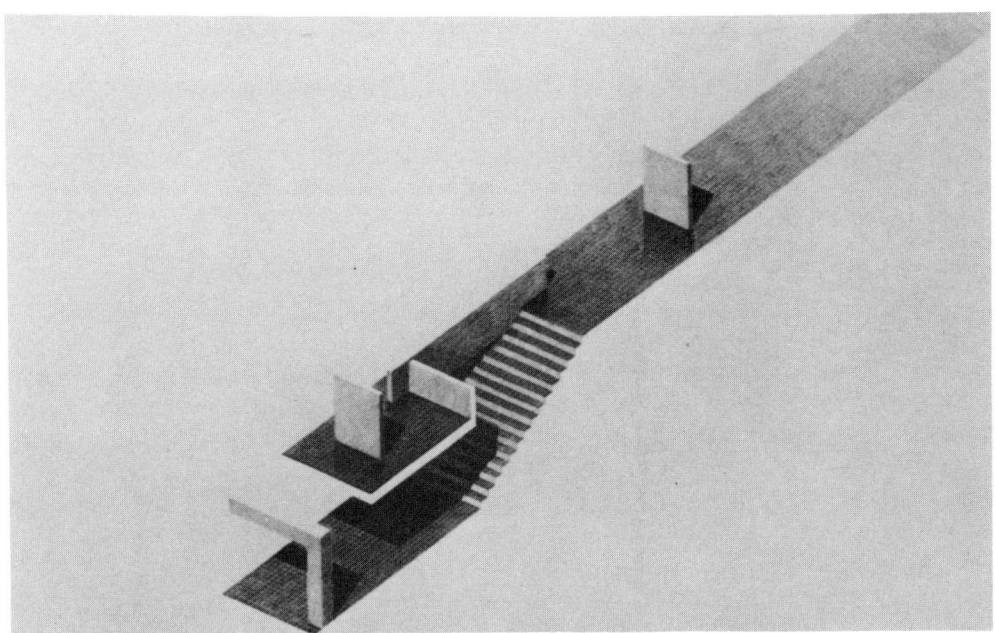
6. Okusu Residence, 1978. Isometric.

with building quickly. They did not concern themselves with how to create a gentle environment for people.

Okumura: Let us return to the earlier question of the importance of the stairway and corridor in your work. What function do they perform, for example, in the Okusu residence (fig. 6)?

Ando: In my architecture, there are usually two formally symmetrical parts, A and B. However, the experience of the inside is completely different from that of the form: while the plan is simple, the paths that people follow within the building are varied and asymmetrical. In post-modernism there is formal variation as well as the varying movement of people. I prefer to use simple forms, and to focus on the mazes created by the paths of people's daily activities. Stairs and corridors fix these patterns; they are places where one cannot move irregularly.

Okumura: This puts a great deal of emphasis on the corridors and stairways; in some instances, in fact, you call them "stage-like." Could you explain what you mean by this?

Ando: Of course houses are a kind of stage on which people live. The manner of entertaining, and the places where people come out, are therefore very important.

Okumura: The stair in the Fuku residence, for example (fig. 7).

Ando: Yes, generally my buildings consist of many small rooms lined up in a row, with the part reserved for ceremony [*gishiki* "ceremony" or "ritual"] being the larger public space. Since the stair is in the public space, the stair/corridor becomes the place for ceremony, the place where the family meets. For example, when you wake up in the morning, you go out, and you meet someone. This meeting place is the most carefully considered space in the house: I pay particular attention to the light and the change it goes through.

Okumura: In the Azuma residence, the use of the corridor is slightly different; it seems to have a stronger connection with nature (fig. 8). Is this related to traditional Japanese architecture?

Ando: The "piece of nature" in the Azuma residence is around forty square meters. To take in nature by building a small garden on a small plot is in itself a ritual activity for the Japanese. Place, nature, and man combined create a kind of ritual. This connection with nature is the most important ritualistic part in much of my architecture. In the Azuma residence it occurs in the exterior space, as in the traditional townhouse style.

Okumura: That is why you always use courtyards.

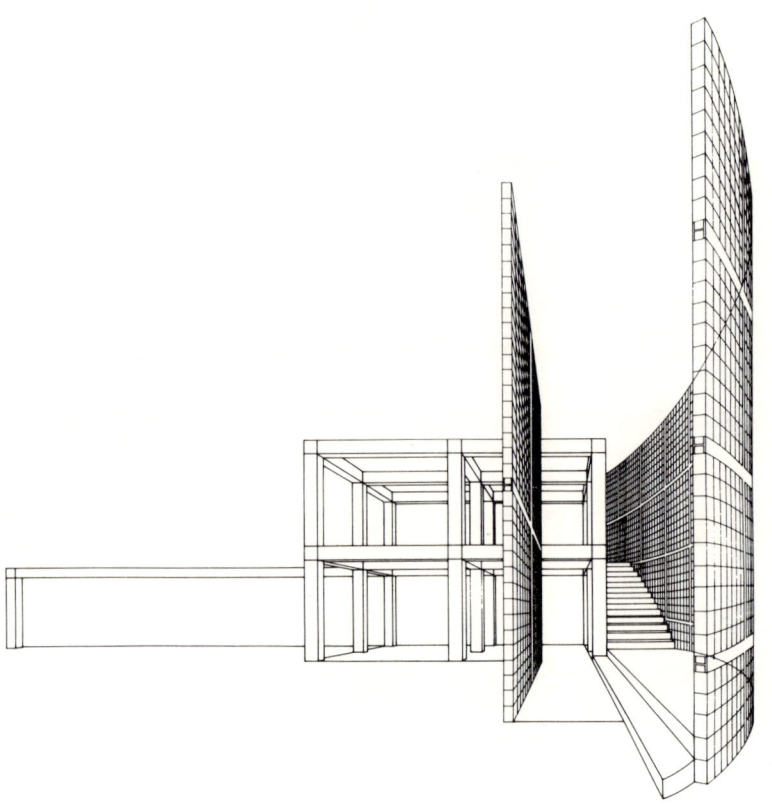

7. Fuku Residence, 1980. Perspective.

Ando: Yes, even in small spaces. You cannot feel nature unless you go outside and expose yourself to it. While nature is important for the community, I also feel that it is important for the individual. If he is able to take in and enclose his own piece of the air, sky, and rain, he will have a much stronger awareness that he is living, that he has been given life.

When a Japanese person opens a low *Fusuma* (sliding door), and sees a tree in fall color, he feels that it is his own fall-colored tree. A person looking at the same tree from a different window likewise thinks that it represents a piece of nature meant for himself. The bit of nature glimpsed through a sightly open window in a tea room is a piece of nature belonging to the two people in the tea room. Traditional architecture incorporates this multi-faceted aspect of nature in a way which is unique to Japan. I think that modern Japanese architecture only makes sense if it incorporates this sensibility. Architects must pay more attention to history, and to the geography and customs of each place and each people.

Okumura: Does that mean that if you build a house in America, the meaning will be lost?

Ando: It would be very difficult to build a house here. I could probably do a shopping center or an art museum, but a house is for people to live in, and because I am not that familiar with Americans, I would probably not be able to do a house. Recently I was asked to do a house in France, but be-

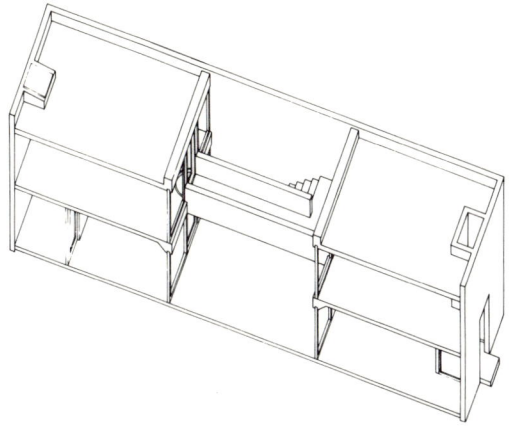

8. *Azuma Residence, 1976. Isometric.*

cause I did not feel that I understood the French people, I declined. My buildings have meaning in relation to their neighborhood, the region near Kyoto. They include historical and cultural information which makes them appropriate for a Japanese person.

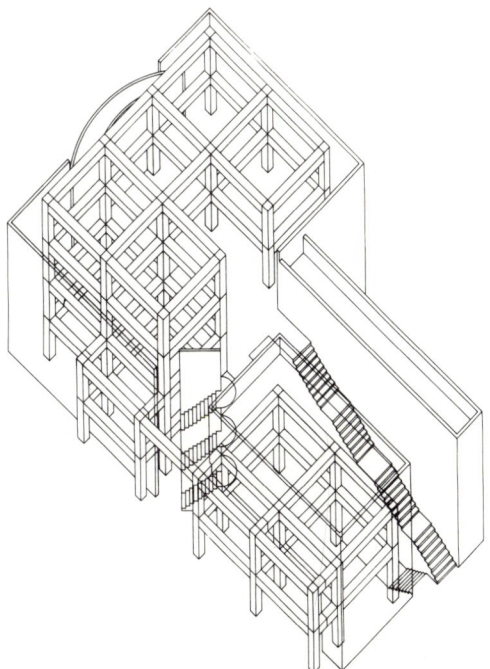

9. *Step Project, under construction. Isometric.*

If you cannot sense the "depth" [*oku-yuki*] or the philosophy of the designer when you experience a building, the architecture is merely an economic activity which does not go beyond simple functional considerations. In that case, the architecture has little meaning for me.

Okumura: You talked earlier about domestic architecture as a stage for daily activities. Do you also apply this idea to a larger urban scale?

Ando: The purpose of architecture is basically the construction of place. The purpose of that place is for people to meet, and this makes up one of the rituals of society. Shopping centers, churches, city halls, and houses are all built for the purpose of assembling or congregation. The problem is the ritual of meeting: how to facilitate the process of meeting, and how to make a place where people might wish to stay.

Okumura: How does your STEP project fulfill the purpose (fig. 9)?

Ando: That project, a multi-storied commercial building, would normally have an elevator. But if you use a stair instead, the people going up and the people going down will have the possibility of meeting: they can stop if they wish to. The stair allows for the movements dictated by individual desire; these cannot be accommodated by a machine. A four storey building such as this often makes several places for the ritual of meeting, something which would not be possible if the floors were separated. A machine is efficient and fast, and can solve a variety of problems. But if you re-solve everything, you do not leave room for the individual's actions.

New York Loft

Peter Wheelwright

A PROBLEM WITH ANALYSIS of any sort is the obscuring of the thing itself. What I see, touch, hear, and smell as I move into and through the loft is most important. These senses are the final arbiters. They provoke thought and feeling, and, consequently, the awareness of place. Nevertheless, it is clear that this project, and, I believe, all architecture, if not actually generated by specific notions of ritual, does involve a ritualistic sense of purpose and an abstraction from human experience.

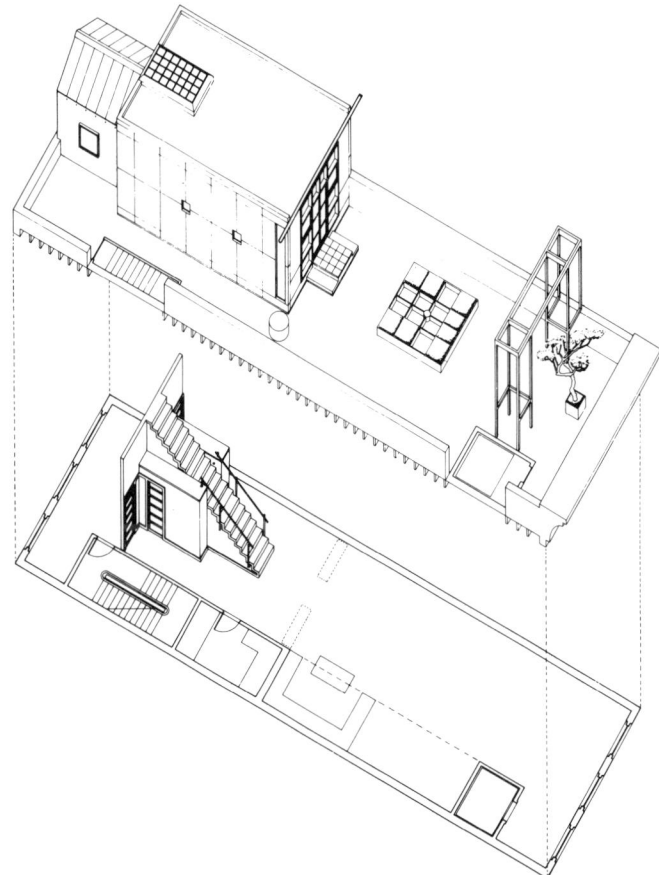

1. *Artist's Loft, New York, 1982. Axonometric view.*

This is a place for making art. The plastic arts have their roots in primitive idolatry, cave paintings, and similar practices, which, if not directly used in religious ritual, were inspired by the same necessity. Indeed, one can consider the artistic endeavor to be fundamentally ritualistic, a humble attempt to place ourselves in some acceptable relation to things unknown and metaphysical.

1. New York Loft. Jeremy Hawker, *Job Captain.* Marthe Rowen, *Assistant.*

2. Artist's Loft. Stair.

The basilican form, with its spare articulation and solemn frescoed wall surfaces, seems an appropriate one in which to house this ritual. Like the basilica, this painting studio is essentially symmetrical, with an "apse" and "nave" (maintaining a strict axiality) and lateral punch windows with a rhythm mimicking that of the colonnade. Although the basilica is best known as an early Christian place of worship (e.g., S. Appollinare Nuovo in Ravenna, Italy), the building type was originally acquired from eastern mystical sects prior to the advent of Christ. This is significant in that pre-Christian paganism exemplifies the relationship of man and ritual in its most essential form. It would seem that the architectonic simplicity of the basilica provides the neutrality and austerity necessary to promote a range of spiritual lives within.

The success of this metaphor depends on recognizing another aspect of ritual and architecture — what I would call "the user ritual." This is a secular rather than a religious ritual, the distinction being determined by the relative priority of the ideal one attempts to attain through the ritual's performance, i.e. great architecture or Eternal Salvation. This inferred user ritual is inherent in the design process and allows the program, the occupant, and the physical matter to come together in the architect's mind with perfect clarity, fitness, and harmony. Initially, the ritual is conceptual and intends the consummate manifestation of the building in terms of a prescribed physical

3. Artist's Loft. Stair detail.

4. Artist's Loft. Studio.

relation to it. The imagined user moves into and through, pauses, senses and considers, is reoriented, passes onward, all in a specific procedure which allows the "materialization" of the building in its ideal and perfect form. The architecture is insistently "viewed" from particular places, at particular angles, and in a particular sequence, thereby enforcing the relevant issues of frontality, forced perspective, symmetry, asymmetry, compression, expansion, and conditions of place.

The relentless axiality and sequential nature of the studio parti is the determinant of this user ritual, a fact which lends itself to a metaphor for the ritual of making art itself. From this perspective, the basilican object becomes the most ephemeral of shelters over the more significant spiritual path. An axial approach leads to the ascent of the stair, framed in a brilliant glow of celestial light from light wells in the floor plane above. Emerging into the "apse" one pauses to consider the primary totems and temple forms of the Manhattan roofscape; then one turns south to the light and continues forth. After momentarily straying from the "way" (left or right of the stairwell), one returns, re-centered, to rest on the mahogany and aluminum dais. There one might witness collected rainwater falling through a slit window at the gutter and splashstone, and contemplate the gardens beyond. At this point also, the sublimity that awaits one at the end of the Journey is captured. Viewed as such, the axial organization and its concomitant detailing (mahogany and aluminum

5. Artist's Loft. Terrace.

occur only and intimately about this axis) can be construed to symbolize a benign and spiritual path to artistic enlightenment.

The making of architecture exists somewhere between primeval instinct and acquired knowledge. Therein lies the source of the vague impulses which direct the selection and organization of forms and details. Simple allusion to basilicae and/or the "way" is not the basis for the architecture here: it should be noted that the specifics of the analogy have been constructed after the fact. What is significant is that the architecture shares a similar intention of creating serenity and spirituality. Is it not the particular quality contained within forms (or ideas) of the past that is of importance rather than the literal forms themselves? Ultimately, all architecture is bound to ritual in that it elicits the awe and wonder that comes from something that suggests more than its physical self.

The ritualized relationship between the user and building is critical. It is this idealized interaction that both determines and is determined by design decisions. Although in reality the ritual initially conceived for the user is unlikely to be performed "just right," it is certain that the success of an architecture will be judged by the degree of variance between the intended ritual and its actual performance and experience. There is not a correct or incorrect architecture: there is only that which stirs the spirit less or more.

■   ■   ■

Peter Wheelwright is committed to the idea that "ritual" does not merely refer to those spiritual and ceremonial acts that the term most immediately evokes, but potentially to all attempts to abstract ourselves and mediate between our condition and that of the world around us. This attitude is expressed on two different levels: the typological, which associates the artist's work-space specifically with the Christian basilica; and the sensual, which emphasizes the importance of architectural quality suggested by a celebration of the user's daily activities. Wheelwright asserts that there is a latent ritualistic aspect to the private and merely habitual, but suggests that architecture is the condition that reveals it. Neither the act nor the architecture alone manifests ritual, but together they produce the scenario in which ritual lies. His argument is similar to Bernard Tschumi's in "Sequences," in which architectural ritual is located in the narrative that links autonomous events and movements with the spaces that they occupy. Unlike Tschumi (who is critical of a generally "discreet restraint that does not reveal the maker's artifices in the final result and favors the certainty of a well-defined axis over the passionate uncertainties of thought"), Wheelwright proposes that "relentless axiality" and symmetry are, in this case, the appropriate means with which to reveal the quality of the activity. While one might challenge his initial assertion that private, secular rituals exist, perhaps the distinctions of ideal and real, symmetry and randomness, prescribed and spontaneous action, are ultimately more significant for the making of ritualistic form than the issues of private vs. public or secular vs. religious rituals.

Hearth Project

Peggy Deamer

THIS PROJECT attempts to address ritual on two levels: the first relates to the content, the second to the form. The meaning of form and content here are specific to the theories of Russian Formalism, according to which form is not taken to be that which "shapes" content, nor that which gives meaning to content. Rather, form *is* the content, i.e., the real subject-matter of art.

According to the Formalists, what was traditionally seen as content — the "image" or the "story" or what we rightfully call the "material" — is merely a "device" for formal manipulation, the secondary excuse and justification for the form. It is at once constant — the material depicted not having changed significantly throughout history, and at the same time varied — the formal structures continually changing the perception of the object. Form, then, is intimately related to the notion of "defamiliarization," whereby content, after receding into the virtual invisibility of habit and over-familiarity, is made perceivable again: a change in form and the use of unconventional structure give the content new value. It is also related to its own self-conscious exposure as form; the success of a work of art depends on the degree to which the "technique" or manipulation of devices is made obvious by the artist.

The *content* of this project is the hearth (an inherently ritualistic object). Fire is the essential element in man's attempt to transcend animal existence, to abstract and thus ritualize his activities. But the hearth is taken merely as a device for the form, the nine square grid. It is the ritual inherent in selecting and exploring this form that is of primary concern. The process by which we choose particular forms is not an isolated, personal, or arbitrary act; it has its own prescribed path and its own history.

The Formalists did not refer to an artwork's dependence on tradition, its lineage, as "ritualistic"; contemporary literary critics, on the other hand, do. Geoffrey Hartman states that the artist participates in ritualistic "rites of passage":

An artist, of course, is a group of one and has little or no ritual authority. Yet art does submit us to ritual and controlled experience of this kind. We are not compelled to participate in it, yet there are those who abide its question....

The ritual process leads ... beyond liminality. A new identity, or re-identification, should emerge. This is not so clear in art because art extends the liminal moment... Art interests us less in the outcome ... than in the passion that attends it ....[1]

The artist provides us with new structures, new conceptual paradigms, but this process of regeneration reaches no endpoint. "The new myth that kills the old, the new form that separates what is dead from what is living, has the value of purification rather than truth." In selecting the nine square grid, I am drawing on one such formal tradition in architecture that is still provocative.

The Design. In each of the four variants, the hearth is subject to a process of defamiliarization that both distorts and defines it; in each case, the nature of the hearth is determined by its role in the formal manoeuvers that change its shape, scale, and implied "source." The chimney is the constant

---

[1] Geoffrey H. Hartman "History Writing as Answerable Style" in *The Fate of Reading and Other Essays* (Chicago: University of Chicago Press, 1975), pp. 109, 110.

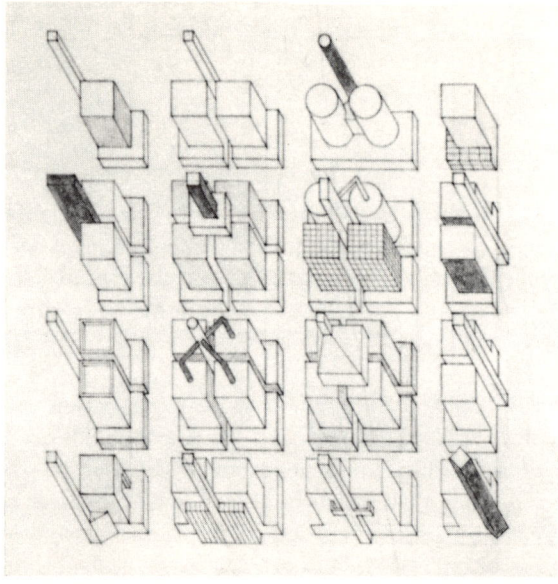

Hearth Project, 1981.   I.

feature that allows these differences to be read. Ultimately, each hearth develops in a manner that implies its own metaphorical associations and historical place. That the nature of the forms which emerge may be culturally determined would support the Formalist concept of the past shaping the present.

I. The centers of each of the nine squares are marked in the attempt to equalize their significance; they are marked by "voids" rather than by objects since centrality is not the issue. The centers of

IV.

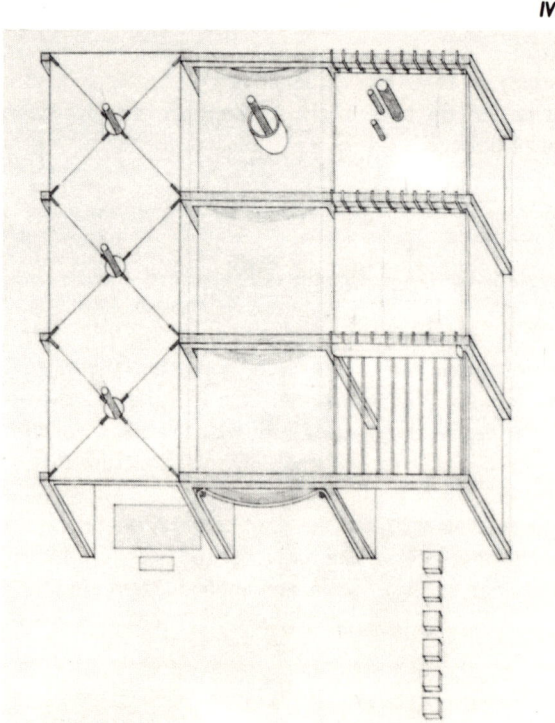

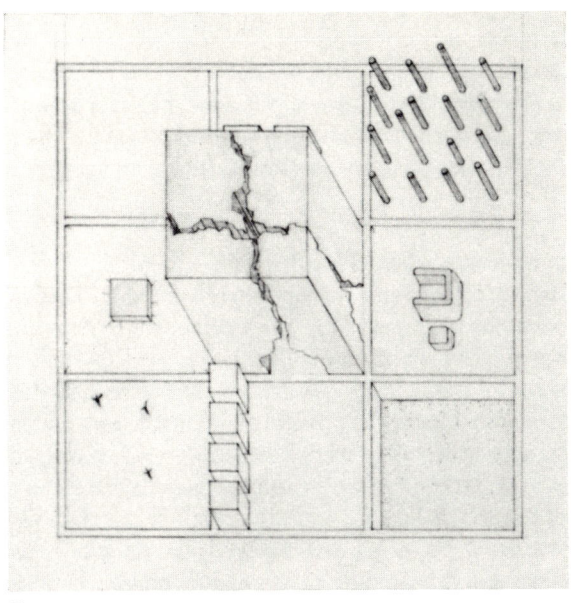

II.

each square set up their own connections, their own "grid," and produce a subdivision of each square into quadrants. Seeing this grid also as empty, but at the same time as positive — as a determining element — leads to a vision of a "street" grid. The project assumes an urban scale. The "hearth," then, is transformed into something factory-like; the chimney becomes a smokestack.

II. The center square is emphasized and the distinction between center and periphery is developed. The center is the hearth. There is a distinction made between those peripheral squares adjacent to

III.

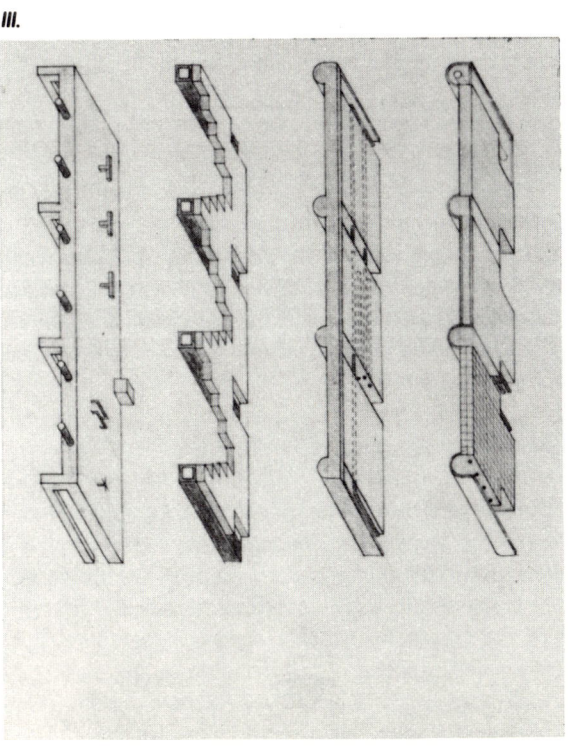

a face of a cube and those tangent to its corners. The four adjacent to the faces become various ways that one can approach, rest by, contemplate, and see the fire; the corner squares become park and garden spaces. The monolithic quality of the cube implies a prehistoric monument, a solid rock whose natural erosion allows both protection and ventilation for the fire. The chimney is not a chimney as such; the cracks allow the fire to escape. Their intersection marks the center of the center square.

III. The four lines which dominate when one axis of the entire grid is emphasized are objectified. These solid walls both separate zones and imply penetration. The flatness of these walls also forces the hearths into odd conditions of compression. They demonstrate different ways that heat is generated, chimneys are engaged, and passage is implied. 1) The heat source of the first wall is hot water. The cut-outs in this wall of water invite penetration. 2) The second wall houses electrical coils; it is essentially an over-scaled radiator. The pockets marking the points of implied grid intersection allow the coil mechanism to be seen and touched and also provide passage through small doors. 3) The third wall is a decorative screen for the hearth and chimneys that lie behind. In this case, the heat source is truly fire, but the wall is not actually structure; the chimneys are the structure for the screen. The configuration of the screen and the openings in it imply passage, but this is blocked by the hearths. 4) The final wall is heated by steam. It is monolithic in quality with no divisions or demarcations other than the repetitive chimneys. The structure, hidden from view, marks the points of the implied grid intersections. The wall is an impenetrable barrier. One is invited to play with the objects attached to its surface. Tactile confrontation replaces passage through the wall.

IV. The three zones implied by the above four divisions are defined and developed as three separate and unrelated axes, three tunnel-like spaces. The structural framework is, however, that of the complete nine square grid. The hearths, whose placements are indicated by the chimneys that poke through their roofs, use real fire, but they participate in their linear and axial spaces differently. In the first case, it is the final element in a series implying procession, but the hearth is not the major object of the series. The second bay also has the hearth placed at the end of its axis, but in this case, it is the only event; it is the goal. In the third bay, the hearths are meant to deny axiality. They emphasize the repetitive potential in this linear space.

■   ■   ■

Deamer juxtaposes two images — the hearth and the nine square grid — whose formal and semantic properties are at odds with each other. The hearth must situate itself on the grid without losing its identity. This is never completely achieved. In (I) it seeks to hold the center, but finds itself repeatedly subdivided. In (II) the monolithic cube dominates the composition, only to be cracked along gridlines. In (III) the chimney-icons become mere markers for points of intersection on the grid. Ultimately the hearth serves the grid. In (I) the chimneys frame its periphery; in (III) the hearth-object becomes a skeletal trace of the grid.

The object/field tension is heightened by the specific nature of the object and field chosen for the project. The hearth is often the center of a dwelling or structure. It sets up a hierarchy of spaces in concentric rings from the (sacred) center point to the remote edges. Movement is directed toward the center. The grid, on the other hand, implies unvarying repetition of its unit (the square) and infinite extension of this monotonous pattern. It establishes an equality and homogeneity of space. There is no one prescribed route; rather, one may follow multiple aimless paths.

In addition to these formal polarities, the hearth and grid reveal semantic differences. They trigger nearly opposite symbolic associations. The geometry of the grid is pure and consistent. From the Roman camp to the Ville Nouvelle it implies order and rationality. Moreover, it symbolizes modern egalitarianism. The grid is populist. It is 640 acres for every American settler. Its geometry is that of a godless world in which men refuse to bow down before authority. The hearth, on the other hand, is a remnant of tribal society, where spirit is an immanent presence in the material realm.

The above oppositions structure the four stages of Deamer's design. In (I) the grid dominates. The image is modern and industrial. This is a city of factories where hearths are furnaces. In (II) the hearth appears to triumph. But despite its size and central location, the hearth is a mute cube that erodes where intersected by the grid. The "parks" are mere geometricized vestiges of nature: barren square lots and limbless column-trees.

Thus (I) and (II) set up two conditions (grid and hearth) whose opposition (III) and (IV) attempt to resolve. The resolution is achieved not by moving from content to form or from form to content, but by allowing the two to affect each other. The grid and hearth are unified by the notion of procession. The repetitive character of the grid suggests possible evolution, sequences where identical conditions are gradually transformed. The hearth implies linear movement toward a culmination point. The sequence of screens in (III) and the three processions in (IV) show how potentialities latent in the grid form lead to a defamiliarization of the hearth. At the same time, the historical forms and metaphorical associations of the hearth determine the character of the resulting environments. Thus, the two ritualistic elements in artistic production — defamiliarization and the reappropriation of the past — generate and guide the design process.

A Napa Valley Winery

Yossi Friedman

THE PROGRAM for the Robert Pepi Vinyard in Rutherford, California calls for an eight thousand case winery (producing both white and red wines), a house for the wine maker, and wine tasting facilities for tour groups. These structures are set on top of bedrock that overlooks the Napa Valley, an area which was, according to local legends, once inhabited by Native Americans.

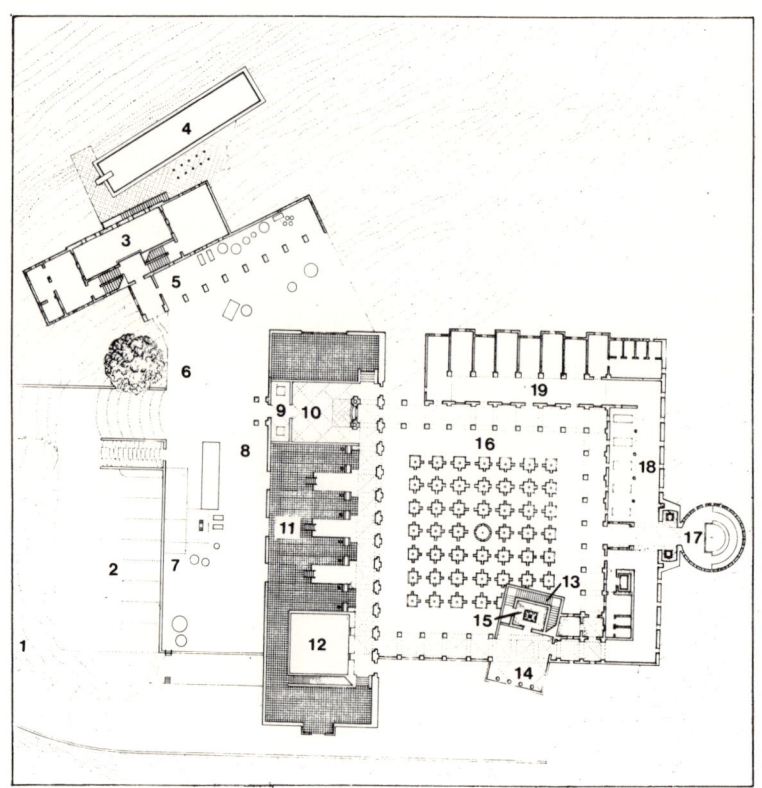

1. Pepi Winery (Master's thesis), 1982. Plan.

1. Vineyards 2. Parking 3. Wine Maker's house 4. Pool 5. Storage 6. Working court 7. Weighing scale 8. Crushing area 9. Entry Vestibule 10. Wine table 11. Fermenting area 12. Bottling area 13. Stair to cellars and shipping 14. Observation deck 15. Wine library 16. Pleasure garden 17. Wine tasting room 18. Dining area 19. Exhibition area

Wine production within a spiritual and bucolic setting creates a unique platform for ritualistic performances. In a society that separates industry (system) from art (imaginative truth), a winery is usually perceived as a factory. The design of the Pepi Winery attempts to maintain the ceremonial observances which have characterized the work of wine makers through the ages. The placement of

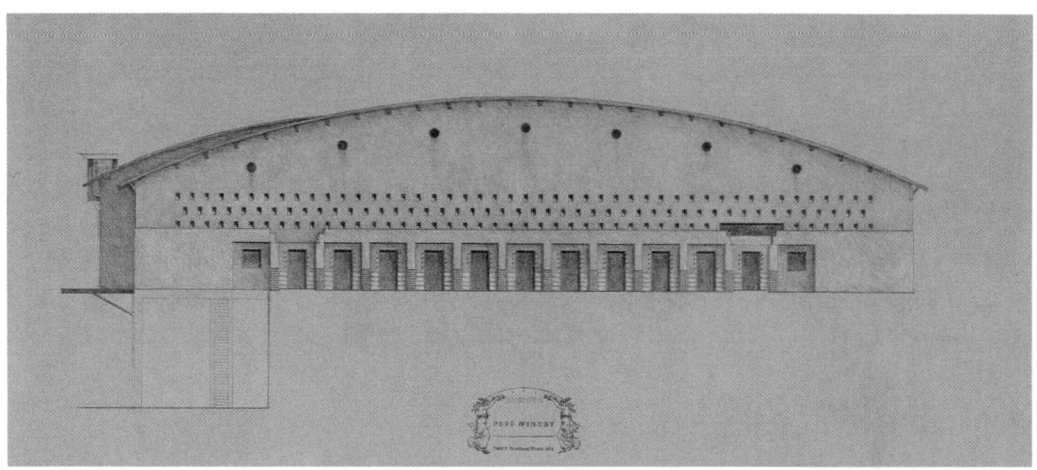

2. Pepi Winery. Court elevation. View toward north.

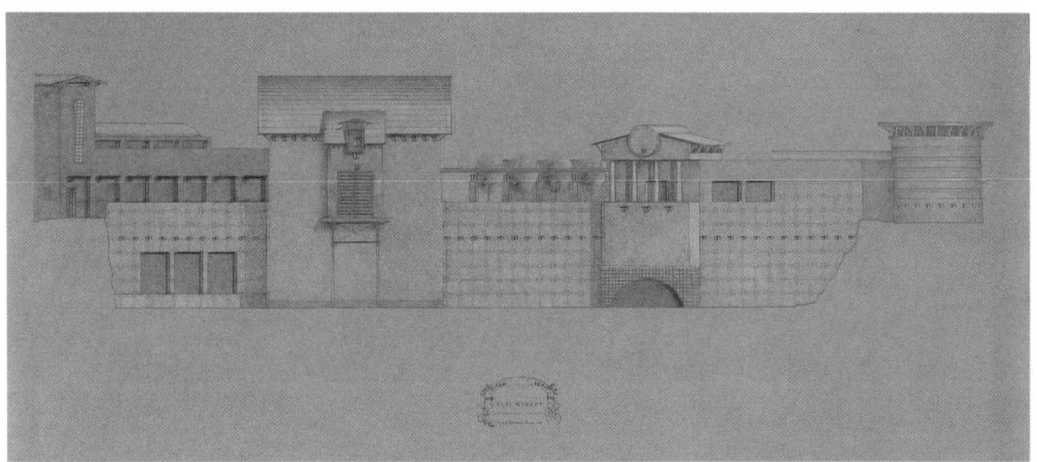

3. Pepi Winery. West elevation.

4. Pepi Winery. Section through court looking south.

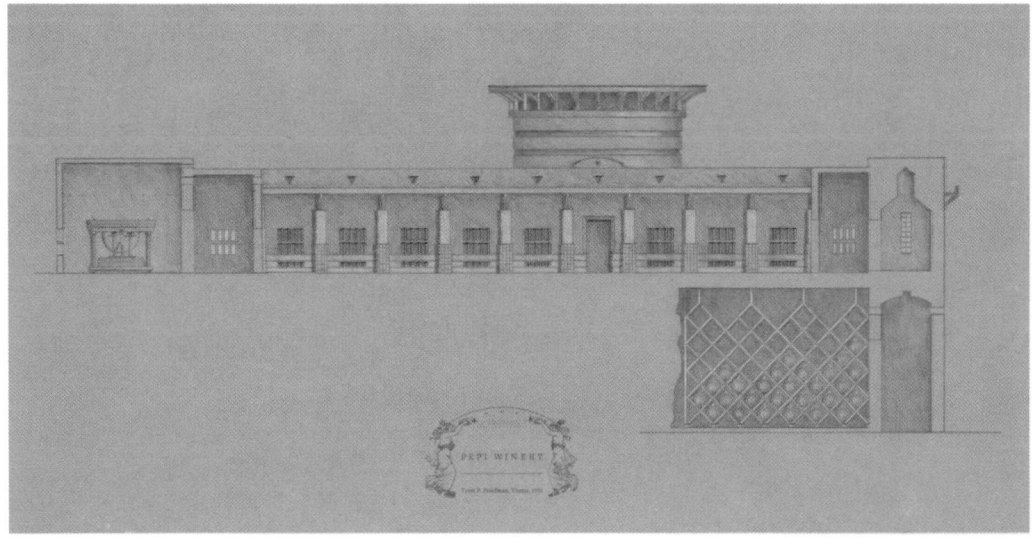

5. Pepi Winery. View from southeast.

architectural elements provides a form which permits the revival of rituals for use in the social exercises of modern assemblage.

The design approach is based on the belief that all rituals contain some variation on the ideas of renewal and transition. Two interacting routes are present. The first route follows the grape from

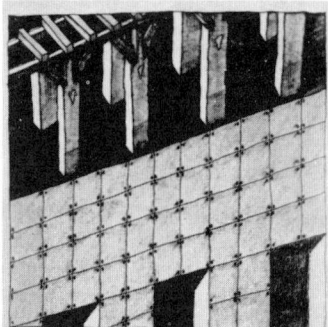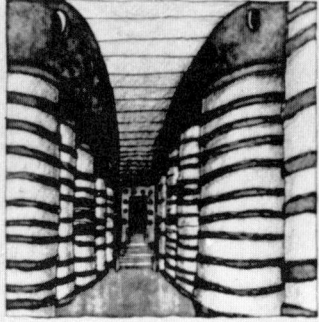

6. Pepi Winery. Preliminary studies.

the vineyards to a working court for crushing and pressing. After this they pass into the fermenting house and finally to the storage cellars below. While the actual processing of wines becomes a critical design issue, the second route enables the visitor to follow all aspects of production. A wine tasting room, an exhibition space, an observation pavilion, and a pleasure garden in the center court — all become a stage for the harvest celebration.

■   ■

> Based in a communal agrarian tradition, the process of wine-making has changed little over time. With the introduction of the tourist to the winery, however, a new path through the plant, distinct from the path of the grape's processing, is created. Focussing on this double route, Friedman explores the ritual potential of the modern winery.

Two courtyard types, the agrarian working court and the monastic cloister, are adopted to serve the different functions: set back-to-back along the spine of the fermentation shed, they create a formal unity while maintaining the distinction between work and leisure. The two paths run parallel through the shed and finally join at the circular cask-like wine-tasting room at the end of the enclosed garden court. In contrast to the relatively understated and loosely defined working court, this court is more systematically articulated; with its dense grid of trees laced together by a Moorish pattern of shallow streams, and its skewed temple on one side of the cloister, it becomes an "inner sanctum," a private place for drinking and contemplation.

While the harvest was traditionally celebrated collectively, the individualized ritual of wine-tasting now claims the center. Nurtured by a consumer society, wine-tasting is ascendent over the archaic activities of communion and celebration. Accepting this present state of affairs, Friedman provides a scenographic backdrop for wine-tasting as a modern ritual.

Passage and Entry [1]
An Artist's Loft

Pe'era Goldman

ORIGINALLY THE LOFT was a single, large, well-lit open space. The owners, an artist and her family, used the front portion of their loft as a studio/dining room/living room/storage area, leaving approximately a third of the total area unused. The intention of the design was to establish a coherent entrance and to distinguish the functions within the entire area. Entry and passage therefore became a major concern.

Upon arrival from the outdoor court of the building, we are admitted to a dark foyer defined by thick storage walls. A celebrated, illuminated glass door, imbedded in a glass wall, acts as the focal point along the entry axis. This axis is continued in the dining room beyond with a deep niche (containing an already existing opening to the kitchen). The sequence is separated from the main room by a thick wall with two openings: a small door admits just enough light to distinguish the foyer, while a larger opening between the dining and living rooms enhances their connection and establishes a sense of intimacy and small scale for eating. The thick wall with its deep openings gives a sense of passage from space to space.

1. Artist's Loft. Deborah Barlow, *Assistant*.

1. Artist's Loft, New York, 1982. Glass door.

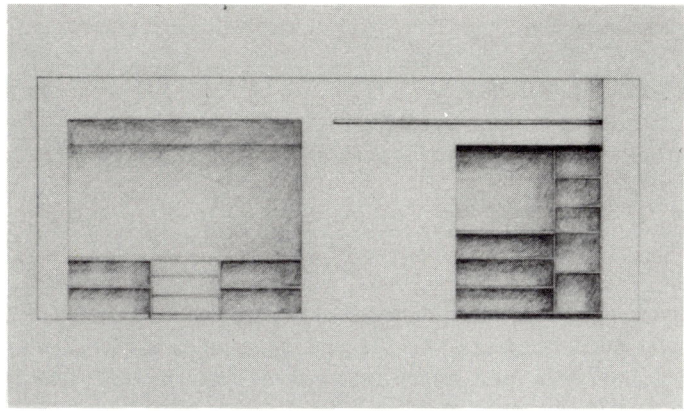

2. Artist's Loft. Foyer elevation

The celebrated glass door is conceived as the real door. At the same time it is part of the glass wall and is strung together with it by horizontal tying lines. These tying lines appear in different materials throughout the design, weaving together such disparate parts as the shelves and lacquered dining

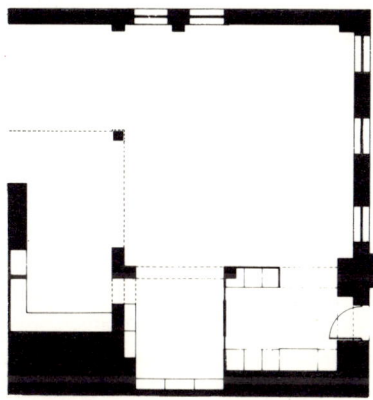

3. Artist's Loft. Plan.

room counters as well as the etched glass entry plane. By absorbing all structural elements within the walls, this horizontal wrapping appears to deny the necessity of vertical support. A further

4. Artist's Loft. Living room elevation. "Deep openings" to dining room and foyer.

ambiguity is brought into play by the door's thick wooden frame, which implies passage through a substantial wall, while in fact only a thin plane of glass holds it in place. The use of both transparent and translucent glass encourages this dual reading of distinction and continuity.

While spatial unity is subtly preserved, then, the rituals of arrival and departure and the specificity of activities are accentuated in the passage from dark to light, from small defined spaces to one large room, and from an axial, articulated sequence of doors and niches to cross-axial deep openings in the wall.

■   ■   ■

Goldman's project investigates the act of passage and the architectural components that constitute it: 1) the plane that defines the transition; 2) the relation that this plane must acknowledge with the spaces on either side; 3) the opening that penetrates and thus defies the plane; 4) the position of that opening on an axis; and, 5) the relationship of that axis to other axes that bind the overall space.

Goldman's formal elements and devices recall those used by the philosopher Ludwig Wittgenstein in his Stonborough House. Wittgenstein explored the dual nature of architectural elements: like the components of any language, architectural elements must exist as part of a system while retaining their individual identities.

The situation is complicated by the fact that each element simultaneously relates to many different aspects of the system (or overall composition); it plays several roles at once. Thus, in Goldman's scheme, the doubled, wood frame of the door both establishes a contrast with the glass plane within which it sits, and provides a visual link to the "frame" in the thick wall that terminates the axis. The dark and light rooms of the entry sequence contrast with each other while both, as small, adjoining rooms, unite to oppose the vast open room on a perpendicular axis to them. In other cases elements of different materials located in different places accomplish the same function. Thus the transparent glass tying lines of the entry plane are associated with the horizontal banding found elsewhere in the apartment.

Finally, a single element can produce different readings, depending on where the viewer is standing. The transparent glass tying lines and the translucent glass of the entry plane produce a contrast of light and dark which reverses as one moves from the dark entry foyer to the lighter second space. And while the glass plane in the dark room glows as a warm element complementing the wood of the walls, in the light room it takes on the opacity and whiteness of the walls of that space.

In both Goldman's and Wittgenstein's designs, the sensuous quality of the elements is never denied. Rather, the heightened presence of the elements, which insistently call attention to themselves, interrupts any single continuous directional movement. The viewer becomes more conscious of his motion through the spaces. Thus one experiences the ritual of passage, while a predictable logic (or single, coherent reading) is denied by the versatility of the elements and the mutability of their relations.

Ritual and the Library[1]

Bruce Abbey and Robert Dripps

OF ALL OF MAN'S INSTITUTIONS, the library represents the codification and elaboration of ritual with a continuity rarely surpassed by any other architectural program. The storing of the collective memory of a civilization and the place of conversation between man and book or man and other men is represented by the Platonic image of a scholar under a tree engaged in dis-

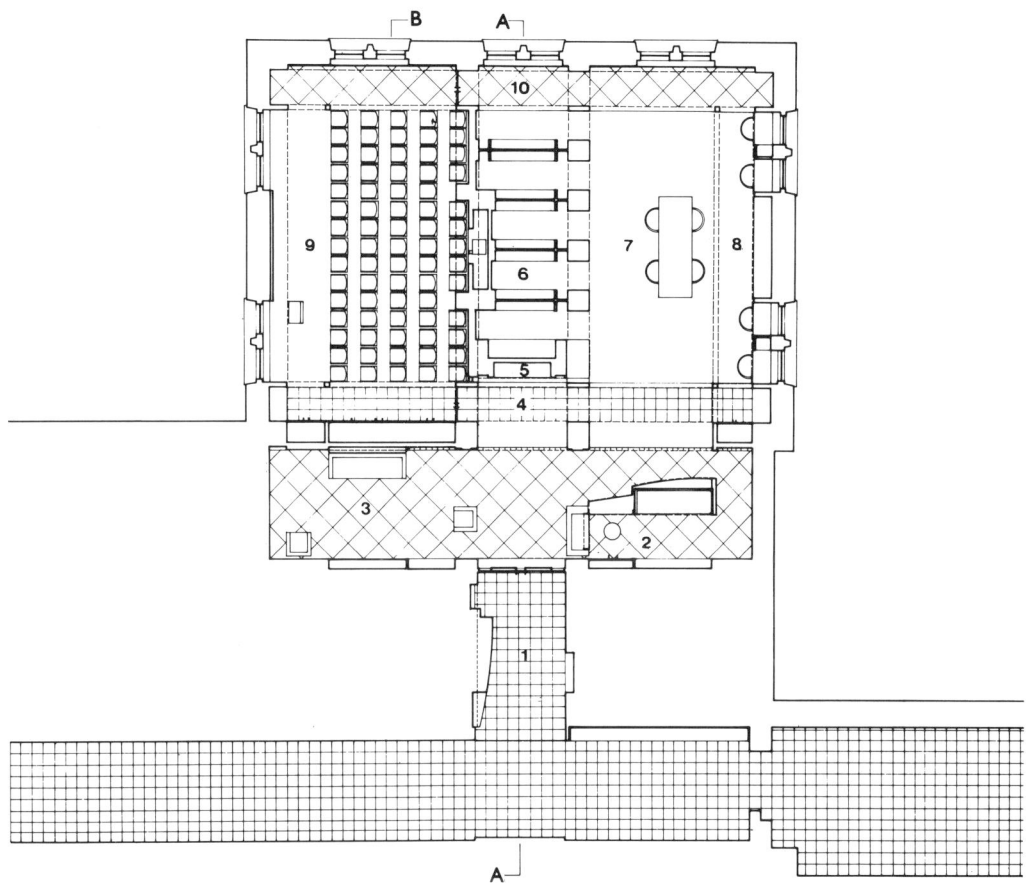

1. Library of Anaesthesiology,
Hospital of the University of Pennsylvania, 1980. Plan.

1. Entry Vestibule 2. Librarian 3. Light Reading 4. Wall Passage 5. Book Chest 6. Stacks
7. Reading 8. Carrels 9. Conference Room 10. Porch

course or walking in a garden enclosed by a colonnade. These images are included in the elaboration of an architectural type that has been developed throughout history. Another image might be that of the ark of the covenant which originally accompanied the Jews during their exodus from

---

1. Library of Anaesthesiology. Gerald F. X. Geier and Keith Loftin III, *Assistants*. Judy Bitting, George Carr, Ruth Gless, Robert McAnulty, and Stacy Oliver, *Model and Drawings*.

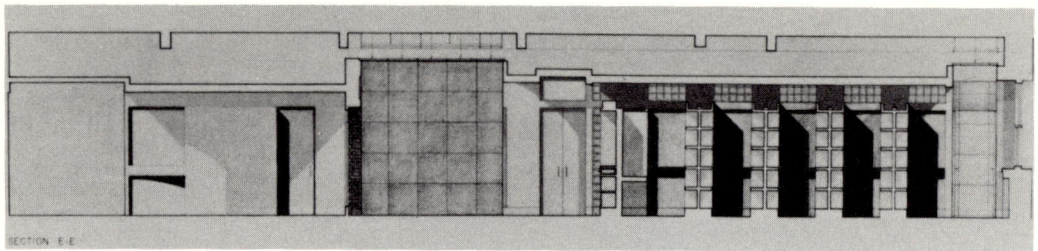

2. Library of Anaesthesiology. Section A-A.

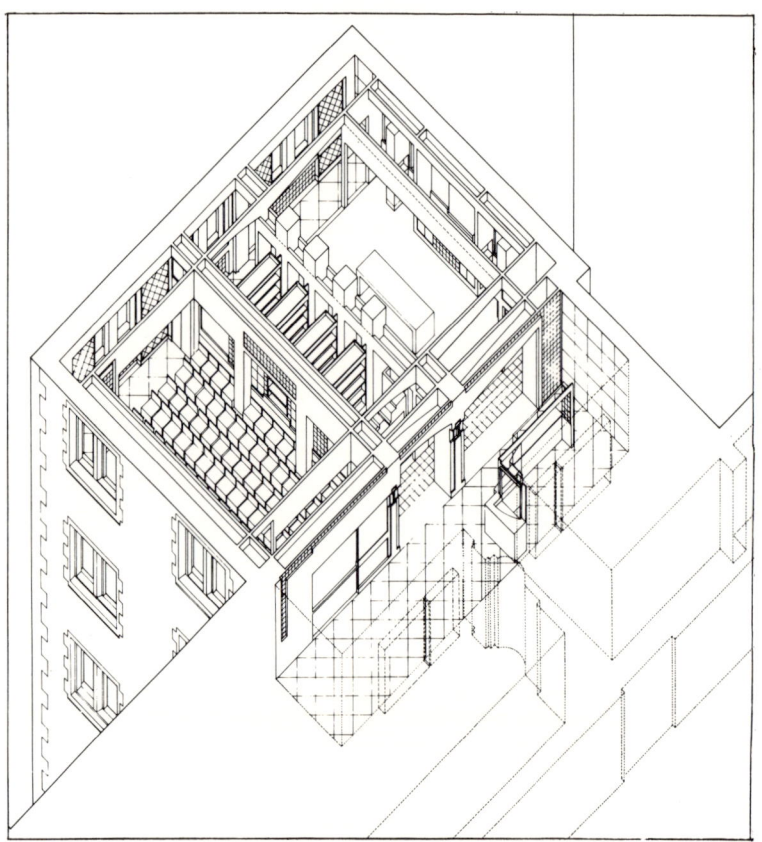

3. Library of Anaesthesiology. Axonometric view.

4. Library of Anaesthesiology. Section B-B.

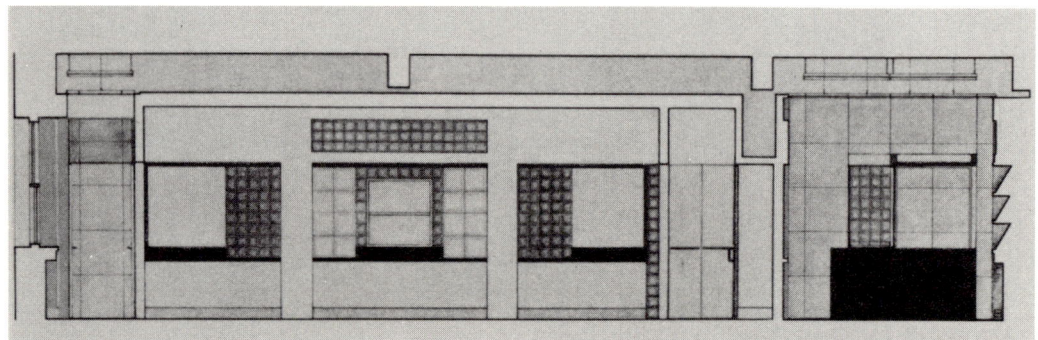

5, 6. Library of Anaesthesiology. Interior views.

Egypt. It is portrayed as a portable book-chest containing the documents and official records of the tribe, and was given an architectural elaboration with a pediment, door, and symbolic carving. This same chest, when placed in the center of an encampment, established a focus, and sense of place. As the stored documentation increased beyond the capacity of a single chest and a fixed location became possible, the collective space was often expressed by a vaulted structure and the stacks as elements of the colonnade. Thus the icon of the bookchest was transformed into a habitable room. Within the library itself, the carrel becomes a further area of ritualized activity. It is at the interface between inside and outside. The location of the carrel near the light is expressive of the intimate relationship of the book to the light, and of the symbolic connection to the world beyond.

In the Library of Anaesthesiology at the Hospital of the University of Pennsylvania the design task was to accommodate these traditional functions of library and study, to provide storage space for a specialized collection, and a meeting room for conferences.

7. Library of Anaesthesiology. Book chest.

A visitor arrives on axis into a space that separates the library from the self-contained world of the hospital. Straight ahead appears the traditional bookchest now containing the card catalogue, the key to the collective memory of the library. The stacks are housed beyond in a vaulted space that is inflected towards the enclosed space on the left containing the meeting room. The catalogue itself inflects to the right towards the ceiling of the reading room with its carrel wall and view of the Philadelphia skyline. Moving through the reading room to the back of the library one arrives at a thin passage that connects the lecture room with the reading area and looks out towards the campus of the University of Pennsylvania. Here, the disengagement from the hospital is complete and connection to the exterior world is made possible.

■   ■   ■

In attempting to consolidate the disparate aspects of the library program, Abbey and Dripps adopt a strategy involving the use and transformation of typologically-based architectural precedents. For example, the structure of the colonnade is used to organize a spatial layering at the periphery of the main rooms, although the colonnade itself is only suggested for its thickness is filled with books. These layers are defined by thick walls and emphasize both the hermetic nature of the library as well as the ritual of entry and procession. In the Library of Anaesthesiology the justification for the formal manipulation of historical models depends largely on the elaboration of meaning through symbol. This suggests an attempt to encourage a heightened experience specific to the library; that is, to invoke rituals which were more clearly understood and more fully supported architecturally in past cultures. In both the ancient Greek and Judaic traditions to which Abbey and Dripps explicitly refer, the location of cultural documents was sanctified and monumentalized architecturally. In the Library of Anaesthesiology, however, the "bookchest" no longer occupies the real center as the bookchest would have historically, but is shifted to the front edge of the space where it functions metaphorically as the library façade. This seems appropriate given the early articulation of the bookchest as a diminutive building as well as this library's location within an existing building. Because of the modified status of ritual as well as the current imperative of typological transformation, the architectural references are here condensed and abstracted.

Mayer House and Alley Theater

Peter Waldman
Text by Peter C. Papademetriou

FUNDAMENTAL EXPLORATIONS OF MEANING lie at the core of Peter Waldman's work, most important of which is a dialectical presentation of opposites, dualities, and inversions. These investigations often involve juxtaposed scales, yet maintain concurrent readings through the conscious transformation of elemental building parts. They are also linked in a phenomenal sense through passage and sequence. Two projects of differing magnitude, one private, one public, and four years apart in conception, illustrate this process.

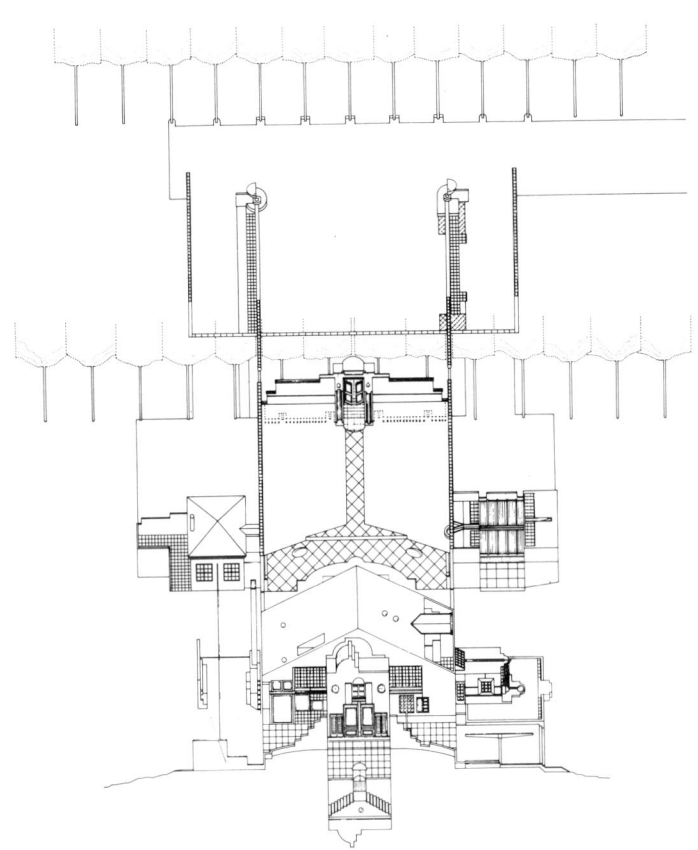

1. Mayer House, Princeton, New Jersey, 1980. Axonometric view.

The Mayer Residence (1978-82) is a private compound for a psychiatrist and his family. The site is at the conjunction of a hardwood forest and a gridded field of mature pines. The solution is the proverbial "hut in the woods" — a highly ordered paradise in a forest clearing. A raised front court

---

1. Mayer House. Andrew Bartle, Tom Bishop, Chris Cowansage, David McAlpin, and John Marusczak, *Assistants*.
Alley Theater. Morris/Aubrey, *Architects*. Peter Waldman, *Design Consultant*. Kent Bowers, Lee Ledbetter, Jim Postell, Douglas Rixey, and Victoria G. K. Rixey, *Assistants*.

2. Mayer House. Front elevation.

accommodating a service yard to the east and an office pavilion to the west reiterates the idealized square of the clearing, and distinguishes the compound from its "natural" setting. The level change is marked by a central portal which establishes a specific beginning for the direction of movement in, through, and out of the house.

3. Mayer House. First floor plan.

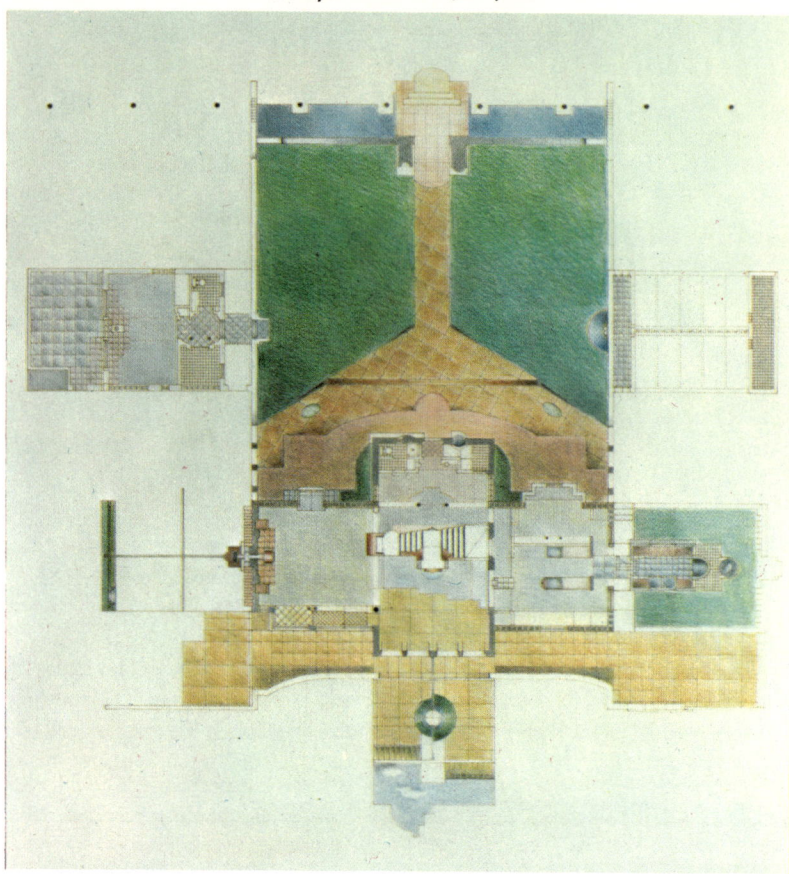

4. Mayer House. Stair detail.

Fundamentally, the Mayer Residence is a two room house with articulated edges. One room is the entry court; the other is the stair-hall, the central space with object within, around which all

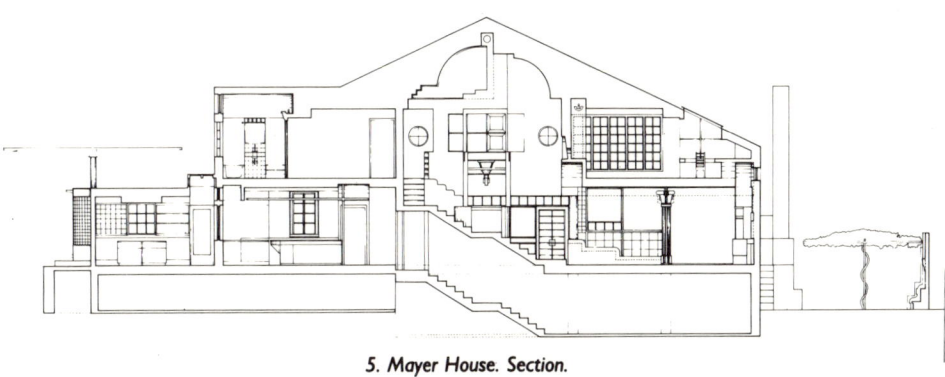

5. Mayer House. Section.

movement is organized. This positive void is given a highly differentiated profile in section which both contrasts with its basic plan shape and penetrates into the simple gable form which is the essential image of the house itself.

6. Mayer House. Psychiatrist's office.

The basic *parti* is the contrast between a more public side, signified by the formal "urban" court, and an informal, private side, defined by the eroded forest edge. The enclosed precinct of the courtyard has a traditional formality recalling the image of the manor house and outbuildings, while the rear extensions into the landscape suggest a modernist sensibility. Although this organization is essentially axial, significant interruptions and elaborated edge conditions extend our actual experience of the sequence.

Axial clarity is enriched by lateral movement, and the interplay is enhanced by articulated layers which stretch the path of the user. Known users are given special, particular, and alternative routes. One precinct comprises a side entry, potting shed/laundry wing connected cross-axially with a combination kitchen/study. A second cross-axis is established by the passage to the separate office. A short landing off the main stair addresses the central void, while a progressively more private master suite of library, bedroom, and bathroom wraps the remaining three sides of the stairwell volume.

Paradoxically it is this most private element, the master bath, which replicates the central section and reads through on the front elevation. Otherwise, the second storey is suppressed, so that major elements dominate and enlarge the scale of the formal courtyard façade. The master bath provides a balcony over the entry, a place where the user can engage the whole of the formal court; pragmatically, a spot from which the owners may welcome arriving guests.

Progression through the threshold below is marked by spatial slots (reinforced by the differentiated treatment of the floor surface). Passing between the twin entry columns, one can see over the squarely centered main stair landing to the garden behind. To *reach* the garden, however, one must move around the stair, and axial passage is again denied at the point of access by the displacement of paired sets of doors to either side of a centered column. This progression accentuates the processes of centering and displacement, of axial and lateral movement. The house may then be read as a continuous whole blown open in the highly figurative central section — the constant datum for all activity, the *axis mundi*.

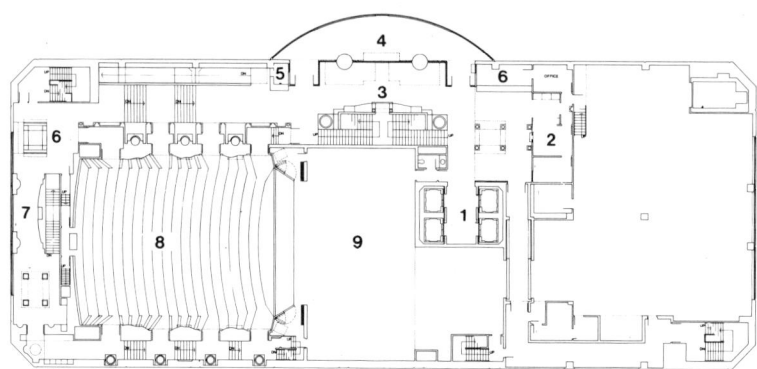

7. Alley Theater, Houston, Texas, 1982. Plan.

1. Vestibule 2. Tickets 3. Main lobby 4. Terrace 5. House manager 6. Concessionaire 7. Back lobby 8. Theater 9. Stage

The Alley Theatre Center (1982-) contrasts sharply in scale, context, and program with the Mayer Residence. A number of specific design parameters were involved, the primary one being that the project was an architecture growing from the inside out. Property adjacent to the existing

Alley Theatre (designed by Ulrich Franzen and completed in 1969) was acquired by the nearby Republic Bank (designed by Johnson/Burgee) for a parking facility. In return, the Alley was to receive a new proscenium theatre and badly needed support spaces. Both were to be inserted in the top of the fifteen storey garage for which many constraints had already been fixed (elevator core locations, a "grand balcony" for the theatre designed as a segmental curve similar to those in the Franzen design, and the overall building envelope of precast and polished granite panels).

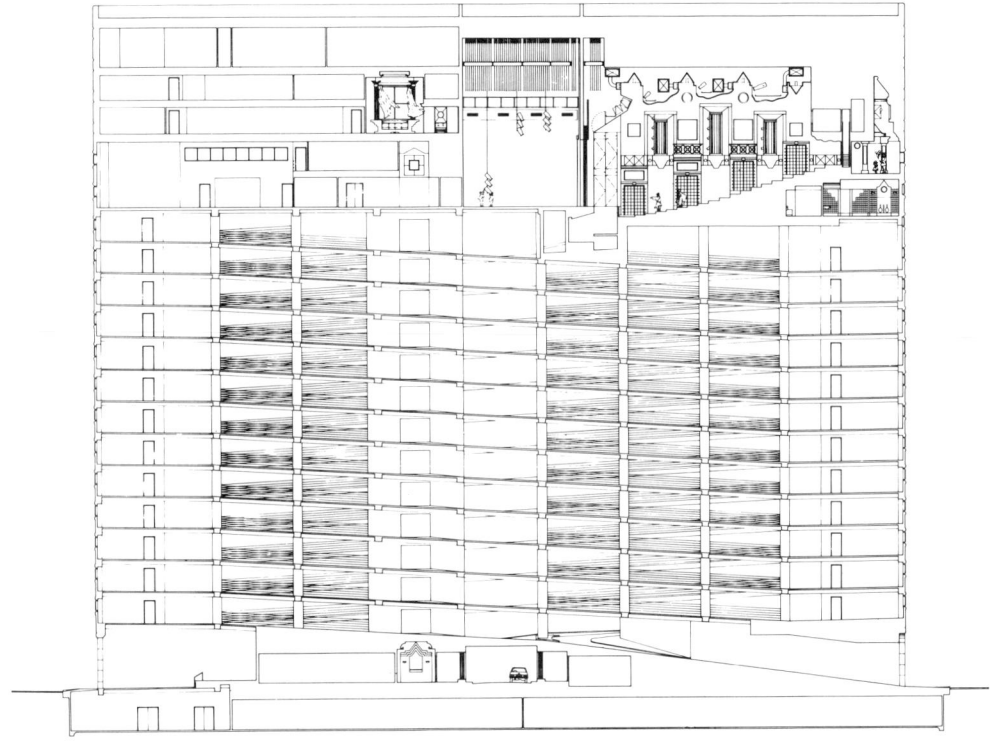

8. Alley Theater. Building section.

Waldman sought to "renovate" the proposed envelope by providing a "crown" to the unilateral treatment of the garage "box." The existing balcony was made more grand by a two-storey "window" to the main lobby, and a small-scale second balcony was projected through from the upper level lounge to centralize and fix its position. This assemblage of elements was capped by a glazed, jewel-like skylight.

The tight planning constraints made it necessary to provide an essentially continuous, linear public space with local episodes. Waldman conceived of this lobby as a street articulated with terraced entry portals, concession stands, and lounge seating. As such, the centrality of this public zone is an experience in time, and not in actual dimension. Its extension lies in the vertical zone of the paired staircases which punctuate the overall linear sequence. Axially oriented to the grand balcony, these stairs have an implied centrality articulated in the convex displacement of the ceiling.

Both monumental and intimate scale coexist in this "accomodating whole." The grand stairs have a balcony-landing where one might pause to look onto the center of things. The giant orders of columns in both the lounge and house (actually prescribed air conditioning duct runs) are played against the gazebo-like concession stands. The passage leading to lower-level restrooms is modu-

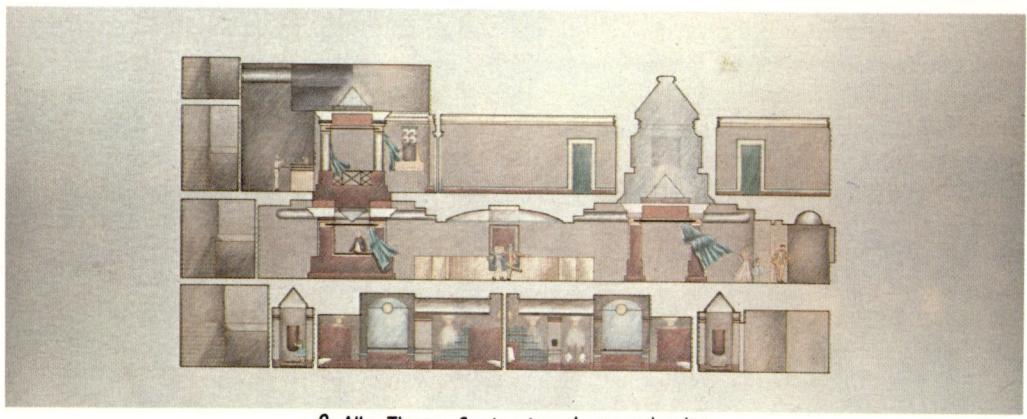

9. Alley Theater. Section through concessionaires.

lated by individual seating niches, including a centrally-located "janitor's chair." This constant dialectical play gives structure to the multiple inversions which characterize the progression of architectural events.

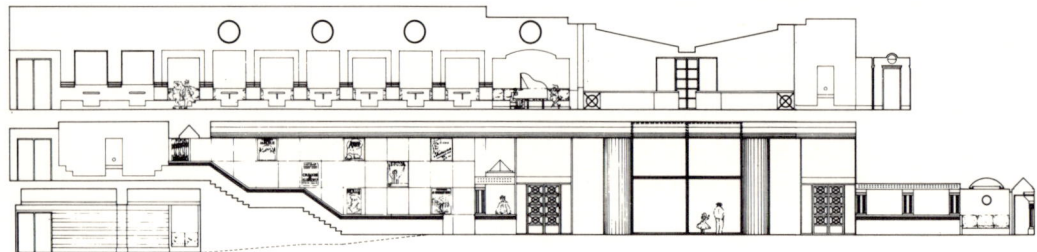

10. Alley Theater. Lounge section.

A complex conjugation of simple phrase and elementary episodes is woven together in these two projects by Peter Waldman. The continuity of the given context provides the reference frame against which specific rituals may be appreciated and connected. Sequence and passage become the glue which binds the juxtapositions into a narrative of experience.

11. Alley Theater. Section through lobby.

Peter Papademitriou's analysis of the Mayer House and the Alley Theatre reveals Waldman's juxtaposition of the ordinary to the extraordinary, translated architecturally into a conflation of varying scales. Waldman himself maintains that "ritual gains significance in the midst of routine; ceremony becomes vital in the context of habit."

Though the theatre project's location in the top portion of a nineteen-floor parking shed was a required part of the program, it seems particularly suited to Waldman's architecture, which repeatedly elaborates the highly specific within the general, the fantastic within the mundane. Like Papademitriou's characterization of the Mayer House as the "proverbial hut in the woods," the theatre, in its celebration of door, stair, street, and stage becomes a sacred room in a profane box. This suggests a longing for an era which Houston never knew. Contrasted with the simplicity of the proscenium, the public entry and waiting spaces become the real stage. Entry and passage are ritualized in their refinement as each is accommodated within a temple-like form. The true ritual occurs, however, in bringing the participant closer to a grand past removed both in time and place.

The Mayer House, as indicated by the drawings, is to be experienced as a progression. Upon arrival from a road through the forest, one feels one has discovered the house. It initially appears as a simple shed in a clearing, yet new precincts are repeatedly established with varying effects on the viewer. The intensity of each successive image erases the memory of the last.

The house elaborates the element of time. One scale of gestures — the static entry court, the simple shed with flat frontal plane and small windows — confronts the occasional visitor. Yet within and around the large scale elements there is an extraordinary amount of detail and elaboration. The spaces and surfaces are intentionally ambiguous and in their restlessness create a dynamic energy as well as a strange disquietude. Throughout the plans, sections, and elevation, symmetries and axes are suggested and then denied. The site itself contrasts an axial organization — where forecourt and backyard, front façade and rear façade are articulated differently — with a centralized one — where the house exists in the middle of a clearing and the stair becomes the event in the center of the house. Perhaps these alternate readings throughout the project suggest the seeming complexity of present day values where rituals are less specific and certainly less universal.

It seems appropriate that the stair becomes the object around which the major spaces of the house are defined. Its central placement beneath the vault, the architectonic sky whose carved sky-light reads as both cloud and sun, reinforces a broader understanding of the stair as the link between earth and heaven. In psychoanalytic literature, the stair represents a mediation between various states of conciousness:

The art of climbing or ascending symbolizes the way towards the absolute reality; and to the profane consciousness, the approach towards that reality arouses an ambivalent feeling, of fear and of joy, of attention and repulsion.... Each of these modes of being represents a cessation of the *profane human condition; that is, a breaking of the ontological plane.*[1]

In the Alley Theatre and Mayer House, context and program direct different solutions yet establish a similar frame of argument. The theatre, in its location within the fragmented world of downtown Houston, is elaborated as an ideal whole in which axes and symmetries are established and maintained. As in a present-day religious rite, memory of a lost period becomes as potent as the icon. The Mayer House, in contrast, posits an architectural fragmentation against an Arcadian setting, the paradisal forest. The house represents a more complex understanding of the modern condition, a dialectical image made possible by an ideal landscape.

1. Mircea Eliade, Myths, Rites, Symbols: A Mircea Eliade Reader *(New York: Harper Colophon Books, 1975), p.240.*

A Tall Tale of Urban Stratification
Men's Club, New York City

John Maruszcak

Actuality is when the lighthouse is dark between flashes. It is the instant between the ticks of the watch: slipping forever through time.

George Kubler, The Shape of Time

THE TALE is of two cities, not of London and Paris or the normative historical city and the city of delirious scenographic dimensions, but the city of the base and the city of the top. The cinematic vertical journey, both up and down, establishes the roof as the site of the inverted city and the new datum to turn Ferris on his head. This inverted city mirrors the imagined juxtaposition of the ivory tower and the "dismantled mountain." The offered panorama traces the map of the habits, routines, and rituals of the vertical and the final paradox of both cities: "the microcosm in a macrocosm."

The head character of state of this cavernous tale is Two Rector, Trinity and Rector Street, N.Y.C. and as such, this lofty companion to Trinity Church provides the major visual limit and laboratorial limits of Wall Street. A consortium of wolves, hedgehogs, bears, and bulls rehearsing a set of directions for Wall Street provides the initial enactment of the attendant programmatic fiction. The collection of contingent polarities and fugitive accomplices yields further evidence for the masquerade of ivory and stone and augments the architectonics of vertical disjunction and solution — no solution's fallacy. As the scaffolding is raised within the archaeology and physiognomy of the roof site, the tale begins again by the penultimate self-referential act; the parody of formal imagistic cannibalism: the lance of the disegno.

1. Men's Club (Master's Thesis, 1980). Top anamorphosis.

2. Men's Club. Garden section.

3. Men's Club. Garden of the Inverted Top.

4. Men's Club. Object and Atmosphere: Garden section.

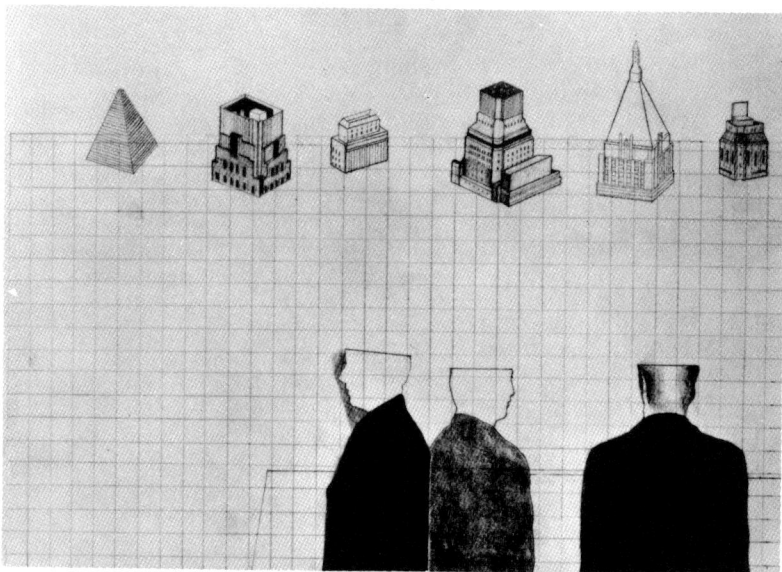
5. Men's Club. Heads of State.

■   ■   ■

John Marusczak's verbal and pictorial fantasy for the penthouse of Two Rector Street is inspired by the landscape of "downtown," particularly downtown at night. The building's location at the tip of Manhattan prompted both the rooftop elaboration as mediator between built and unbuilt and the lighthouse references. Unlike the familiar man/nature plan dualities, Marusczak explores the verticalization of figural spaces and the poetics of the horizon.

His "dismantled mountain" or inverted pyramid represents the most explicit reference to building in the design, yet even this suggests further possibilities as a hung valley or a fertile triangle. The diverse images never actually crystallize. Fragments evolve into fragments which simply coexist, rather than achieving any recognizable resolution. The design is no longer like an organism, for wholeness is only a hypothesis. What is self-evidently unified is the single element itself. The images are an attempt more to structure a process than to represent a building, and the existing base functions solely to elevate the rooftop illusion.

Water Folly

Gustavo Bonevardi

A RITUAL is not a habit. A ritual can be an act or a series of actions abstracted from their original everyday purpose. A ritual act is materially useless. What remains is the shadow of the act. As in a ballet, only the symbolic aspects are retained, as a stylized version of reality. A baptism does not physically cleanse. The sprinkling of a handful of earth on a coffin does not bury.

Rituals are reinforced by accroutrements such as tools or costumes. But again, these are useless. Like an Egyptian pharaoh's staff and whip, they are only representations of functional objects, too small and fragile to be put to use.

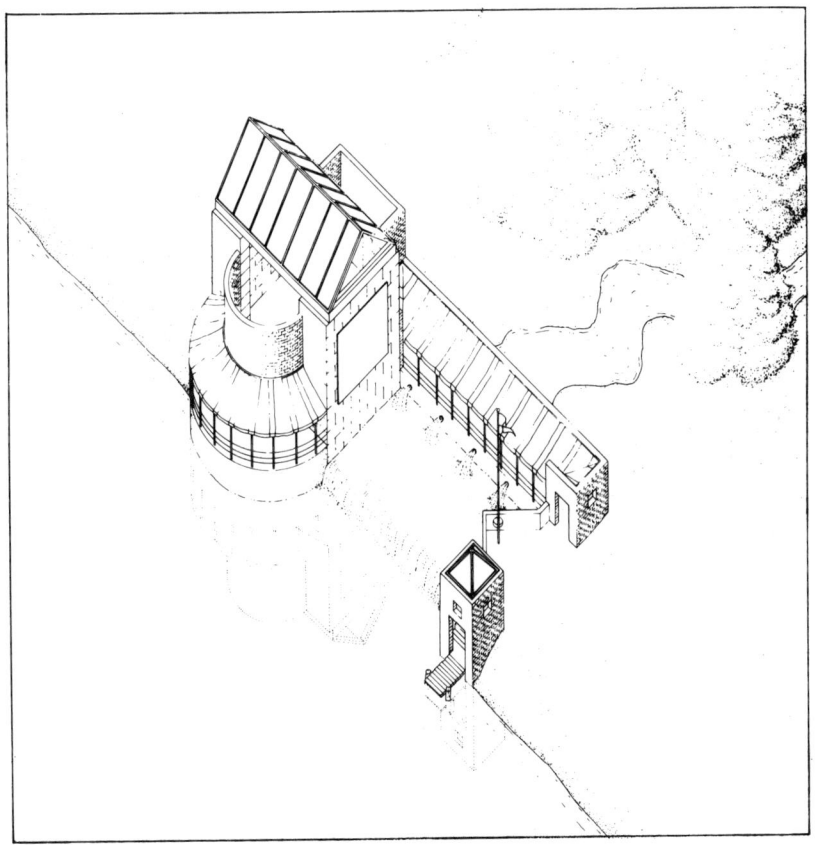

1. Water Folly (project), 1982. Axonometric view.

Rituals can be acts which are performed for a particular result (marriage), or they can be commemorations of events or processes (Easter and harvest rituals). Commemoration often takes the form of reenactment, as in the Christian eucharist.

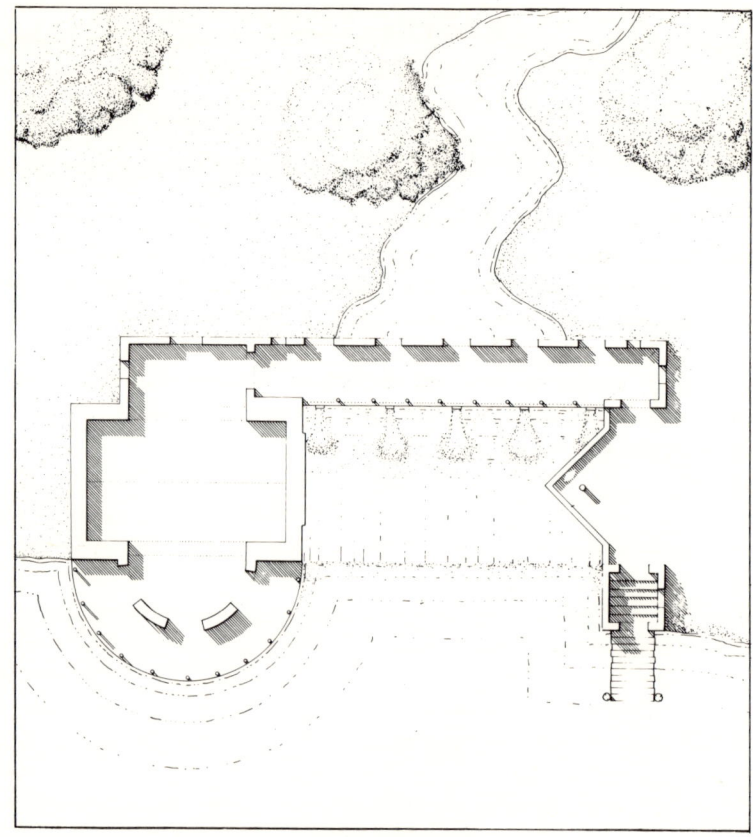

2. Water Folly. Plan.

In the same way that ritual need not always have a practical function, architectural types can also lose their functional purpose and become purely symbolic. In this project there is just such a discrepancy between the functional intent suggested visually, and the actual use of the elements.

3. Water Folly. Elevation.

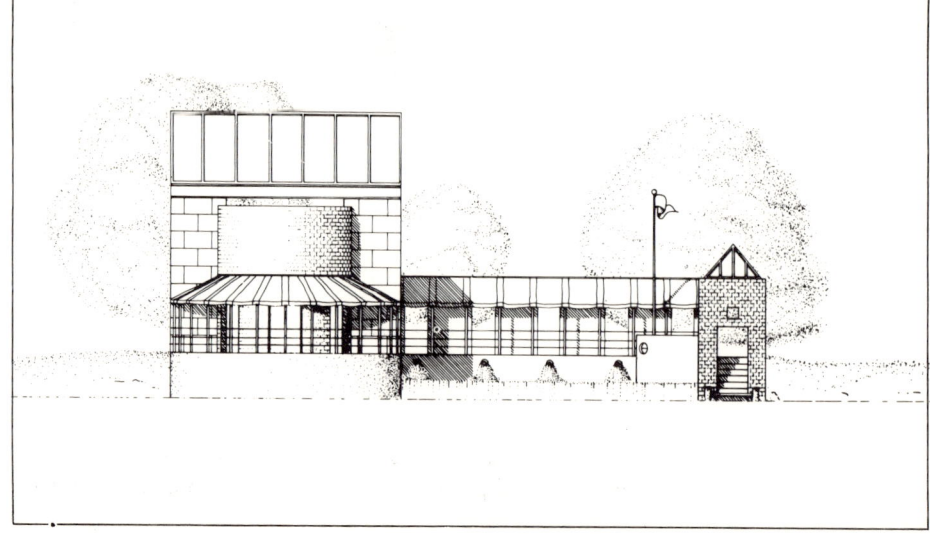

In its formal structure the project is ostensibly organized around a central processional axis established through the gate (between the stairtower and the end of the loggia), the forecourt, and the pediment of the pavilion. In practice, however, the circulation is deflected at each point by a perpendicular reorientation. One cannot pass through the gate, and the court is unoccupyable since it has become a water terrace. The pavilion does not provide shelter. In this way the architectural types create a folly of disappointed suggestion.

The visitor arrives by boat, disembarks by stair, and at the balcony resembling the bow of a ship sees his goal, the pavilion. He then starts on another journey by crossing the water at the point where it is transformed from river to pond. Upon arrival at the pavilion, the visitor is reoriented by the formal change of axis. The journey concludes in a retrospective view from the belvedere back to the point of origin.

■   ■   ■

Employing one of the most archaic ideas of ritual, the demarcation of an event in the landscape, Bonevardi transforms nature into architectural form. While the resulting structure does not create an explicit ceremony, it does establish a monumental condition that brings forth the most diagrammatic and formal components of ritual. Manipulation of nature is at the root of ritual: man's ability to impose his will on the landscape paradoxically memorializes his separation from the environment.

The project marks the juncture between a river and a body of water, establishing the uniqueness of the place and thereby its transformation into a structured domain. In addition it enforces a sequence of movements with the central pool as the point of rotation. The exact meaning of the particular events along the path may elude us, but ultimately ritual is brought into being because the structure cermonializes its own existence, the act of its own construction.

Ancient Mesopotamia and the Foundation of Architectural Representation[1]

Peter Carl

In this article, an extract from a three part essay, Peter Carl examines the relationship between the representation of myth and ritual in architecture and the interpretation of the past. Claiming that the myth and ritual elements of a society are related to its need to sustain a dialogue with its primitive origins, Carl distinguishes between a weak and a strong form of that dialogue according to the degreee to which myth and ritual are embodied in its culture. The strong form, which he illustrates using the example of Ancient Mesopotamia, involves both the faithful interpretation of the past, and the application of that understanding to the present. In contrast, the weak form declares a loss of faith in the present, so that the past is idealized, thereby serving as a form of compensation for the absence of a living tradition. This is accompanied by a vision of authorial originality which sanctifies a free appropriation of imagery according to self-assigned principles.

The problem of trying to establish a ground for the meaning of architecture is constituted within the long-standing belief that architects are necessarily forced out of their area of expertise in order to confront the truth claims of architecture itself. Theory can lead, according to Carl, to what Heidegger and Ricoeur call a "forgetting of Being"; in particular, it can obscure the function of symbolic elements and ritual. Yet lack of expertise can be turned to advantage. Carl's theoretical sensibility is firmly hermeneutical: understanding is always built out of a combination of prejudgement and openness; we must learn what questions to ask, and how to ask them.

■   ■   ■

The modern concern for symbols implies a new contact with the sacred, a movement beyond the forgetfulness of Being which is today manifested in the manipulation of empty signs and formalized languages.

Paul Ricoeur, The Conflict of Interpretations[2]

FROM AS FAR BACK in history as evidence permits us to judge, it has apparently been necessary for civilized society to sustain a dialogue with whatever is conceived to be its primitive origins.[3] This dialogue is distinguished by a weak and a strong form. In its weak form the past is idealized: noble savages populate utopian Golden Ages. Little is declared but a loss of faith in the

---

1. This article has been excerpted from an unpublished essay whose basic theme is the relation of architecture to the cultural representation of the unity of the cosmos. The excerpt, the first of three chapters, offers an account of this relation in a mythically embodied society. In chapter two an estimation is offered as to the present character of that relation. Chapter three outlines an interpretive direction, concentrating on the contemporary city.
2. Paul Ricoeur, "The Hermeneutics of Symbols II," *The Conflict of Interpretations*, (Evanston: Northwestern University Press, 1974), p. 319.
3. The list of people to whom the argument is indebted extends, in the original, to over fifty names. Within the confines of this extract, the absolutely minimum acknowledgements include: Joseph Rykwert, for original inspiration; Professor Frank

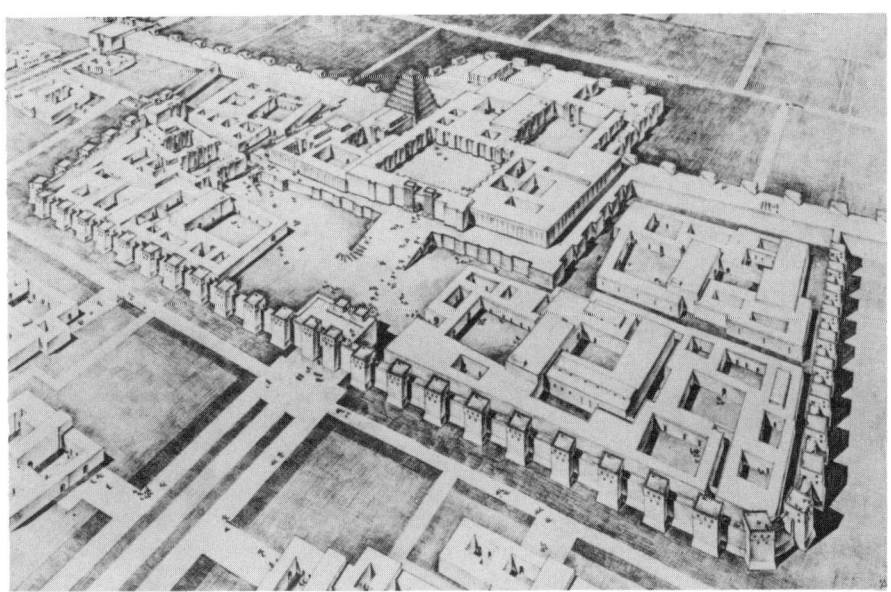

1. Khorsabad. View of temple-palace compound.

present. In its strong form, precisely the opposite is declared — the past is the basis for the faithful transmission of a tradition. It stands as an exemplum or a paradigm by means of which the essential meanings of a society are preserved for the purposes of interpreting the present. Nevertheless both attitudes require that the past be re-presented; and the superficial formal similarity between these two representations promotes the belief that idealization satisfactorily compensates for the absence of a living tradition. Nothing could be further from the truth.

In the weak form of dialogue, the past stands as a challenge to the present; in the strong form, the present is meaningful *only* as a re-interpretation of the past. In the weak form, the reliance upon representation is total — so much so that the present attains a status equivalent to the past, and soon enough it dissolves into an unresolveable field of potential significations. In the strong form, representation itself is not thematic. Rather it is the "invisible" medium — like sentence structure in a text — which enables the ethical/political/religious (not in fact usefully separated categories in such circumstances) core of the society to be revealed *to* the society.

In the weak form, authorship of any given representation is personal, necessarily an allegorization of original creation, and in competition with it. In the strong form, authorship is comparatively insignificant (certainly in personal terms) and constitutes rather a re-interpretation of what had been established primordially.

Since, however, representation is the only available means of revealing, the radical opposition of what is revealed in each case becomes significant. In the weak dialogue, authorship becomes a performance before a society relegated to a more or less appreciative background. Authorship itself becomes the way of life at all levels of representation. By contrast, representations within a tradition constitute re-affirmations and re-interpretations of the original situation of wholeness.

E. Brown, for establishing what constitutes the interpretive field; Dr. Bernard Frischer, Bunny Harvey, and Frank Muhly, for invaluable conversations and contributions; Dean Anthony Eardley, for the opportunity to teach a course on the architecture of the Ancient Near East; Professor Colin St. John Wilson, for the opportunity to develop the discussion to its present stage; and Dr. Dalibor Vesely, whose influence upon the overall argument is most substantial of all. In thanking these people, they are absolved of any burden of agreement with what I have made of their inspiration.

Indeed the insistence upon individual freedom in the first case does not *inherently* relieve society of the threat of a profusion of more or less compatible versions of "freedom," and therefore of the threat of anarchy. The second case inherently situates personal freedom in respect to the primary orientation and specific possibilities of the culture.

Provisionally, at least, it appears that a disembodiment with respect to the past institutes, or supports, a more general disembodiment. So much is the import behind Heidegger's characterization of embodied society as a "being for one another in history."[4] In the society grounded in an idealized, and therefore disposable, past, we have observed that neither of the two terms of Heidegger's expression are fulfilled. In this light, our original distinction between a weak and a strong interpretation of the past suggests that we are distinguishing ultimately between culture disembodied and embodied.

● ● ●

In this essay, I would like to give some account of the relation between representation and the whole in a mythically embodied society. I wish to consider the architecture of ancient Mesopotamia because it constitutes the earliest formulation of the full complex of themes regarding the city and myth, a complex which Jacobsen has summarized as "the cosmos as state." This form of city became the inspiration or point of departure for most subsequent ancient cities in the West. The contribution of Egypt lies in other areas; the Egyptians were not originally predisposed towards city-making as was Mesopotamia. With regard to dating, the earliest cities appear with writing, at approximately the end of the fourth millenium B.C.

My interest here is with establishing a reasonable approximation of the whole in respect to the issue of embodied representation.[5] The series "house, temple, temple-palace, city, city-state, empire" constitutes a chronology and a hierarchy of scale; but more importantly, it refers to a progressively more articulated and differentiated reformulation of the primordial experience of dwelling in a mythically embodied society: what we may term the "cosmic house."

The house, at its most basic level, is a residence with a father at its head, who also acts as "priest" of the domestic cult. Although densely grouped from Neolithic times onwards, houses appear to betray an individual's tie to the earth, in respect of agriculture, animal husbandry, and the proto-magical techniques of cooking, etc.[6] It is invariably a courtyard house. With a single annulus of rooms surrounding the central opening, the dwelling is completely internalized. The celestial orientation of the courtyard seems to have been recognized in the temple, where secondary rooms similarly frame the main chamber of worship (fig. 2).

---

4. I cannot locate this precise expression; but the essence of it is found in *Being and Time* I.IV.26, I.IV.41, II.V.74 (Oxford: Basil Blackwell, 1978).
5. The list of works in this area is obviously vast. The best general introduction is still *Before Philosophy: The Intellectual Adventure of Ancient Man*, by Henri Frankfort, et al. (Baltimore: Penguin Books, 1946 73). Two more works by Frankfort are invaluable: *The Art and Architecture of the Ancient Near East* (Harmondsworth: Penguin Books Ltd., 1970) and *Kingship and the Gods* (Chicago: University of Chicago Press, 1948). Others who have contributed to my formulation of the problem of representation in Ancient Mesopotamia are Thorkild Jacobsen, Samuel Noah Kramer, A. Leo Oppenheim, James Mellaart, Leonard Wooley, Walter Andrae, S. Lloyd, and E.A. Speiser.
For the most part, these authors have relied upon the following for their understanding of myth and religion: Rudolph Otto, C. Van Der Leuw, E. Cassirer and L. Levi-Bruhl. Mircea Eliade has been my basic guide in matters of religious symbolism and iconography. General sources: *Patterns in Comparative Religion* (London: Sheed and Ward, 1958); *The Sacred and the Profane* (New York: Harper Torchbooks, 1979). On the smith-shaman: *The Forge and the Crucible* (Chicago: Harper, 1962.) On the question of the order of the cosmos: *Cosmos and History* (New York: Harper, 1959). Beyond these, I have relied upon certain portions of the writings of E. Voegelin, M. Heidegger, and H.-G. Gadamer.
6. Frankfort stresses that the Mesopotamian city "must not be conceived as a contrast to the open country. The city was but a settlement of people who were largely agriculturalists themselves." *Kingship and the Gods*, p. 411.

The temple is the residence of its god, for whom food is prepared, a bed is made, etc. Here the *ensi*, or ruler-priest, enters into dialogue with the god, either through direct propitiation (prayer, sacrifice) or through dreams. The *ensi* typically leaves a statue of himself in the presence of that of the god, their expressions and postures eloquently speaking the mood of the encounter (fig. 3).

In its role as house of discourse with the god, the temple is both aloof and receptive with respect to a theophany (literally god-appearance). The experience of aloofness derives from the belief that cosmic order prevails, ultimately, as profound and remote. The temple is positioned upon a hill, which establishes a vertical centrality. The celestial symbolism of this hill is most literally presented in the seven-tiered ziggurat at Babylon, where, according to Herodotus, each tier was colored after its appropriate planet. Quite likely, this hill came to be seen as a shamanistic ladder to heaven (a planetary journey). This hill is also the earth. It provides access to the underworld and is the tomb of the god. In Mesopotamian relief and sculpture, the hill is the standard manifestation of deity (along with the crown of bull-horns, etc.). The temple on its hill is often described in texts as heaven and earth, as the center of the cosmos. The collection of symbolic properties exhibited by the temple (of law, abundance, prophecy, etc.) is the essential property of cosmic order (fig. 4).

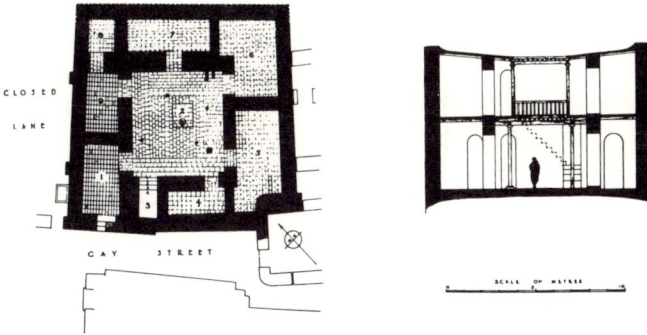

2. House No.3, Gay Street; Ur. Plan and section.

The experience of receptivity derives from the belief that while the cosmos appears universally, significant discourse transpires between gods and men in the setting of the god's house. Within the temple the *ensi* is received in the presence of the god. The face-to-face encounter leading to understanding, the stasis of revelatory awe, or the epiphany, to use the generic term, is the fundamental experience of the entire setting. To the Mesopotamians, not only people but animals, rivers, plants, stones possessed wills and could be addressed. But any notion of order, in its deepest sense — pertaining to the historical totality of earth and sky, gods and men — was unthinkable without the assured promise of direct and effective discourse with the deity.

3. Statues of gods, ensis, and priests from Abu Temple, Tell Ashwar.

Thus the tension between aloofness and reception is the necessary correlate of epiphany. On one hand the temple is heaven and earth and needs to display the primary attributes of the cosmos. It is a setting appropriate to deity, suitably adorned, and separated from the world of men. On the other hand, it is only through the god's residing in the town where he is worshipped that he could be approached.

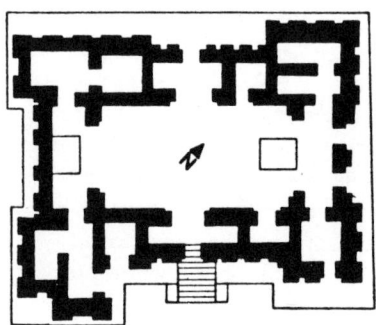

4. Temple VII, Eridu. Plan.

It will be observed that the epiphanic posture accounts as well for the manner in which the temple is approached, and the manner in which the crucial elements are positioned. Movement in the presence of the deity becomes regularized and deliberated, intimating its connection to other sacred movements (e.g., procession and dance). The ritual route is carefully delineated, with attention paid to straightness, to turning, to arrival. Points of passage — doors, steps, etc. — mark what is essentially an initiation. The positioning of ritual elements reconciles the corners and walls of the house with the decorum appropriate to the ceremonial level of each movement. The statue of the primary deity, for example, stands with his back to the wall, the very manifestation of epiphany, gazing at the supplicant. The statue is sometimes raised and framed, like the temple itself (although, properly speaking, the temple represents the positioning of the deity).

This fore-gazing from the wall characterizes epiphanic inhabiting, and animates perceptions of the temple as a deity, capable of giving oracles or flying across the depths. Indeed one may properly, if slightly awkwardly, speak of a "housification" of the cosmos — through residing, the cosmos is made available to propitiation.[7]

What cannot be stressed too often is that re-presenting is re-enacting. The cosmic house re-enacts the primordial experience of dwelling. It provides the setting appropriate to a dialogue between inhabitant and deity. The apparently perplexing multiplicity of cosmic centers in Mesopotamia has nothing to do with false pride or an inability to count, but rather with the necessity for any temple (read "city" as well) worthy of the name to reinstate the primordial situation of order. With the recognition that the temples retained attributes of the earliest reed temples, we observe a five-fold bonding in the cosmic house: in respect of earth, sky, gods, men, and history (fig. 5). Indeed re-enactment is the central motif of ritual time — which constitutes a progressive re-interpretation of the cosmic cycles.

The design and, symbolically at least, the construction of the temple must also be understood as a re-enactment. The most vivid description we have of this process is found in an account left by Gudea, *ensi* of Lagash (c. 2125 B.C.). When the Tigris fails to flood, Gudea repairs to the temple.

---

7. See, for example, the description of Enlil's temple at Nipur in the Hymn to Enlil (found in Samuel Noah Kramer, *History Begins at Sumer* [Garden City: Doubleday, 1959], pp.91ff).

There the god Ningirsu appears to Gudea in a dream.[8] The god appears as a gigantic winged man divinely crowned, whose body rises from the floodcrest. He is framed by recumbent lions (all this is the standard imagery of theophany). Ningirsu commands that his temple be rebuilt. Dawn appears at the horizon. A woman, carrying a gold stylus and a clay tablet inscribed with stars, razes a building plot. A warrior then sketches the plan of a house upon a tablet of lapis lazuli (fig. 6). Gudea's account documents a long process which leads eventually to the preparation of the site, purification of the city, and subsequent construction and dedication of the temple.

5. *Gypsum trough, thought to be from a sanctuary, Uruk, showing archaic reed hut/temple at center.*

Thus the temple is pre-given by the god. It is sited and oriented celestially and then terrestrially. Actual construction proceeds in a similar way. The first baked-brick is prepared and then set in place by the *ensi* (in what has become our corner-stone laying ceremony). A recess in the purified earth beneath this brick contains a small deposit of artifacts. Among these is a plaque depicting the building of the temple by the *ensi* (fig. 7). The pragmatics of temple-construction, needless to say, involve a vast social and economic organization of laborers, trade, and so forth. However, as with all other activities of the city, the sheer scale and coherence of such an effort testifies more to divine focus than to any procedural de-sanctification in "construction," as contemporary practice might suggest.

6. *Statue of Gudea as Architect, with tablet inscribed with the plan of a temple. A stylus is aligned with the right edge. A scale, with graduated increments, is inscribed across the top.*

This is not to intimate, however, that the artisans and laborers participate in the divine revelation. On the contrary, the preservation of sanctity necessitates that this experience remain with the *ensi* and his priests. Indeed the entire process from dream revelation to ritual fabrication situates the

---

8. Ancient god of natural life and, at Lagash, bringer of the floods and rain-storms, the violence of which latter allows him also to be seen as a god of war — the chief deity at Lagash.

7. Plaque showing Ur-Nanshe carrying clay to mold first brick, with dedication.

ensi within the extremely ancient tradition of the artificer smith-shaman. This tradition comprises a host of "creative" activities: from magic and healing through crafts to poetry, dance, and music.

The smith-shaman is most easily understood as a medium through whom divine inspiration becomes bodily ritual. Thus many of the details of what we have called the epiphany in the cosmic house find their source in this tradition. As a result of their too-intimate affiliation with the divine and of their apparent appropriation of creativity, these figures suffer an ambivalent status in subsequent cultures (for example the Biblical Cain, a city-builder whose name translates "smith," is portrayed as the murderer of Abel, the "shepherd"). The smith-shaman is the bearer of the mystery of divine source, which enables only him to re-present order, in the form of ritual re-enactment.

The temple-palace and the city must be considered together. Roughly, a proportional relationship prevails between temple and temple-palace on the one hand, and the temple-palace and the city on the other. The level of sanctity of each, however, devolves successively from the temple.

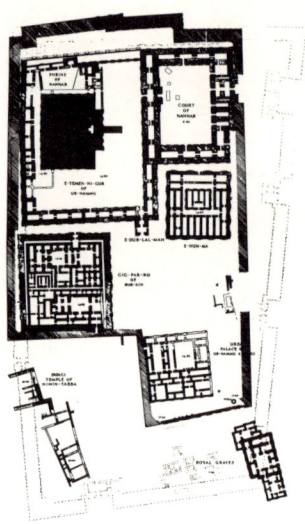

8. The temple-palace compound at Ur, Third Dynasty.

Architecturally, what in earlier times had been at best a large house adjoining the temple precinct (figs. 8, 9, 10), has become in the later period a proper palace organized together with the temple into a unity of their own. Insofar as the orientation of the palace is typically coordinated with that of the temple, and as the two together are so distinguished from the surrounding town, one may speak of the differentiation of the temple to include the palace. The city consequently displays the characteristic "fried egg" plan, in which the temple-palace compound establishes mythical centrality for the town and surrounding countryside.[9]

In fact the temple-palace compound is not only the religious and political center of the city but the center of it's administration as well. The city is conceived as an "estate," managed by the *ensi*. The digging of canals, agriculture, the fermentation of grain to produce beer (which considerably antedated wine), education, the conduct of trade and war, the administration of justice (the Code of Hammurabi being its most memorable legacy), the organization of crafts, and so forth are all the concern of the *ensi* and his staff. All of these "civic" activities are correspondingly sustained in cult.

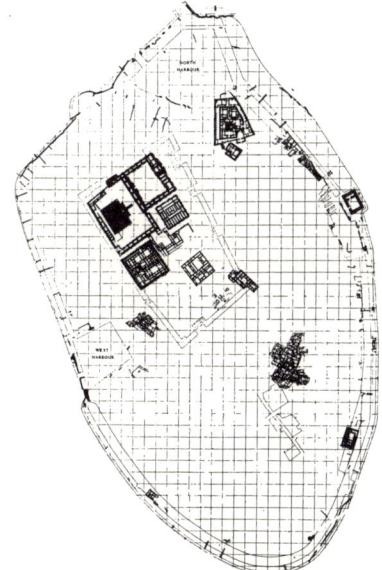

9. City of Ur. Plan.

Jacobsen has identified a middle period in the development of Mesopotamian myth in which something of a politicization of the gods may be identified.[10] From this derives his conception of the cosmos as state. The titulary god of the city (in Babylon, Marduk) is seen to prevail with the counsel of the other gods. I severely understate the complexity of the situation, particularly with regard to the reconciliation with more ancient material in the myths. The point is that symbolism of order begins to incorporate a redistribution of theophanic dialogue within the cosmos.

The grouping of gods within the temple (which will later become a grouping of temples within the temple-palace compound) is re-enacted in the structure of the organization headed by the *ensi* in the management of the estate. The estate is effectively the property of the titulary god. The mode

---

9. Oleg Grabar points out that there are basically two traditions with respect to the positioning of the temple-palace in relation to the city. The first is central; the second is across the defense wall. The city of Ur is an example of the first; Khorsabad, of the second. I've not found an interpretation of the problem which prevents us here from considering them as two versions of the larger symbolism of centrality.
10. Thokhild Jacobsen, *The Treasures of Darkness* (New Haven: Yale University Press, 1976). It is worth mentioning the oft-repeated caution that the Mesopotamian *ensi*, unlike pharoah, was never considered a living god.

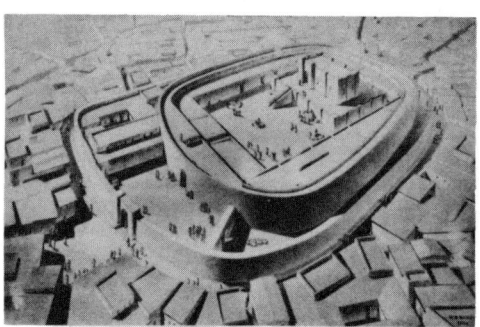

10. Khafaje, temple oval, showing separation of temple precinct and proto-palace.

of dialogue remains founded in the unique relationship between the *ensi* and the gods, however. The re-interpretation of face-to-face conversation into a communal speaking-the-order is nonetheless significant. As a form of interpretation, it must be understood as a reconstitution of the primordial order, and absolutely characteristic of mythic societies. That the transformation itself might lead to a radical independence of the realms of deity and man cannot be examined in detail.

According to Frankfort, the main gate between the temple-palace compound and the town is the site of conversation (of the appearance of the *ensi*, as it were) between them, being used variously for pronouncements, for justice, as a market, and so forth. He thus interprets this gate as an anticipation of the agora and forum in democratic societies. This reading seems apposite when one considers that the temple-palace compound is to this gate what the acropolis (arx) is to the agora (forum) in respect of content, ceremonial position, and orientation.

Cosmic order, and thereby the city, is re-founded annually in what has come to be called the New Year's Ceremony. It is the most important ceremony pertaining to the city. Performed over a period of several days it takes place at the height of the dry season. The titulary god is presumed "lost," or, equally metaphorically, "dead." The declared purpose of the ceremony is the restoration of the god to his temple — in fact, the restoration of theophany. Original creation is given in the *Enuma Elish* (so called after the opening words of the Akkadian version) and this myth is the basis for re-enactment. As in everything else, the *ensi* is the leading participant. Indeed he undergoes a form of initiatory trial in the course of the ceremony.[11]

It is important to recognize that all the discussion concerning centrality is not a matter of stability as stasis, but rather as cyclic recurrence. This relation of dramatic consequence, or temporal fulfillment, to the larger order is even seen in the characteristic form of poetry and prayer. The events of historic succession or of liturgical purpose are superimposed upon subtly modified, repeated affirmations which are chanted in choral fashion. Just as one finds this mode of representation in ceremony, procession, and, presumably, dance and music, so it is found in the architecture of the temple-palace compound.

By way of demonstration, it is necessary first to recall that the twin themes of the temple — house and ritual — are consummated in the theophany. In referring to the temple-palace compound as a "differentiated templa," I am concerned to indicate how precisely this thematic is sustained. Quite simply, the role of the secondary rooms which frame the chamber of worship in the temple is extended to develop suites of secondary rooms which are themselves orchestrated about the primary

---

11. The best study of this ceremony is found in *Kingship of the Gods*, chapter 22.

rooms of the palace. Ritual movement is similarly differentiated to the level of the palace. As with the organization of the city in relation to the temple-palace compound, and the temple-palace compound in relation to the temple, so it is even with the architectural "details" in relation to the epiphanic recess. We see a hierarchical presentation of the proposition found in procession, poetry, prayer, etc. The primary event is supported by repetitions of secondary affirmations.

To understand the phenomenon as a formal principle is to miss the point. Rather it must be considered a manifestation of the primacy of re-enactment to representation generally. The general affiliation of affirmation with being accounts for the belief that such repetitions enhance the power and vitality of a presentation. In these societies, the continuum described by Merleau-Ponty, from gesture to speech to more articulated forms of representing, is most apparent.[12]

Thus in poetry the repeated sentence supports (or "affirms") the narrative. In architecture, the repetitions of house culminate in the cosmic house; or a rhythm of wall buttresses "supports" the walls housing the chamber of worship; or the several doors, each multiply recessed, prefigures the epiphanic recess; or the numerous flights of steps — eventually bonded to the ziggurat itself — are fulfilled in those "supporting" and giving access to the statue of the god. The comparatively late appearance of global symmetries (validated for the modern period by the effective symbolization in perspectivity of the transaction between subject and object) can only be accounted for as a secondary symbolization of the means by which theophany is differentiated — and, no doubt, of the need to do so (see Appendix One).

The city-state and the empire correspond, in the first case, to an organization of villages about a dominant city (together of course with temples, fields, canals, etc.) and, in the second, to a similar organization of cities. There is little to add to the basic conception of centrality except what devolves from the sheer increase in scale. For example, the New Year's Ceremony at Babylon includes the ritual visitation of the major deities of its cities, the statues of whom are transported to Babylon for the ceremony. On the other hand, with the advent of empires the size of Assyria, a conception is instituted which will find its ultimate expression in Rome — "an empire of cities with a city at its head," in Frank Brown's apt phrase.[13] The attributes of centrality pertinent to a single city are elaborated across the full extent of the inhabited world. Expressions like "King of the Four Corners of the Universe" are susceptible to literal interpretation.[14]

Among the more enduring legacies of this transformation in scale is the correlative shift in status, and therefore representational character, of the *ensi* in relation to the king and then to the emperor. The architectural consequence of this is seen in a growing independence of the palace from the temple. Significantly, the throne room acquires certain characteristics borrowed from the chamber of worship in the temple. The propitiatory gestures of subject to ruler had in any case always related to those of the *ensi* to his god. The difference is then one of degree, but still important enough.

---

12. Maurice Merleau-Ponty, *The Phenomenology of Perception* (London: Routledge & Kegan Paul, 1962).
13. Frank E. Brown, *Roman Architecture* (New York: Braziller, 1976), p. 30.
14. The expression "four corners" is commonly understood to be a manifestation of a belief in a bi-axial or at least quadrate universe. This rendering seems suspiciously indebted to Descartes. The expression suggests to me the four corners of a room, which better corresponds to the experience of cosmic unity as an interior. It further gives the sense of cosmic house as a more pervasive theme. The temple is not invested with total symbolic power; rather it is the most direct manifestation of the "sitedness" of the cosmos, and the agency of its celebration. There is no question that the celestial axis of rotation is represented as the "north-south" arm of a central cross in terrestrial squares and circles. A detailed determination of the nature of symbolic mapping in general is, however, beyond the scope of this essay, which deals less with specific motifs than with the basics of the relation between representing and ordering. The sense of the matter is given in Joseph Rykwert's *The Idea of a Town* (London: Faber and Faber, 1976).

The eighth century B.C. palace of the Assyrian emperor Sargon II at Khorsabad displays the motif in a highly developed form (figs. I,II). The temple-palace compound is positioned across the perimeter wall of the city. Were the line of the wall to be drawn through the palace, the ziggurat would occupy the western intersection; the throne room occupies the center with its court extending to the eastern side of the palace. The wall which bonds this court to the throne room is faced with the famous winged bull-gods and what are called "genii." These in turn are flanked by a long procession of men bearing offerings. The winged bull-gods and genii are in fact carefully knitted together to compose a frame for the tripartite portal (one major opening and two minor to either side) leading to the throne room. They display two orientations — one facing the court, and the other in the plane of the wall facing the doorways (see Appendix Two). It appears that the visitor made a right-angle turn upon entering the throne room, a movement derived from temple entry.

The order of the cosmos is continually renewed. To an outsider, the cosmos appears as a multiplicity of primarily religious representations which reconcile the essence of social and natural life. The cosmos is in fact the whole order, and its order is in its wholeness.

Nature appears in two primary dimensions — heaven and earth. Further, each manifests itself first in transitory, immediate phenomena and then in permanent, more profound phenomena. The immediate phenomena of the earth are the rivers, the plants, the animals. The immediate phenomena of the heavens are basically those of the weather — the most prominent being the explosive Mesopotamian storms. The profound phenomena of the earth are, first, the mountains, and then the plains and seas. Within the earth is the netherworld; from the earth regeneration occurs. The deepest stratum is the abyss of dark waters, *Apsu*. The profound phenomena of the heavens and those of the celestial realm are the sun and the moon, then the planets, and finally the stars, most permanent of all. The several levels of celestial movement (diurnal, monthly, seasonally, annually, etc.) are observed as "appearances" on the eastern horizon; the stars "present" appearing as re-affirmation. The whole is understood to be moving about a cosmic axis of rotation (whose 26,000-year precession they knew) passing through the (then) pole stars. When the ecliptic dips in winter, those stars which fail to appear above the horizon are thought to have sunk in the "waters of the deep" (*Apsu*) where in any case the poles of the cosmic axis are located.[15]

The myths are too richly interwoven and infused with parallel motifs for one to declare absolutely the contribution of specifically celestial and specifically terrestrial themes to the overall symbolic picture. However, in general it can be said that cosmic centrality as an issue of the representation of nature speaks of the reconciliation of the celestial axis of rotation with the earth mountain. The comparative reluctance of the earth to renew itself with the precision of celestial cycles, the apparently limitless capacity for the laconic, ever-revealing stars to become a sort of eternal symbolic map, and the primacy of order itself as the essence of how the cosmos "appears" all account for the relative pre-eminence of heavenly deities.

The cosmic house is understood to provide for dwelling in centrality. It is positioned upon the hill which, in its dual symbolism, reconciles celestial and terrestrial centrality. Gods and men sustain this centrality. Society's institutions and artifacts have meaning only in terms of this centrality. The exchange between sustaining and meaning is the essence of re-enactment.

The phenomena of the lived world are experienced as a territory, as a realm of the multiple appearances of particular beings which accumulate in an overall Being. Centrality is a symbolization of

---

15. For those with the determination to cope with what the authors describe as their "medieval" presentation, there is a wealth of material on celestial symbolism in G. de Santillana and H. von Dekend, *Hamlet's Mill* (Boston: Gambit, 1974.)

that experience as a unity of the cosmos. Affirmation of unity is the experience of ordering. In this, order itself "appears." The consistency and repeatedness of affirming reveals how intimately order dwells with chaos, how implicitly fragile is order. It is pertinent that chaos, as the condition prior to the institution of order, is not a formless void in the sense given by intergalactic space, but rather an aqueous latency — a murky silence of water and silt.[16] It is primary substance deprived of any means of appearing. Appearing then exists in symmetry with ordering, and each increment of appearance declares an equivalent increment of chaos. Centrality declares the bondedness of unity, which is experienced as an "interior" (of fellowship and ritual) walled against a peripheral vastness of unformable chaos. It is for this reason that the notion of empire is so problematic — in its literal vastness, it proposes to banish chaos or, more likely, to include chaos within order.

This series of relations may be summarized: ordering transpires as the multiple re-enactments, the appearing representations; ordering institutes the appearance of centrality; centrality declares the unity of the cosmos; the cosmos stands as the unity of the whole, as Order's manner of appearing and its ground.

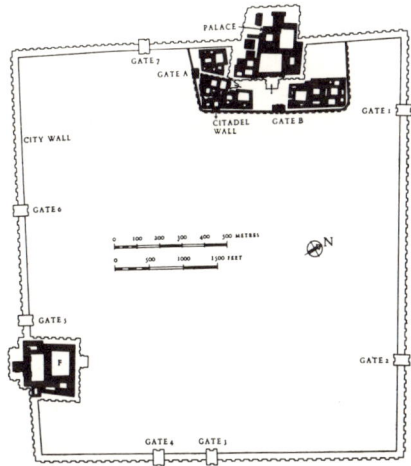

11. Khorsabad. Plan of city.

The ancient documents do not yield so objective a presentation. Even the *Enuma Elish* takes all of this as an assumption, at best. The myth's concern is with the refracting of watery chaos into the personalities of original creation, their role in the initiatory battle to be fought by the titulary god, and the manifold virtues of the god and his order subsequent to victory. The myths generally present fragments of "nature" in terms of ineluctably determined yet — to us — psychologically intractable chains of association.[17] To be sure, mood and purpose are for the most part clear; but the effect of seemingly arbitrary association masquerading as certain cause has prompted the appellation "mythopoeic" for this way of representing. Those scholars who use this term see its source

---

16. One version of the situation prior to the creation of heaven and earth is given in the opening passage of the *Enuma Elish*, which I abbreviate here: "When there was no heaven, no earth, no height, no depth, no name; when *Apsu*, the first begetter, was alone ... when there were no gods; when sweet and bitter water mingled together ... the gods were nameless, natureless, featureless ... in the waters gods were created, in the waters silt precipitated...." Translation by N. K. Dandars, from *Poems of Heaven and Hell from Ancient Mesopotamia* (Harmondsworth: Penguin, 1971).
17. For the Mesopotamian mythographers, the main virtue of distinctions and classifications seems to be their susceptibility to poetic combination.

in the "I-Thou" relationship which prevails between humans and everything else. This relationship is of course fulfilled in theophany.

Eric Voegelin observes a crucial aspect in the structure of the symbolic whole. He emphasizes the role of mutual analogy. A reed, for example, presents itself as a water-plant in the lush marshes, as an element in the construction of the ancient reed hut, as a flute or pipe, as the instrument which produces writing, and so forth. Its array of powers enter into association with the related powers of other objects and events. The cumulative effect is an infinite network of analogies — the multiplicity of the power of the cosmos. On this basis, Voegelin rightly asserts that the ancient cosmos was *tensionally* closed, as against "the fundamentalist fallacy of imagining the cosmos of primary experience to be *spatially* closed."[18]

Thus my original presentation of the symbolization of nature as a sort of architectural section through the cosmos fails to give the sense in which the cosmos is experienced by its inhabitants (who are in any case part of the cosmos). Indeed there is no Mesopotamian equivalent, in any of its languages, for the Greek term "cosmos."[19] Rather the potential volatility of the symbolic structure of lived reality is mediated by intracosmic gods and men towards the most profound manifestations of stability-as-recurrence. The city itself effectively summarizes the nature of things: the tendency of diversity towards chaos is stilled by the rhythm of re-affirmations which are in turn fulfilled in that dwelling in centrality which provides for theophanic discourse.

As we have seen, what is now called representation originates in ritual re-enactment. Actors do not perform a ritual; rather they are performed by it. A ritual is unconcerned about specific personalities, and is not the subject of invention or authorship. Stability and meaning reside in the closedness of ritual with respect to the eternality of gods and the cosmos. On the other hand a balanced exchange prevails between the necessity of performers to the ritual, and the necessity of ritual to the society. The performers participate in the self-revealing autonomy of the ritual. Furthermore, in respect to the tensional bonding of mutual analogies, we perceive that the reconciliation in representation of the essence of social and natural life (in fact understood as the religious, ethical, political, social, natural — i.e. the mythical — core of what the cosmos as a lived reality stands for) prevails as a dialogue between them. This is experienced as a broad continuum of transformations of "nature" in the reciprocity between the sustaining of unity and the meaning of society's institutions and artifacts.

---

18. Eric Voegelin, *The Ecumenic Age* (Baton Rouge: Univ. of Louisiana Press, 1974), p. 77.
19. It is possible here to present only the barest outline of the true state of affairs. Since all subsequent interpretation "begins at Sumer" (Kramer), the Sumerian version is given. The Sumerian word for "universe" is *an-ki*, which translates "heaven-earth." In between is *lil*, a word connoting movement and expansion. It apparently refers to a conception of atmosphere or air which is contained within heavenly bodies as well. These last possess the additional attribute of luminosity. Apsu, the abyss of the primeval sea which engendered the cosmos, also surrounds an-ki. From Apsu appears the cosmic mountain, in which heaven and earth are united. Subsequent to the separation of heaven and earth, the cosmos appears as an affair of men and nature mediated by intracosmic gods. The harmonious order of the cosmos is contained within the more than one hundred "me's," or divine laws. These range in their subject matter from lordship and godship to the craft of building and musical instruments, from the exalted shrine and kingship to prostitution and wisdom. Of the hundreds of Sumerian deities, the four primary are An (heaven), Enlil (air, the chief deity), Enki (earth), and Ninhursag/Ninmah (mother of living things, and quite possibly to be associated with the earth or the primeval sea in earlier times). This arrangement fails to take into account earlier and later interpretations, or the variations from text to text. For example, one account states that, after the separation of heaven and earth, An carried off heaven, and Enlil, earth. In *History Begins at Sumer*, pp.76ff., from which this summary was taken, Kramer gives the usual interpretation of this state of affairs. Not being philosophically inclined, the mythographers were interested less in causation in their subject matter than in the process and appearance of lived (mythical) reality. The truth of this however, seems to have prevented any deeper interpretation of what criteria for precision were important. Thorkild Jacobsen, in *Treasures of Darkness*, provides a very good description of the basic changes in mythic orientation between the fourth and first millenia in Mesopotamia.

Appendix One

If the temporal aspects of centrality have already been mentioned, the notion of centrality as a matter of place perhaps needs similar clarification. Le Corbusier's amusing depiction of a primitive tent-shrine fully informed by Beaux-Arts geometry certainly tells us more about Le Corbusier, child of the Enlightenment, than it does about primitive man — or his geometries. This is ultimately a very complex problem concerning the relation between Order, as a fulfillment of lived reality, and geometry, as a non-arbitrary, sufficient symbolization of Order. The question is posed at this level by Husserl in his "Essay On The Origin of Geometry."

For primitive man, geometry (literally earth-measure) only began to attain its current theoretical understanding with Euclid. As Joseph Rykwert reminds us, the relation between visual pattern and ritual must countenance taboo, habits of walking and dancing, of sitting and of reaching, bird and animal tracks and leavings, celestial movements, accidents of local topography, human and animal faces and bodies, the physiognomies of plants and stones, and so forth. Even as late as the Renaissance and Baroque periods, what we now call geometry possessed a profound symbolic content. Kepler, as is well known, considered his astronomical discoveries to validate "our magnificent temple of God ... God, like a master-builder, has laid the foundation of the world according to order and law ... God from the very beginning and purposely has selected the curved and the straight for stamping the world with the Divinity of the Creator ...."[20]

Dalibor Vesely demonstrates that the project of Durand may be taken to represent a crucial late stage in a long history of architectural theoretization and de-mythization. Here architecture presents itself as a collection of disembodied elements made wholly available to the compositional instrumentalities of axis and grid. (Indeed the term "axis" is inappropriately applied to architecture prior to the development of analytical geometry in the work of Desargues, Descartes, and then Monge). The emptiness of the proposition is observed by Anthony Vidler in the ease with which it supports the eclecticist fantasies which effectively terminated the Classical tradition.

The efforts of modern artists such as Le Corbusier to re-invest this instrumental, theoretical geometry with some form of symbolic content (rooted, on the one hand, in standardized measurements taken from an ideal body, and, on the other, in naive psychologisms concerning form, matter, and space) have only served to confuse the issue. The good intentions are undermined by the magic by which they might attain fulfillment, since the essentially theoretical character of the modern use of symbols deprives them of any real participatory content. For example, the reliance upon the value-free neutrality of "space," as the a priori to all considerations related to architecture, institutes a profound symbolic contradiction. Space is a theoretical substitute for the continuity of lived experience. It leaves all symbolic pretentions trapped within the representational object, since the conceptual realm of space declares a distrust of the shared, cultural experience which might support the symbol. The tendency on the part of more recent artist-architects to ground their symbolic speculations in psychology, art history, sociology, anthropology and so forth only increases the theoretical disjunction, and can hardly establish a proper ontology of the symbol.

In any event, as these matters pertain to Ancient Mesopotamia, the relevant understanding of centrality is obtained in that culture's general orientation towards the affirmation of unity. The concern to sustain unity as a matter of wholeness doubtless accounts for the reluctance to indulge in generalized manifestations of symmetry. Quite simply, architecture was not conceived to be a matter of exemplary objects which might symbolize the whole order (cf. Appendix Two); rather it participated significantly in the broad spectrum of symbolic manifestations. As the reed appears in several realms of existence, from the natural to the ritual, so architecture cannot reasonably be detached from culture as a radically separate category of knowledge and experience. For reasons of brevity I have only suggested the nature of architecture's ultimate ambivalence to the modern mind. The relation between house and ritual provides both the ground for specificity and the origin of associative extension.

I am ultimately concerned here with identifying what might be called the ontological ground of architecture in Ancient Mesopotamia. I have concentrated upon ritual architecture because of its participation in the more profound levels of the symbolization of unity. Speaking a myth or a prayer constitutes the most significant plane of discourse in a hierarchy of planes of discourse. These correspond to a more or less equivalent hierarchy of human situations. Similarly architecture establishes settings appropriate to these situations. So much underlies mythic compactness as a style of thought and as a realm in which Order appears. Present culture quite obviously aspires to a higher degree of articulatedness than that found in mythic representation. This aspiration has introduced certain impediments to an equivalent understanding of how contemporary architectural representation corresponds to the ontological ground, and this is the subject of the unpublished second chapter of this essay. In the third chapter I undertake to address this problem; but insofar as the relation between setting and situation might still be regarded as fundamental to such an interpretation, see the introduction to *Architecture and Continuity* by Dalibor Veseley.

With regard to the problem of symmetric dispositions in Ancient Mesopotamia, it is necessary to point out that initially one finds such arrangements in pottery, symbolic reliefs, and sculptural groups. Their subsequent appearance in the more elaborated forms of temple and ziggurat remains confined to those sacred situations and is generally understood to be a matter of

---

20. J. Kepler, *Mysterium Cosmographicum*, Tubingen, 1596, quoted by W. Heisenberg in *The Physicist's Conception of Nature*, transl. A.J. Pomerans (London: Hutchinson, 1958), pp.73, 74, 80.

184 THE PRINCETON JOURNAL

potential symmetries and alignment — or the deliberate avoidance of alignment — grounded in the fulfillment of rhythm, rather than anything related to symmetric composition as it is commonly understood. Furthermore, these sacred situations retain their contingent relationship with their supporting elements in an amorphous hierarchy of situations which ultimately fades out somewhere beyond the laborers in a distant irrigation canal before re-appearing at the horizon. With certain limited exceptions, so much could be said for the appearance of large-scale symmetries in the western city, until the affiliation of theoretic and artistic speculations approximately 3,500 years later.

Appendix Two

This wall (fig. B) deserves mention in relation to what eventually becomes the *scenae frons* in the classical theater to which it exhibits a number of interesting parallels. Among these are the iconography of the ruler's palace, the tri-partite doorway centrally focused, the proto-columnar arrangement of the sculptures, and the overall status of the wall in relation to the court. In both cases we are discussing what might be termed an epiphaic wall, a wall-of-appearance or revelation, frontally regarded. Although the wall at Khorsabad antedates the earliest *scenae frons* by several hundred years, and a number of agencies of transmission could be offered, a substantial dialogue with the East is difficult to support between the "orientalizing period" (Corinthian Ware) and Hellenistic times. For the purposes of these remarks, I wish to assume only that they are related in terms of the similarities noticed. The problem is worth exposing by virtue of the remarkable persistence in architecture of the frontally regarded wall which supports intimations of appearance or revelation as the vehicle for what constitutes a fundamental experience of architectural representation. The full development of the motif in the antique can be seen in the post-Hellenistic *scenae frons*, in which the wall is composed of a superimposition of aediculae (see fig. D). As such, the wall presents two contradictory themes: first, it is a wall, a surface against which the realm dominated by it comes to rest; second, it is a window which does not release the view to what lies behind, but rather confers the property of revealing upon what transpires before the wall. The late *scenae frons* is composed almost entirely of architectural elements which institute a hierarchy of framing: the niches for statuary (exemplary existence in the wall), the aediculae, and the wall itself. The three, and, in a later stage of elaboration, occasionally five portals are the primary points of passage or emergence in the wall, although provision was made in earlier structures for the appearance of the *deus ex machina* in a manner similar to temple pediments.

Were the wall at Khorsabad to be regarded as part of this tradition, its most notable difference from the post-Hellenistic, or Roman *scenae frons* is that the winged bull-gods and genii in the former perform a role similar to the architectural elements in the latter. Evidence seems to encourage the view that there is a continuity of theme to be observed here. The column is vastly more rare in Mesopotamia than in Egypt or later in Greece. If one takes a very broad historical perspective, the following sequence might be proposed.

The earliest arrangements of animals in formal groupings present nature (or the aspects of nature and divinity carried by particular animals) as ordered. Configurational order in artifacts represents cosmic order with respect to stability and to the transformation of stone, bitumen, lapis lazuli, ivory, gold, etc. into an entity with a higher level of existence; it is alive enough to sustain the belief that the god is present in his image. The shrines at Catal Huyuk present bulls, rams, leopards, etc. bonded to the setting of the house in an early (ca. sixth millenium) manifestation of what we have called "the housification of the cosmos" (see fig. A).

It is through the agency of secondary symbolism that such figures are made available to the imperial setting of the palace at Khorsabad. A late stage in the proposed sequence points towards the *scenae frons*: the throne room at Persepolis is essentially an enlargement of the Ancient Near Eastern Temple, except that the interior chamber is now a hypostyle hall (see fig. C). Each of the one hundred columns carries a roof beam on the back of twinned bull-gods, positioned on top of the unique tree-of-life/Egyptian lotus capital. The decrease in scale combined with critical positioning give the sense of how the sequence marks the shift in representational means and intent.

I see in Persepolis a significant stage in the sequence of secondary symbolizations of architectural order. Persepolis, begun by Darius I in 518 B.C., constitutes a singular event, in which there seems to prevail a dominating reliance upon representational techniques. From an architectural point of view, at least, the notion of King of the Four Corners of the Universe seems to have been interpreted in terms of the representational proclivities of whatever peoples dwelt in the (four-cornered) empire. So much is apparent in appellations such as "The Gate of All Countries" and in the pride with which Darius lists the contribution to the building of Susa of artisans from all over the Eastern Mediterranean. In any event, the increased demands for breadth of reference seem to have met the requirements for unity by the dual device of reducing the use of specific symbols and of distributing the few primary motifs throughout the whole. The complex is almost entirely composed of roughly square hypostyle chambers positioned with respect to ramps and terraces. If the presence of celestial themes must be inferred in the distribution of the order of the throne-room throughout the complex, the remnants of the cosmic mountain are certainly present in the ramps and terraces.[21] Architecture here manifests itself as the essence of

---

21. Frankfort, in *Art and Architecture*, presents the main events and a summary of the discussion surrounding both Khorsabad (pp.127 ff.) and Persepolis (pp.348ff. — both references are to the soft-cover version). However, his figure 168, a line-drawing of the wall in question, is incomplete; for the full restoration, consult the excavation report: G. Loud, *Khorsabad I and II* (Chicago: University of Chicago Press, 1936), p.38.

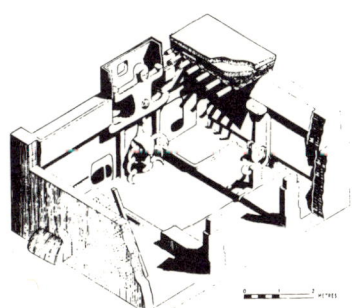

A. Shrine VI.A.10 at Çatal Hüyük, ca. sixth millenium B.C.

B. Khorsabad. Wall of court leading to throne room; reconstruction by Botta. The elevation omits the left minor portal and the remainder of the orthostats to its left. Eighth century B.C.

C. Persepolis. Throne room; reconstruction by Chipiez. 518–460 B.C.

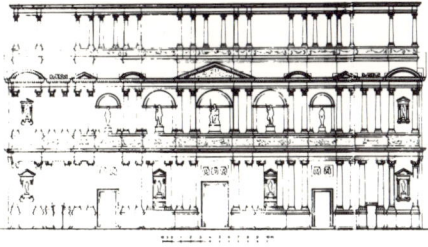

D. Ephesus. Scenae Frons, elevation. Roman Period.

E. Façade of Palazzo Branconio dell'Aquita, by Raphael. Drawing usually attributed to Parmagianino.

F. Façade of former Piazza Impero, Casa del Fascio; G. Terragni.

what cosmic representation of empire might adequately encompass. It may similarly be taken to respond to the dilemma of empire, in which the celebration of unity is ranged against the cosmos itself.

Architecture, now elevated to an exemplary representational status, has become the primary agency by which the cosmic house may appear. The progressive sublimation of the original diversity of this setting will allow architectural ordering to stand for symbolic ordering generally. In time, architecture will come to be understood as "orders" which are susceptible to compositional arrangement, or ordering. The possible experiences appropriate to the architectural setting become determined by the presence of architectural elements (window frames, portals, colonnades, etc.) in the representational proposition at hand. It is on this basis that the late *scenae frons* is more than a tedious collection of too-often repeated architectural elements. A transaction is instituted between a spectator and revelatory order, declared as a confrontational extreme. At this point, the *scenae frons* may be seen to be a secondary symbol for the original participation in ritual, the antecedent of drama.

Whatever the case, the subsequent affiliation in the Renaissance of the dramatic, revelatory wall with the picture plane ensured the reliance upon this form of confrontational ordering and revealing well into the present day (see figs. E, F).

The significance of the confrontation itself resides on the status of legitimate *appearing in the world*. This manner of architectural ordering presents the cosmos in the form of a sublimated cosmic house, a self-sufficient symbol for order in the larger sense. It provides appearing in a revelatory object on man's terms, and available to his manipulation and design. Appearing itself becomes limited to looking — but it is, however, an empty stare, an architecturally reticulated gaze into multiple vacant windows. The wall becomes a wall against the plenitude of the world's appearing behind it. This much at least is declared in the neurotic character of the wall itself, and its recurring tendency to engage in the possibility of its own dematerialization. The investment in monothematic symbolization simply cannot support the requirements of richness and diversity, whatever the virtues of availability to manipulation. Certainly the effective architectural symbolization of unity cannot be consigned to such limited means. The drama of lived reality requires participation in, and preservation of, the world as a whole, as a cosmos.

Illustration Credits

Deamer: All photographs by William Taylor. *Fernandez*: 1: Drawing by Stephen Corelli after a diagram in J. W. Fernandez, *Fang Architectonics* (Philadelphia, 1977), fig. 4; 2: Drawing by Ellen Dunham after a diagram in Fernandez, fig. 8. *Graves*: 2-5: Charles McGrath; 6: Proto Acme Photo. *Gans*: 1: Photograph by Herbert Migdoll: Courtesy of the Joffrey Ballet; 2: Photograph by Larry Craven; Courtesy of the Dean Dance and Music Foundation; 3: Photography by Lois Greenfield; Courtesy of the Dean Dance and Music Foundation; 4,5: Reprinted from Cyril W. Beaumont, *Ballet Design, Past and Present* (New York, 1946), p.4; 6: Reprinted from George R. Kernodle, *From Art to Theatre* (Chicago, 1944), fig. 59; 7: Photograph courtesy of The Pace Gallery, New York; 8: Photograph by Rudolph Burkhardt; Courtesy of Leo Castelli, New York; 9: Photograph by James Klosty; Courtesy of Cunningham Dance Foundation, Inc. *Goldman*: 1: Fred Cohen; 2,4: William Taylor. *Corelli*: 3: William Taylor. *Agrest and Gandelsonas*: All photographs courtesy of Diana Agrest. *Wheelright*: All photographs courtesy of Peter Wheelwright. *Vidler*: 1,2: Drawing by Ludmilla Pavlova, after a diagram by the author. *Maxwell*: 1: Reprinted from O. C. Le Corbusier, *Oeuvre Complète, 1910-1929.*, (Zurich, 1960), fig.67; 2: Reprinted from Marcel Duchamp, *Salt Seller: The Workings of Marcel Duchamp*, Michel Sanouillet and Elmer Peterson, eds., (New York, 1973), p.176. *Marosi*: 1: William Taylor; 2: Norman McGrath. *WilliamsTsien*: 1: Courtesy of Tod Williams; 2: Steven Falatko. *Ando*: 1: Photograph by Yukio Futakawa. Reprinted from *Tradition and Creation in Japanese Architecture* (Tokyo, 1972); 3: Photograph by Tomio Ohashi; 4: Photograph courtesy of Tadao Ando, Architect and Associates; 5: Photograph by Tomio Ohashi; 6: Reprinted from *Stage Design 8106*, p.49. *Plattus*: Reprinted from Inez Scott Ryberg, *Panel Reliefs of Marcus Aurelius* (New York, 1967), fig. 9a; 2: Reprinted from Ena Makin, "The Triumphal Route with Particular Reference to the Flavian Triumph," *The Journal of Roman Studies*, vol. XI (London, 1921), pp.24+25; 3: Reprinted from Filippo Magi, *I Relievi Flavi del Palazzo della Cancelleria* (Rome, 1945), tavola I, fregi A; 4: Reprinted from Gilbert Charles-Picard, *Les Trophées Romains* (Paris, 1957), pl.2; 5-16: Reprinted from Andrew Martindale, *The Triumphs of Caesar by Andrea Mantegna* (London, 1979), pls.68,69,70,72; 17: Reprinted from *Monumenti Inediti Publicati dell "Instituto di Corrispondenza Archaeologica,"* vol. V (Rome, 1849-1853), tavola VII; 18: Drawing by Diana Noya after a map reproduced in Robert Payne, *The Roman Triumph* (London, 1962), p.118. *Moya*: 2: William Taylor; 3: Courtesy of Frank Moya. *Waldman*: 2,7,8,12: Courtesy of Peter Waldman; 3,5,6: Y. Futagawa and Associates, Photographers. *AbbeyDripps*: All photographs courtesy of Bruce Abbey and Robert Dripps. *Marusczak*: All photographs courtesy of John Marusczak. *Friedman*: All photographs by Doug Paschal and William Taylor. *Carl*: 1: Reprinted from G. Loud, *Khorsabad: The Citadel and the Town*, vol. II (Chicago: University of Chicago Press, 1938), frontispiece, courtesy of the Oriental Institute of the University of Chicago; 2: Reprinted from *The Antiquaries Journal*, vol. VII, no. 4 (October, 1927), plate XLI; 3: Reprinted from Henri Frankfort, *Oriental Institute: Discoveries in Iraq 1933-1934* (Chicago: University of Chicago Press, 1939), figure 13; 4: Reprinted from *Sumer*, III (1947), figure 3; 5: Couresty of the author; 6: Reprinted from Samuel Noah Kramer, *History Begins at Sumer* (New York: Doubleday, Anchor, 1959), figure 7; 7: Reprinted from E. de Sarzec and L. Henzey, *Découvertes en Chaldée* (Paris, 1884-1912), plate 2; 8: Reprinted from *The Antiquaries Journal*, XIV, No. 4, (October, 1934), plate XLIX; 9: Reprinted from L. Woolley, *Excavations at Ur* (London, 1934), figure 6; 10: Reprinted from P. DeLougaz, *The Temple Oval at Khafaje* (Chicago: Chicago University Press, 1940), frontispiece; 11,12: Reprinted from G. Loud, *Khorsabad: The Citadel and the Town*, vol.II (Chicago: University of Chicago Press, 1938), plate 69; plate 2 (reconstruction by Charles Altman); A: Reprinted from J. Meilaart, *Çatal Hüyük* (London: Thames and Hudson, 1967), fig. 40; E: Reprinted from *The Complete Works of Raphael*, fig. 73, courtesy of the Instituto Geografico de Agostini, Novara; Reprinted from Bruno Zevi, *Giuseppe Terragni*, p.74, fig.7.

Frontispiece reprinted from Wieland Schmied, *Caspar David Friedrich* (Koln: DuMont Schauberg, 1975), p. 29.

Contributors

Bruce Abbey: B. Arch., Cornell University, 1966. M. Arch., Princeton University, 1971. He is an Associate Professor at the University of Virginia and Co-Chairman of the Division of Architecture. He maintains a private practice in Charlottesville, Virginia. **Diana Agrest** graduated from the University of Buenos Aires School of Architecture and Urbanism in 1967 and from 1967-1969 attended the Ecole Pratique des Hautes Etudes and the Centre de Réchérche d'Urbanisme, both in Paris. She taught at Princeton University from 1971-1975 and currently teaches at the Cooper Union School of Architecture and the Institute for Architecture and Urban Studies where she is a Fellow. She is a principle in the firm Agrest and Gandelsonas, Architects in New York City. **Tadao Ando** is a self-taught architect from Osaka, Japan. In 1980 he received the Award of the Architectural Institute of Japan. He was a guest lecturer at Princeton University in the spring of 1983. **Gustavo Bonevardi**: B.A., Sarah Lawrence College, 1982. He studied at the Institute for Architecture and Urban Studies and is currently a second year graduate student at Princeton University. **Peter Carl**: B.A., Princeton University, 1968. M. Arch., Princeton University, 1974. He has taught at the University of Kentucky and is currently a Fellow of the College of Architecture, Cambridge University. **Alan Colquhoun** received his degree in architecture from the Architectural Association, London, in 1949. He has taught at the Architectural Association, Cornell University, University College, Dublin, The Polytechnic of Central London, l'Ecole Polytechnique Fédérale de Lausanne, and the University of Virginia. He is presently a Professor of Architecture at Princeton University and a principle in the firm Colquhoun and Miller, Architects in London. **Stephen Corelli** studied at the University of Toronto and the Architectural Association, London. He received his M. Arch. from Princeton University in 1982. **Peggy Deamer**: B.A., Oberlin College, 1972. B. Arch., Cooper Union, 1977. She has taught at Cooper Union and the University of Kentucky and is currently a Ph.D. candidate in architecture at Princeton University. **Robert Dripps**: B.A. Arch., Princeton University, 1964. M. Arch., University of Pennsylvania, 1966. He is an Associate Professor at the University of Virginia and Co-Chairman of the Division of Architecture. **James Fernandez**: B.A., Amherst College, 1952. Ph.D., Northwestern University, 1962. He has taught at Smith College and Dartmouth College and is currently a Professor of Anthropology at Princeton University. **Yossi Friedman**: B.F.A., Rhode Island School of Design, 1979. B. Arch., Rhode Island School of Design, 1980. M. Arch., Princeton University, 1982. **Mario Gandelsonas** studied at the University of Buenos Aires School of Architecture and Urbanism and from 1967-1968 at the Ecole Pratique des Hautes Etudes and the Centre de Réchérche d'Urbanisme in Paris. He is a Fellow at the Institute for Architecture and Urban Studies where he teaches theory and design, and is a principle in the firm Agrest and Gandelsonas, Architects in New York City. He was a visiting critic at Princeton University in the spring of 1981. **Deborah Gans**: A.B., Harvard College, 1978. M. Arch., Princeton University, 1981. **George Gintole**: B. Arch., Cooper Union, 1976. M. Arch., Princeton University, 1980. He has taught at the University of Virginia, the University of Texas at Arlington, Rice University and currently teaches at the Graduate School of Design, Harvard University. **Pe'era Goldman**: Diploma, Bezalel Academy of Art and Design, Jerusalem, Israel, 1973. M. Arch., Princeton Univeristy, 1978. She taught at Princeton University from 1980-1983 and is presently teaching at the Technion-Israel Institute of Technology in Haifa, Israel. **Michael Graves**: B.S. Arch., University of Cincinnati, 1958. M. Arch., Harvard University, 1959. Fellow, American Academy in Rome, 1960-62. Honorary Doctorate, University of Cincinnati, 1982. He has taught at the University of Houston, the University of California at Los Angeles, the University of Texas at Austin, the University of Maryland, and the New School for Social Research in New York. He is Schirmer Professor of Architecture at Princeton University where he has taught since 1962. He maintains a private practice in Princeton, New Jersey. **Steven Harris**: B.A., New College, 1972. B.F.A., Rhode Island School of Design, 1975. M. Arch., Princeton University, 1977. He has taught at the Institute for Architecture and Urban Studies, the University of Texas at Austin, and is currently an Assistant Professor at Princeton University. **Erich Marosi**: B.S. Arch., McGill University, 1975. B. Arch., McGill University, 1976. He is currently a third year graduate student at Princeton University. **John Marusczak**: B. Arch., Cooper Union, 1977. M. Arch., Princeton University, 1980. He has taught at the University of Miami, Carleton College, and Catholic University. He is currently an Assistant Professor of Architecture at the University of Texas at Arlington. **Robert Maxwell**: B. Arch., Liverpool School of Architecture, 1949. He has taught at the University College of London and the British School in Rome. He is currently Dean of the Princeton University School of Architecture. **Fernando Montes** received his diploma in architecture from the Faculty of Architecture, Catholic University of Santiago and now practices and teaches in Paris. He has also taught at the Royal College of Art in London, at the Rhode Island School of Design, and was a guest lecturer at Princeton in the Spring of 1982. **Frank Moya**: B.A. Arch., Princeton University, 1980. M. Arch., Princeton University, 1982. **Toshio Okumura**: A.B., Harvard College, 1980. He is presently a third year graduate student at Princeton University. **Peter C. Papademetriou**: B.A. Arch., Princeton University, 1965. M. Arch., Yale University, 1968. He has taught at Carnegie-Mellon, the University of Texas at Austin and is currently an Associate Professor of Architecture at Rice University. **Alan Plattus**: B.A., Yale University, 1976. M. Arch., Princeton University, 1979. He is presently an Assistant Professor of Architecture at Princeton University. **Bernard Tschumi**: Dipl. Arch., Eidgenossische Technische Hochschule, Zurich, Switzerland. He has served as a Visiting Professor at Princeton University. He is currently a Visiting Professor at the Cooper Union School of Architecture and maintains a private practice in Paris. **Billie Tsien**, B.A., Yale University, 1971. M.Arch., U.C.L.A., 1977. She has taught at the Cooper Union School of Architecture and the University of Miami, and she is an associate with Tod Williams and Associates, New York City. **Anthony Vidler** received his degree from Cambridge University in 1965. He has taught at the Architectural Association, the University of Kentucky, Yale University and Institute for Architecture and Urban Studies where he is a Fellow. He is a Professor of Architecture at Princeton University where he has taught since 1965. **Peter Waldman**: B.A. Arch., Princeton University, 1965. M.F.A. Arch., Princeton University, 1967. He has taught at Princeton University, the Rhode Island School of Design, the University of Miami, the University of Virginia, the University of Cincinnati, and Harvard University. He is currently an Associate Professor of Architecture at Rice University. and maintains a private practice in Houston, Texas. **Peter Wheelwright**: B.A., Trinity College, 1972. M. Arch., Princeton University, 1975. He is a partner in the firm Anderson/Wheelwright Associates in New York City. **Tod Williams**: B.A. Arch., Princeton University, 1965. Cambridge University, 1966. M.F.A. Arch., Princeton University, 1967. He has taught at the Institute for Architecture and Urban Studies and is presently an adjunct Professor of Architecture at Cooper Union. Fellow, American Academy in Rome, 1983. **Judy Wolin**: B. Arch., Cornell University, 1968. M. Ed. Architectural History and Theory, Yale University, 1971. She has taught at Princeton University and Harvard University and is currently an Associate Professor of Architecture at the Rhode Island School of Design.

Patrons

Broadacre Management Company
Michael Graves, Architect
Hugh Hardy
Mary Wistar O'Connor *in memory of Benjamin Wistar Morris*
Robert B. O'Connor *in memory of Howard Crosby Butler*
Joseph E. Seagram & Sons, Inc.

The Princeton School of Architecture
Princeton University

•   •   •

Sponsors

Hobart Betts Associates
G. Mitchell Bourke
Marjorie Bourke
Hank Bruce
Peter W. Charapko
F.C.L. Associates, Inc.
Geddes Brecher Qualls Cunningham
Lawrence Haines
G. E. Kidder-Smith
Charles Lagreco
David M. McAlpin
Martin and Jones Architects
Robert Venturi
Tod Williams

Donors

Bruce Abbey
Arthur Cotton Moore Associates
George Baird
J. F. Bull
William O. Burwell
Harold Caufield
Sho-Ping Chin
Peggy Deamer
Alfred De Vido
Neville Epstein
Gustav E. Escher III
Colder Florance, FAIA
Jeremiah Ford III
Frederick G. Frost, Jr.
José R. Gonzalez-Barahona
Steven W. Henkelman
Elizabeth Hicks
Stephen A. Kaufman
Henry A. Jandl *in memory of Mercedes Labatut*
Holt and Morgan Associates
Doug Kelbaugh
John Lawson
Peter Lokhammer
J. C. Mancuso
Dr. and Mrs. Nesbitt
Eugene M. Packin
Harlow Pearson
Chester Rapkin
Burton Romberger
Hugo Roomann
Abraham Rothenberg
William Short
Stephen Synakowski
Max Underwood
Peter Wheelwright
Tim Wood

THIS FIRST VOLUME OF *The Princeton Journal: Thematic Studies in Architecture* was designed by Stephen Falatko and printed in an edition of 3000 by *Hallowell & West* at Andalusia, Pennsylvania. The typography is based upon letters invented by Eric Gill at Capel-y-ffyn, Wales, in 1927.